D1713402

Deliverance and Submission

Evangelical Women and the Negotiation of Patriarchy in South Korea

Harvard East Asian Monographs 309

Deliverance and Submission

Evangelical Women and the Negotiation of Patriarchy in South Korea

Kelly H. Chong

Published by the Harvard University Asia Center
and distributed by Harvard University Press
Cambridge (Massachusetts) and London, 2008

Printed in the United States of America

The Harvard University Asia Center publishes a monograph series and, in coordination with the Fairbank Center for Chinese Studies, the Korea Institute, the Reischauer Institute of Japanese Studies, and other faculties and institutes, administers research projects designed to further scholarly understanding of China, Japan, Vietnam, Korea, and other Asian countries. The Center also sponsors projects addressing multidisciplinary and regional issues in Asia.

Library of Congress Cataloging-in-Publication Data

Chong, Kelly H., 1964-
    Deliverance and submission : evangelical women and the negotiation of patriarchy in South Korea / Kelly H. Chong.
        p. cm. -- (Harvard East Asian monographs ; 309)
    Includes bibliographical references and index.
    ISBN 978-0-674-03107-4 (cloth : alk. paper)
        1. Evangelicalism--Korea (South) 2. Middle-aged women--Religious life. 3. Religion and sociology--Korea (South) 4. Middle-aged women--Korea (South) 5. Women's studies--Korea (South) 6. Korea (South)--Religion. I. Title.
    BV1642.K6C46 2008
    275.195'083082--dc22

                                                                                2008032964

Index by Mary Mortensen

♾ Printed on acid-free paper

Last figure below indicates year of this printing

18 17 16 15 14 13 12 11 10 09 08

For my mother and father,

Dongyaw Chong and Hanchae Chong

Acknowledgments

I must begin by expressing my deepest gratitude to all of the people with whom I have had the privilege of meeting and talking in the course of my fieldwork. Although their names have been altered in order to ensure anonymity, I particularly thank the women whose stories grace the pages in this book; they generously shared their time and a part of themselves to make this book possible. I am also greatly indebted to my various sponsors within the churches for their cooperation and willingness to assist me in this research at every step of the way. I express special, heartfelt thanks to the two assistant pastors of my two primary research sites who, though they must remain anonymous, opened their church doors and supported this research; without them, this book could not have been written.

At the University of Chicago. I owe an enormous debt to my advisor, Martin Riesebrodt, whose incisive intellectual direction and unstinting support and enthusiasm for this project from its inception was key to its unfolding. Martin has remained a wonderful colleague and friend through the years since graduate school, guiding me professionally and intellectually at critical junctures. I would also like to thank Leslie Salzinger, whose feedback, critiques, and advice regarding gender issues always turned out to be just what was needed. I am also grateful to her for lending her ear when I needed it, and kindly providing assistance on all kinds of matters over the years. I sincerely thank Mary Brinton for her support for this project and for expanding my horizons with regard to gender issues in East Asia. Finally, I would like to thank Bruce Cumings for his valuable insights regarding Korea, many of which proved to be an even greater asset to my analysis than I had anticipated, and for his continued friendship over the years.

I must convey my gratitude to the several institutions that have financially supported my research. This includes the USIA/IIE Fulbright Fellowship, which sponsored my fieldwork in South Korea. The Blakemore Foundation supported language study in Korea. The Martin Marty Center for the Advanced Study of Religion at the Divinity School and the Center for East Asian Studies, both at the University of Chicago, provided write-up grants during the dissertation stage. I owe special thanks to the Korea Foundation for granting me both a dissertation fellowship and an advanced research fellowship; the latter enabled me to pursue additional research for this project and take leave from teaching to complete the book manuscript. The New Faculty General Research Fund from the University of Kansas also aided in this effort. I also thank the Institute for the Advanced Study of Religion at Yale University and Harvard Divinity School for their post-doctoral fellowships.

My sincerest thanks go to the many colleagues and friends who have generously spared the time to read and comment on my work and encouraged me in various ways over the years. I thank Ju-Yeon Chong, Gerald L. Curtis, Hilary Dunst, Andreas Glaser, Chi-Young Koh, Mary Ellen Konieczny, Loren Lybarger, Dawne Moon, Mary Ann O'Donnell, Jaesoon Rhee, Fabio Rojas, David Smilde, R. Stephen Warner, as well as the 1999–2000 members of the Martin Marty Seminar at the University of Chicago Divinity School (led by Frank Reynolds and Clark W. Gilpin) for reading and providing feedback on various parts of my drafts. I especially thank the 2003–2004 fellows of the Women's Studies in Religion Program at Harvard Divinity School, a program directed by Ann Braude, for the wonderful scholarly exchanges we shared. I also thank Bob Antonio, Shirley Harkess, and the members of the Hall Center gender workshop at the University of Kansas for reading portions of my manuscript.

I must acknowledge a number of individuals in Seoul for their invaluable assistance in helping to facilitate my fieldwork and research;

these include Dr. Yong-Hak Kim, the late Dr. Linsu Kim, Dr. Yi Man-Yŏl, Dr. Sang Jin Han, as well as the staff members of various departments at Yonsei University, Ewha University, and of the National Council of Churches in Korea. I owe a special debt to Moon-Sook Lee for her wonderful friendship and her deep insights about Korean Christianity and women's issues. Stateside, special thanks go to Timothy Lee for offering useful research contacts and insights about Korean Christianity, particularly at the beginning stages of this research, and for generously responding to my numerous, pesky queries through the final stages of book preparation. I would also like to thank Nancy Abelmann for her particularly astute evaluation of my book manuscript and for being supportive of my various research endeavors over the years.

I would like to express my appreciation to my editors at the Harvard University Asia Center. I especially thank William Hammell for his skillful copy-editing and for his patience and even-handed handling of the book production process through its publication. Finally, I thank the anonymous reviewers of my book manuscript and articles related to this research for helping to make this a far better book than it would otherwise have been.

This book has been a long journey and my most profound gratitude goes to friends and family members close to me who have supported my scholarly endeavors—financially, morally, emotionally—from my earliest years. I would sincerely like to thank my long-time friends Hilary Dunst and Jaesoon Rhee both for the many stimulating conversations we had regarding gender, Korea, and Christianity and for their emotional support during difficult times. Special thanks are due to my aunt and her family in Seoul for providing me with a home away from home during fieldwork; the value of my aunt's assistance in matters big and small while I lived in South Korea cannot be measured. Last but not least, I must express my deepest appreciation and love for my husband and partner Cornell H. Fleischer, who not only read, edited, and commented upon innumerable versions of this manuscript, ever without a word of complaint, but served as a tireless sounding board and cheerleader for this project.

I must end with the acknowledgment of the two individuals who are most responsible for making this book a reality: my mother Chong Dongyaw and my father Chong Hanchae. The infinite sense of gratitude and debt I feel toward them are beyond words. I cannot imagine being blessed with parents who could have been more supportive, patient, and loving through all of my academic endeavors; it is only because of their unwavering support, both practical and emotional, and their unshakable belief in me over the years, that this project was able to reach its conclusion.

Contents

List of Tables   xiii

Note to the Reader   xiv

Introduction   1

1   Entering the Field: Protestant Evangelicalism in Korea   14
    A Brief History   *15*
    The Contemporary Picture: Beliefs, Practices, and Culture   *24*
    Setting and Method   *32*
    A Note on Ethnography   *39*

2   Women's Conversion and the Contradictions of
    Contemporary Gender and Family Relations   48
    The Economic "Miracle" and the Quandaries
      of Compressed Development   *53*
    The Ideology and Structure of Neo-Confucian Patriarchy   *58*
    Changes and Contradictions in Family
      and Gender after World War II   *63*
    Women's Domestic Dilemmas   *74*
    Conclusion   *80*

3   Search for Release, Search for Healing:
    Deliverance through Spiritual Practice   82
    Pathways to Conversion   *84*
    "Opening-Up" the Self   *95*
    The Power of Surrender   *99*
    Love, Forgiveness, and Empowerment   *104*
    Conclusion   *109*

4 Negotiating Women's Space:
   Community, Autonomy, and Empowerment   110
       From "Helpmate" to "Kitchen Herd" 112
       Women's Space, Women's Community 117
       In Quest of Recognition: God's Work and Status Rewards 121
       Confidence and Fearlessness: Toward Internal Transformation 126
       Self-Cultivation and Learning 131
       Conclusion 133

5 Bargaining with Patriarchy:
   The Politics of Submission and Gender   135
       Domesticating Willful Women:
           The Evangelical Ideology of Family and Gender 136
       The Paradox of Submission 148
       Conclusion 170

6 Women's Redomestication and the Question of Consent   171
       The Two Sides of Religious Power 171
       Explaining Consent 176

   Conclusion   188
       Women and Evangelicalism in South Korea:
           Blessing or Burden? 189
       The Politics of Resistance and Consent 194
       Of Women, Gender, Modernity, and the Future
           of Korean Evangelicalism 196

Reference Matter

   Notes   203
   Bibliography   239
   Index   257

Tables

1   Educational Attainment in South Korea and Taiwan,
    1970–1990   65
2   Employment Status Distribution by Age among Urban
    Married Women in South Korea and Taiwan   71

Note to the Reader

All translations in this book are my own, unless otherwise indicated. In transliterating Korean words, I employ the Revised Romanization system; however, I have retained the McCune-Reischauer system for names of Korean individuals and authors, place names, and other types of proper nouns. All personal names are given in Korean order (with family name first), unless the individual's name is more widely known in another form (e.g., Syngman Rhee).

Deliverance and Submission

EVANGELICAL WOMEN
AND THE NEGOTIATION OF
PATRIARCHY IN SOUTH KOREA

INTRODUCTION

As one rides the train in the evening in Seoul and looks out of the window as the scenery races by, one can observe a most striking sight: countless red neon crosses dotting the hilly landscape like thousands of fireflies. Watching these bright red crosses blurring by, one is left to wonder how there could be so many churches in one place; crosses seem to be atop every other building on the cityscape, all fiercely competing for attention. Walking around some of Seoul's residential neighborhoods, one seems to find a church practically on every other block—some in majestic stand alone structures, and others as storefront operations occupying a floor or a section in one of the gray, generic office buildings ubiquitous to the city.

For anyone visiting Seoul, these initial visual impressions of the city help to capture something of the unique reality of Seoul's religious landscape. Present-day Seoul is a city of churches, the numbers and density of which would not fail to provoke amazement in any observer. First introduced from the United States in the late 1800s, evangelical Protestantism—to which I will refer herein simply as evangelicalism—began its vigorous expansion in South Korea starting in the early 1960s, exploding in the 1970s and 1980s.[1] Membership numbers for evangelical churches, which constitute the vast majority of Protestant churches in South Korea, have surged, from a little over 500,000 adherents in the 1950s to 6.5 million by 1985, growing more than ten times in three decades. As of 1997, the number of Protestants was estimated to be over 12 million, over 21 percent of South Korea's population, with over

33,000 churches around the country and about 40,000 pastors (Gallup Korea 1998: 164–67). Together with Catholics, estimated to comprise about a third of the Christian population, Christians now constitute the largest religious group in South Korea.[2]

South Korean evangelicalism, however, has not only distinguished itself for its impressive rate of growth, but for the size of its churches, some of which are now the largest in the world. South Korea currently boasts the world's largest congregation, the Yeoido Full Gospel Church, and the world's largest Presbyterian, Baptist, and Methodist congregations.[3] South Korean evangelicalism, just as importantly, is notable in another respect: the particular fervor and devotional enthusiasm with which many of its adherents seem to approach the religion. Reflecting what one scholar has called its "intensely practical and devotional bent" (Lee 1996: 234), South Korean evangelicals have developed a dedication to a range of devotional practices—such as frequent and fervent prayers, strict observance of the Sabbath, dedicated Bible study, regular tithing, and revival meetings—with an intensity difficult to match anywhere around the world.[4]

A fascinating phenomenon in and of itself, the remarkable success of evangelicalism in post–World War II South Korea has drawn a number of efforts by scholars to explain its "puzzling" nature.[5] Echoing the analyses of some earlier works on the growth of Protestantism in Latin America,[6] many of these studies have tended to offer broad historical or macro-sociological explanations, locating the causes of evangelicalism's ascendance in South Korea within the dislocating socio-cultural conditions generated by the "late-late" developmental and industrialization process of the 1960s and 1970s. According to these explanations, the appeal of evangelicalism for many ordinary Koreans lay in its capacity to provide a kind of spiritual and material "refuge" for those suffering the effects of innumerable social and economic ills, including poverty, despair, and a sense of urban anomie. Evangelical churches helped by offering community, practical aid, enduring values, and hope through the prospect of other-worldly salvation.

Although useful as a starting point for thinking about the success of Korean evangelicalism, these macro-level explanations succeed only in offering us a limited understanding of the South Korean evangelical phenomenon. Very few of these studies are rooted in an on-the-ground analysis of the converts' experiences and the conversion processes that can help to capture both the uniqueness and complexities of South Korean evangelicalism and its distinctive success in East Asia. The effort to understand the special character and impact of Korean evangelicalism, in particular, has been marred by a persistent neglect of the experiences of women. Not only do women constitute the majority— estimated at anywhere between 60 to 75 percent—of the Protestant population, but their fervent spirituality, institutional dedication, and evangelical zeal have been the driving forces behind the expansion and maintenance of Korean evangelical churches.

Based on sixteen months of ethnographic fieldwork in two evangelical churches in Seoul, this book attempts to correct this lack of attention by investigating the meaning of—and the reasons behind— the involvement of contemporary middle-class women in South Korean evangelicalism and tracing the consequences of their conversion. Utilizing an ethnographic mode of research and analysis, an approach that allows us to capture the unique character of Korean evangelical women's religiosity by attending closely to the women's own words, experiences, and perspectives, this study not only brings to light the relevance of women to Korean evangelicalism but helps provide a fuller picture of the success of the evangelical movement in South Korea.

In addition to incorporating the dimension of gender into the analysis of Korean evangelicalism, this focus on women has another key aim: addressing the important sociological question or the apparent "paradox" of the involvement of women in contemporary conservative-fundamentalist religious movements. The growing attraction to, and support for, many varieties of conservative-fundamentalist religious groups among women around the world has become an increasing focus of attention in recent years. From studies of women in American evangelical and fundamentalist groups to Pentecostal women in Latin America and women of traditionalist Islam, a growing body of literature attempts to explicate this important global phenomenon. Why are so many women, across classes and cultures, enthusiastically joining and supporting religions that advocate patriarchal structures of authority and morality, and therefore, seem designed to perpetuate their subordination?

Owing to a unique set of historical and social factors, Korean evangelicalism has, over the last century, developed into a highly patriarchal religion, one that embraces both theologically and culturally a highly conservative, in many cases fundamentalist, belief system (Lee 2006; Hong, Won, and Kim 1966; Ro and Nelson 1995). In regard to gender and family relations in particular, a majority of Korean evangelical churches espouse a traditionalist model that upholds female submission and conventional gender roles—a model that is rooted, as we will see, in an amalgam of Confucian and evangelical conceptions of the ideal family and gender order. In spite of this, contemporary Korean women, many of them well educated and self-identified as middle class, participate in this religion with a degree of fervor and a sense of dedication difficult to observe in many other locales. By interrogating the tensions and "paradox" implied in the attraction between this rigorously patriarchal religion and a class of "modern," well-educated women, this study of middle-class Korean evangelical women, then, offers a fruitful opportunity to examine further the meaning of contemporary women's involvement in religious traditionalism, promising a deeper understanding of its dynamics and appeal.

An inquiry into the question of contemporary women's attraction to religious traditionalism is an endeavor that engages some of the most important and enduring sociological questions. With regard to religion, it directly addresses the long-standing debate on secularization and the question of religion's role in the modern world, especially in relation to modernizing social transformations across societies. With regard to gender, it sheds light upon the varied nature of women's engagement with contemporary patriarchies, the dynamics of changing gender relations, and the creative means by which women negotiate the challenges of modernity and social change. Through an examination of the unique engagement of middle-class women with the evangelical religion in South Korea, this book will show both how these issues play out in the context of modern South Korea, and consider how the South Korean case illuminates the issue of women and religious traditionalism in general.

Among the important issues central to women and religious traditionalism with which this book is concerned—the relationship of religion to modernities, the nature of religion's role in contemporary women's struggles, and the dynamics of the conversion process—a question of particular interest is the understanding of the complex and contradictory impact of traditionalist beliefs and practices on the lives of women, as well as the patterns of resistance and accommodation in women's engagement with religious patriarchy. With regard to South Korea in particular, this book not only clarifies the place and workings of the evangelical religion in contemporary society by elucidating the dimension of gender, but also, by depicting the struggles of women in the context of their daily lives, offers another important window through which to view South Korea's recent socio-cultural transformative processes and its engagement with modernity.

Women and Religious Traditionalism: Power, Agency, Resistance

When I embarked on this study of Korean evangelical women, I benefited from a growing body of emerging research on women and traditionalist religious movements that had begun to provide a wealth of valuable insights into the topic. Collectively, one major contribution made by these studies has been the examination of women's motivations for joining traditionalist religious groups. Analyzing the actions and choices of women within the sociological and historical context of each society, these studies suggest that the involvement of contemporary women in patriarchally-oriented religious groups can be seen in large part as a reaction to the problems and challenges generated by the forces of modernity and modernizing socio-cultural transformation that have affected different societies, especially those affecting family and gender relations.[7]

For instance, in studies focusing on conservative-fundamentalist religious groups in America such as evangelical/fundamentalist Protestantism and Orthodox Judaism, various researchers have discovered that the attraction of middle-class women to conservatively-oriented religions is motivated in part by the perceived "failures" of feminism and the values of modern individualism to bring women stable domestic life, meaningful relationships, and a sense of identity.[8] Given that many of these women are joining groups that articulate the problems of family, gender, and sexual and social morality as central concerns, it is clear that these issues reflect the focal concerns of women. In works focusing on Latin American evangelicalism, the major finding is that the growing involvement of lower-class women in evangelical or Pentecostal religions in many Latin American countries is driven by severe social and economic dislocations stemming from rapid societal changes, and represents efforts by women to cope with the economic insecurities and the breakdown of family structures brought about by these changes.[9]

In addition to illuminating the motivations behind conversion, these studies further contribute by revealing the significance and impact of these religions on the lives of women. Across societies, traditionalist religions appeal to women as important sources of support as women struggle with economic difficulties and domestic upheavals; these religions, for instance, offer material, social, and spiritual resources to aid women achieve stability in these spheres. But because traditionalist religions also advocate conservative beliefs regarding gender, they have been viewed as oppressive to women. By revealing the actual complexities involved in women's religious engagements in different societies and religious traditions, many recent studies have helped challenge such conventional interpretations. One central insight here has been that contrary to simply functioning as a source of oppression for women, religious patriarchy can actually serve women in surprising ways—namely, as "flexible resources" for negotiating gender relations and pursuing domestic interests and as vehicles in women's gender and domestic struggles.

Explorations of American evangelical and fundamentalist women, for instance, have shown that women's accommodation to the church's conservative teachings on gender, especially the ideology of "submission," cannot be seen as a simple capitulation to patriarchy, but rather as an effort to re-negotiate gender relations and achieve marital stability, especially by reforming men.[10] Scholars such as Judith Stacey (1990) have, moreover, directed our attention to the often "conscious," "strategic," and "instrumental" nature of such efforts, highlighting the importance of women's agency. Others have called attention to the discrepancy that exists among women between formal ideology and actual practice.[11] Indeed, more recent studies on evangelicals have not only underscored such discrepancies—a work by Gallagher and Smith (1999) labels this "symbolic traditionalism and pragmatic egalitarianism"—but have highlighted the diversity that exists among evangelicals with regard to their church's ideology of submission (Bartkowski 2001).

Going beyond the analysis of traditionalist religions as resources in women's efforts to negotiate patriarchal relations, many of these works have also brought to light some of the "liberating" aspects of traditionalist religions, pointing to the ways in which these religions open up spaces for subtle forms of dissent and resistance on the part of women against patriarchal structures. Research on American Orthodox Jewish women (Davidman 1991; Kaufman 1989), for example, has highlighted the unexpected ways that orthodox religious beliefs and practices serve as a vehicle of empowerment for women, not only in the ways these beliefs help women reconstitute stable identities and kinship relations, but also through "feminist" reinterpretations of traditionalist ideology that valorizes womanhood and reaffirms female power.[12] Outside of the American setting, works on Latin American Pentecostal women have been especially notable for emphasizing the liberating potential of traditionalist religions, especially as a resource for raising female status and subverting patriarchal relations within both domestic and religious spheres.[13] Calling attention to the "revolutionary" potential of Colombian Pentecostalism for reforming gender roles, Brusco (1995), for example, has gone as far as to call Colombian evangelicalism a "revolutionary" and "strategic" form of women's collective action that has been even more effective than Western feminism in raising women's status and altering gender role behavior.[14]

In addition to illuminating the factors that shape women's decisions to embrace religious traditionalism, this body of work, then, has made important contributions in helping us better understand the surprising ways traditionalist religions are relevant in the lives of women. Their major contribution lies in uncovering the phenomenon that while conservative religions, across societies, serve as important instruments in women's efforts to deal with domestic and social instabilities, they are also availed by women in an array of creative and unexpected ways, including as sites of gender negotiation and resistance. By emphasizing the issues of women's dissent, agency, and the complexities inherent in the operations of religious power, these studies have helped problematize the view of traditionalist religions as monolithic sources of gender domination, as well as of women as simple "dupes" of false consciousness, moving our understanding of traditionalist religions in sophisticated new directions.[15]

By capturing and delineating the nature of and meaning inscribed in the religious beliefs and practices of Korean evangelical women, this study significantly expands our perspective on these issues, opening up new avenues for understanding. The Korean case accomplishes this by affirming some of the current findings as well as challenging them in important ways. As we will see, the dynamics of religious engagement of the women found in this study, while displaying some commonalities with women in other cultural settings, are also distinctive, both in the ways evangelicalism is appropriated by these women and its consequences, offering significant implications for altering our current understandings of women and religious traditionalism.

To begin, this study will show that Korean women's motivations for religious involvement are driven by a distinctive set of gender dilemmas that are generated within the historical, structural, and ideological context of a unique patriarchal system and its contradictions. This not only influences directly the character of women's religious engagement, but its impact on their lives. In particular, the Korean case highlights the complex interplay that holds between the "liberating" and "oppressive" dimensions of women's religious engagement and its consequences—a situation that poses interesting challenges to current interpretative frameworks regarding women and religious traditionalism.

I begin my argument by suggesting that the motivations behind conversions of evangelical women must be understood within the framework of a complex set of problems affecting contemporary family and gender relations—which I broadly describe as crises or contradictions of modern patriarchy—that have been generated by the tumultuous social and cultural transformations in post–World War II South Korea. The reasons for and the anatomy of this crisis are highly complex, but they have their roots in the growing contradictions between the powerful social and economic transformative forces that are rapidly liberalizing the wider culture as well as the subjectivities of women, and a social system that continues to uphold key patriarchal structures at the level of both society and family. This system of modern patriarchy, however, does not simply represent the survival of "tradition" but one that has been reconfigured and reconstituted within the contemporary social context by political design, primarily through the efforts of a patriarchal-developmental state concerned to ensure social stability in the process of nation-building. For the generation of married middle-class housewives investigated in this study, many of whom are caught in a welter of objective and subjective contradictions induced by the fluctuating and conflicting topography of "tradition," "modernity," even "post-modernity," this situation has given rise to a highly challenging set of tensions and dilemmas, especially within the domestic sphere.

One major thrust of my argument is that the church participation of evangelical women found in these pages can in many ways be seen as a response to these crises and contradictions of the contemporary South Korean gender and family system, an effort on the part of women to cope with and resolve an array of domestic and personal conflicts stemming from the predicaments posed by modern patriarchal relations. Although I believe that this cultural crisis does pose a number of dilemmas that are broadly common to women across classes in South Korea, my main concern in this book is to examine and illuminate the nature, meaning, and consequences of this crisis for middle-class women in particular, and their responses to them. Indeed, despite some of the basic cultural and experiential similarities shared by women across different social groups that I have observed throughout this research, the specific differences reflected in the situations and predicaments of women along class lines—as related especially to the divergences in class-specific gender ideologies, power structures, and how these ideologies are actually practiced and lived—render the experiences of middle-class women in many ways distinctive and suitable for separate analysis.

Although I make no claims that the women's actions are driven solely by conscious or instrumental motives, I demonstrate that many of the women in this study seek and experience their churches and the evangelical belief system for the ways they help them cope with their domestic distress and suffering. I have found, for instance, that the churches help women deal with their domestic situations by providing ways to pursue spiritual healing and a sense of empowerment, and by offering a space in which to experience a measure of psychic and social autonomy from the family. As such, the Korean evangelical church can first and foremost be seen as a vehicle in women's struggle for deliverance from gender oppression, even for resisting patriarchal authority.

Despite the liberating impulse that is clearly evident in women's religiosity, the engagement of Korean women with evangelical beliefs and practices, however, is at the same time characterized by acute contradictions that symbolize the significant tensions between their desire for liberation from the patriarchal structures and an impulse toward acquiescence. Indeed, along with their efforts at resistance against the patriarchal system through the spiritual and social spaces provided by the church, as well as through their creative engagement with religious patriarchy, we also find among many women a striking willingness to accommodate to the church's ideologies of gender, especially as a strategy for resolving their domestic contradictions. Exploring these tensions, which are revealed through a complex interplay of emancipation and subordination, resistance and accommodation, will be a major focus of this work.

Attending to the tensions in Korean evangelical women's religiosity poses interesting theoretical challenges to the problem of women and religious traditionalism. I contend that the recent interpretative emphasis on "resistance" and "liberating" dimensions of women's engagement with religious patriarchy has been fruitful; but at the same time, it has deflected attention in some crucial ways from other central dynamics of this engagement. In particular, the crucial problems of patriarchal power and domination tend to be elided, along with the thorny issue of women's assent to patriarchal structures and authority. Although the recent scholarly attention to the dimensions of protest or resistance in women's actions has been valuable for achieving a more thorough understanding of the nature of women's engagement with religious traditionalisms, the acute tensions that exist between "resistance" and the more accommodative aspects of women's actions—aspects that raise questions both of the ambiguity of women's intentions/subjectivities and the consequences of their actions with regard to patriarchy—have been explored less thoroughly.[16]

In important ways, these interpretive approaches reflect and draw on recent developments in social scientific and feminist theorizing, developments that have been characterized by a distinctive concern with and emphasis on the issues of agency, resistance, and praxis in the analysis of subordinate groups. These theoretical approaches, broadly characterized as "poststructural" and influenced by the ideas of such thinkers as Michel Foucault (1990), Antonio Gramsci (1992), and Raymond Williams (1973), pivot around "de-centered" conceptions of power, where culture is a field of both the inscription of and resistance to power (Rubin 1996). Furthermore, this line of theorizing draws its inspiration from what Sherry Ortner (1984) has labeled "practice theory," a form of theorizing that emerged in the 1980s that embraces a more "action-based approach" to analyzing human behavior centered on the "doing subject" (seen as an active strategizing/calculating agent) and what Ortner calls the "strategic model" of human action.

Although these approaches have been extremely valuable in comprehending the complexities of human actions and motivations, the engagement of women with religious patriarchy is a complex matter, the particular dynamics and effects of which must be understood as shaped within specific socio-historical contexts and regimes of patriarchy. The Korean case demonstrates that we must comprehend not only the motivations behind women's turn to religious traditionalism, but also the particular forms of their religious engagement and its consequences as products of each society's specific socio-historical processes—of social change, modernity, and the structure and logic of gender/family relations—that give shape to the distinctive gendered subjectivities, motivations, and interests of women.

Hence, this book will be concerned with one final crucial issue: the question of women's "consent" to patriarchy. The issue of consent, in general, remains an undertheorized problem in gender studies (Anyon 1983; Baron 1991; Barrett 1997). Although there has been a great deal of attention in recent years in the human and social sciences to the issue of resistance among the subordinated—revealing a tendency toward what Abu-Lughod (1990) refers to as the "romanticization" of resistance—there have been far less serious explorations of the question of consent, that is, why the "oppressed" would assent to and participate in perpetuating their oppression and subordinate status, even while they resist such oppressive structures.[17] This study will investigate women's consent through a close, socially contextualized analysis of the Korean family/gender system, namely, the configurations of the dominant gender ideology and the workings of power within this gender and family regime. Attending, then, to how women's subjectivities, motives, and interests are formed and configured within such a structural context, we will move toward understanding the complex investments made by many contemporary middle-class Korean women regarding patriarchy, and the workings of their feminine agency.

In Chapter 1, I present a brief overview of the history and character of Korean evangelicalism and describe the fieldwork setting and my research methods. In Chapter 2, I offer an analysis of the larger sociological/cultural context and conditions within which evangelical participation of Korean women might be understood, particularly the recent transformations in the social and cultural milieu that are responsible for the important alterations in the relations of family and gender in South Korea. After elucidating the character of the Korean Neo-Confucian family/gender system and its transformations through intensified engagement with Western modernity and the forces of globalization, I describe how some of these changes have helped destabilize the current patriarchal system and have heightened the conflicts and contradictions within family and gender relations.

In Chapters 3 and 4, I present my observations and analyses of some of the central dimensions of women's evangelical beliefs and practices, which I argue constitute the primary forms of evangelical women's response to their domestic contradictions and conflicts. In these chapters, I focus on the dynamics of the spiritual and institutional aspects of women's religious participation, showing how these serve as central vehicles in women's efforts to negotiate—and even resist—the restrictions and injuries of the contemporary family system.

In Chapter 3, I focus specifically on the spiritual aspect of women's gender struggle and its role as a resource in enabling women to transcend and find relief from domestic suffering and oppression; I show how this occurs mainly through spiritual healing, which offers women not only a release from suffering but a sense of empowerment that helps them reconstitute their identities. Chapter 4 focuses on the institutional aspects of women's religious participation, and the role this participation plays in helping them negotiate their domestic lives by providing a sense of social and psychic autonomy. Through dedicated church participation, women often appropriate the church as a social space in which to carve out a measure of autonomy and independence from the constraints of the domestic sphere and from their husbands. This is accomplished by making the church a focal point of social interaction and female-centered community, as well as a site in which to pursue "learning" and limited kinds of self-achievement and fulfillment.

In Chapter 5, I turn my attention to women's engagement with traditionalist ideologies of gender and family as articulated by the church, particularly their responses to the church's efforts at female "redomestication." Focusing in particular on the dynamics and meaning of women's accommodation to the ideology of submission/obedience, especially as a strategy for negotiating their domestic situations, I show that submission must be seen as a complex process characterized by attempts at accommodation and resistance. In Chapter 6, I explore the larger implications of this dynamic on the religiosity of evangelical women and then address the issue of "consent" to religious patriarchy. Here, I examine some of the major motivations behind women's normative consent to the principles of patriarchal relations, especially as they relate to women's interests and gender subjectivities as these are embedded in and shaped by the ideological, structural, and power configurations of the Korean family/gender regime.

ONE

Entering the Field:

Protestant Evangelicalism in Korea

When I was a little girl growing up in Seoul in the early 1970s, I lived in a house that was located directly across the street from a large Presbyterian church. In the landscape of my early memory, this church looms quite large; not only did this church visually dominate the view from our windows, but my family would wake up every morning to the sounds of hymn singing and of fervent prayers that began at dawn. When I went back to this neighborhood in my visit back to Korea fifteen years later, our old house, to my disappointment, had long since been torn down and was nowhere to be seen, but the church, the place where I made my first acquaintance with Christianity, had been rebuilt into a gigantic modernist structure at least five times larger than its previous size and was thriving as never before.

In my mind, the remarkable development of this church from my childhood neighborhood symbolizes, in many ways, the impressive development of Protestantism as a whole in South Korea, the only East Asian country in which Protestantism, or Christianity in general, has experienced such spectacular success. As mentioned in the Introduction, Korean Protestantism has undergone extraordinary growth since the 1960s; the present chapter will provide a more detailed look at the evolution of Korean evangelicalism in order to better understand its current form and character, then move on to a discussion of the setting for my research and my approach to fieldwork.

A Brief History

The history of the Protestant mission in Korea officially begins in the mid-1880s with the arrival of a small group of American missionaries.[1] To understand the success of Protestantism in Korea, it is important to grasp first how the religion started and took root during this initial phase of expansion through the efforts of Western Christian missionaries, who, their industrious efforts notwithstanding, were the fortunate beneficiaries of a highly favorable set of political, social, and cultural circumstances for missionizing that held in Korea.

By the latter half of the nineteenth century, Korea was becoming known widely around the world as the "hermit kingdom" because of its centuries of self-imposed isolation. But in a world characterized by increasing imperialist aggression, resistance was becoming futile; Korea was finally forced to open itself to the world, first through the Ganghwa Treaty with Japan in 1876, followed soon by agreements with the United States in 1882 and a number of European nations. Korea soon became a battleground upon which the expansionist ambitions of its three neighboring powers—Japan, Russia, and China—were played out, with Japan annexing Korea in 1910 as its colony for the next 35 years. This early period, which ushered in the demise of a small but proud country with several millennia of history, was one of the most difficult and tumultuous in Korea's history. The Yi dynasty (1392–1910), which had been in power for about five hundred years, was wracked by various domestic problems—among them political corruption and factionalism—and was unable to withstand the internal and external forces that were pressing it toward collapse.

Unlike the persecuted Catholics who preceded them by a century, the Protestant missionaries made their entry into Korea under conditions that were highly advantageous for missionizing efforts.[2] Of these, the most important was the fact that the missionaries found themselves among a populace broken up and ground down by chaos and sociopolitical upheaval, and who were open and receptive to new religious messages, especially those coming from the West. This receptivity was driven by several factors. By the time the first group of American Protestant missionaries arrived in Korea two years after the signing of the diplomatic treaty with the United States, the Korean government, for the sake of its national survival, had already abandoned its isolationist policies. Along with this, a dramatic shift in attitudes and sentiment was occurring among the Koreans, especially among the elites, in regard to the outside world and the West. Despondent over the plight of the country, which was increasingly being attributed to the "backwardness" of Korean society and culture, many of the country's establishment elites came to welcome and embrace Western knowledge and culture as vital to national interests and survival. This had significant consequences for the missionaries.

Besides profiting from the opportunities provided by Korea's internal problems, the missionaries benefited from the positive perception of Protestantism among many Koreans as a conduit of Western learning and modernity. Indeed, as various aspects of the traditional culture, particularly Confucianism, were becoming delegitimized and viewed as the culprit for the nation's woeful plight, many Koreans welcomed the Protestant religion for its potential as an "enlightening" influence on Korean society.[3] To account for Protestantism's favorable image and reception in Korea, we must, in addition, consider another important factor: whereas Christian missions in other parts of Asia, such as Japan and China, were associated with American imperialist ambitions, Protestantism's acceptance in Korea was facilitated by the fact that the United States was not perceived as a threatening force, but rather as a remote and benign presence lacking in imperialist designs on Korea.

The missionaries focused their efforts in Korea on three major areas: church-founding, medical work, and education (D. Clark 1986: 8). Direct church-establishment and training of a native pastorate were primary concerns to the missionaries, but medicine and education were two important vehicles through which they pursued evangelization.[4] Working as medical doctors and teachers, the missionaries built modern hospitals and educational institutions, winning many converts across social classes.[5] They also engaged in extensive social welfare work among the poor. The schools taught children letters, science, as well as Scripture, and served in particular as centers for spreading Christian teachings. These schools became the loci of education for the Korean literati, who often turned to Christianity to learn English and Western knowledge. A large numbers of Korea's elite and leaders were educated in mission schools (D. Clark 1986: 8).

Indeed, because of the ready acceptance of Western culture and Christianity by the members of the country's upper class, it can be reasonably argued that the initial success of Protestant missionizing in Korea lies in its acceptance by the elites. Harking back even earlier, one observer (Hunt 1980: 82) notes that the Protestant mission in Korea indeed "began with the court." This refers, of course, to one of the most oft-told events from the lore of early Korean Christian missions: when Horace Allen, the first Presbyterian missionary to Korea and a medical doctor, managed to win the favor of the royal court by healing a serious injury of the reigning queen's nephew, an important figure within the Yi government.[6] Earning the gratitude of King Gojong with this feat, Allen was appointed as the King's personal physician and given permission in 1885 to open and operate a small hospital—which later became the renowned Severance Hospital in Seoul—enabling Protestant missionary work to begin in Korea without persecution.

To comprehend the success of Protestant missions in Korea, however, we must not only understand Protestantism's appeal to the elites, but its immense appeal to the ordinary population. Although Protestantism was attractive to the elites for its association with Western learning and modernity, it seems to have been for the destitute, illiterate, and exploited masses a particularly meaningful vehicle for dealing with poverty and despair. In addition to the welfare work the churches were carrying out among the poor, evangelicalism, with its simple and unequivocal message of salvation in a better afterlife and deliverance from pain and suffering in return for devotion to God, seems to have had a powerful appeal for the ordinary people. In fact, early missionary writings are replete with accounts of the extraordinary spiritual receptivity of the Korean people during this period. The following observation by a missionary provides one example:

We found the country in a very ready condition and people everywhere who seemed simply waiting for an invitation to come into the church, and as never before ready to buy books and to listen to the preached Word. . . . It was not necessary to go out to seek an audience. All that we had to do was to stay quietly in our rooms at the inns and we would have a constant succession of inquirers coming to us. We often could not get the rest we needed on account of the large number of inquirers. (Bull 1906: 168–69; quoted in T. Lee 1996: 36)

Another missionary wrote:

The general unrest and lack of something to which they may cling is causing
the people to turn to the Missionary and the message he has; and they are
trying to find out if we have something which they can trust. On my last visit
to the country I often heard the expression, "Uijihal got domochi Eobso"
(There is altogether no place to lean on).

(Moose 1906: 51–52; quoted in T. Lee 1996: 35)

Not surprisingly, the missionaries considered Korea an evangelistic bo-
nanza. Aware of the exceptional receptivity of the common people, the
missionaries consciously pursued from the beginning a policy designed
to target the poor, and particularly women, who were seen as the oppressed of the oppressed. Also vital to the missionaries' efforts to reach
the ordinary people was an early translation of the Bible into the native
vernacular—using the native Korean alphabet *hangeul*—and its aggressive dissemination.[7]

Many converts were won through the technique of rural itineration,
in which the missionaries and local volunteers spread out across the
country, opening small stations in all the provinces.[8] Importantly, a
great number of converts were also gained through a series of highly
spiritual revivals that swept the nation at the turn of the twentieth century, including the first Great Revival of 1907 in Pyongyang and the
second in 1909.[9] In particular, the 1907 revival is seen as a watershed
event in the history of Korean Christianity, an event that supposedly set
much of the tone, character, and "religious habits" of Korean Protestantism (G. Han 1994: 58; Moffett 1962: 52). Occurring during a time of
great national crisis—Korea finally became a protectorate of Japan in
1905 after Japan pushed both China and Russia off of Korean soil—
these revivals seem to have held powerful attraction for people from all
walks of life (I. Kim 1985; Martin 1990; Suh 1985).

An additional reason that should be mentioned behind the success
of Protestantism in Korea, both in the past and today, has been the
particular effectiveness of the tradition and practice of institutional self-
reliance, both financially and in terms of local leadership. Following
a missionizing method—called the Nevius Plan—that emphasized the
principles of self-government, self-support, and self-propagation, the
missionaries encouraged Koreans to pursue church plantings and expansion through tough self-reliance.[10] In addition to the churches' ef-

forts to be independent from foreign funding and leadership, the practice of aggressive lay evangelism by ordinary members, as is evident today, was also central to the expansion of Protestantism around the country.[11] Indeed, the special "evangelical zeal" of Korean Christians, together with the self-reliance of Korean churches, is often considered one of the primary reasons behind Korean churches' rapid expansion (see also B. Kim 1985: 70; J. Kim 1996: 169).

From these early days, women played a central role in evangelizing activities. Not only were women the most responsive and enthusiastic of converts,[12] but once converted, they often became especially active as *jeondo buin*, commonly known as "Bible women" (but literally translated as "evangelizing lady"), whose central tasks were evangelism and church work.[13] Initially trained and employed by female missionaries who had no choice but to rely on women to reach other women, these Bible women were a vital part of the itinerant evangelists who traveled the country not only selling Bibles, teaching catechisms, and spreading the Gospel, but visiting the sick, teaching other women how to read, and giving them practical instruction on matters such as health and hygiene. Though clearly subordinated in status relative to men within the church and frequently denied due credit for many of their accomplishments, female evangelists were instrumental in founding scores of new churches throughout the country.[14]

In the earlier phases of the Japanese occupation (1910–45), Christianity gained a new kind of legitimacy and following among the Korean people as it became associated with an emerging nationalism, especially among the elites. Embraced with particular enthusiasm by young Western- and Japanese-educated reformers impatient to set Korea on the road to modernization and independence, Christianity was adopted by many Korean intellectuals as a political vehicle of nascent Korean nationalism. Although the Korean nationalist struggle was neither endorsed nor opposed by the conservative missionaries, who endeavored to remain neutral for fear of antagonizing the colonial government,[15] some Korean Christian leaders were prominent in societies organized to awaken Korean resistance to colonization, and the church itself was seen by many as a refuge from Japanese rule. Many notable anti-Japanese freedom fighters were Christians.[16] Despite the missionaries' official policy of non-interference, these resistance activities gave Christianity and Christians an association with and prominent place in anti-Japanese efforts and the nationalist movement.

In the course of the Japanese occupation, Korean Christianity continued to expand, though, subject to systematic repression by the Japanese authorities, it suffered several bouts of decline.[17] The Japanese, apprehensive about the subversive potential of Christianity and the humanitarian efforts being made by the missionaries on behalf of Koreans, engaged in efforts to cripple the church and co-opt the missionaries throughout the occupation; their efforts to extirpate Christian associations and related educational institutions intensified after the 1930s.

In South Korea, as we will see, Protestantism began to experience its most dramatic expansion in the 1960s, some time after the liberation from Japan on August 15, 1945. Before we discuss this important period, we must first pay brief attention to what occurred in the decade after the Korean War (1950–53), as the events in this period had a significant impact on how Protestantism subsequently developed in Korea. The years following the liberation were supposed to be a period of reconstruction for the Korean church, as it attempted to reconstitute itself after the Japanese occupation and the ensuing Korean War; unfortunately, though, the 1950s were filled with strife and crisis for Korean Protestantism. Although the church was now largely independent of missionaries—most of them were forced to leave Korea toward the end of the Japanese occupation—it now had to cope with the legacy of Japanese policies regarding the church and the national division brought about by the Korean War. While Christians were being systematically repressed in North Korea by the communist regime, the church in South Korea underwent internecine conflicts and denominational schisms over theological matters, regional and personal rivalries, and other practical issues that are still felt among the churches today.

One of the major sources of this virulent intra- and interdenominational strife is the issue of the Shinto worship during the Japanese occupation (T. Lee 1996: 120; Oh 1995: 187). As part of its "cultural assimilation" policy in Korea, the Japanese colonial government began attempts in the 1930s to impose Shinto on the entire Korean populace.[18] Claiming that adherence to the Japanese state religion was a patriotic act and not a religious one, the Japanese authorities tried to impose the observance of Shinto ceremonies in all Christian churches and schools. Although many Christians resisted this decree—leading to the forced closure of many churches and Christian schools—others, often as whole denominations, were pressured to comply.[19] After the liberation, the conflict between those who supposedly resisted the Japanese policies and those who supposedly complied became one of the bitterest struggles and schisms within the Protestant church.

One legacy of this strife is the resulting intradenominational schisms that gave rise to numerous and painful divisions within some of the denominations that stand to this day. For example, the Presbyterian denomination was bitterly torn between "resisters" and "collaborators" after its forced capitulation to Japanese pressure in 1938. Between 1951 and 1959, the original body of the Presbyterian church split several times over Shinto and other issues, resulting in the present-day existence of four major Presbyterian denominations—one liberal, two conservative, and one ultra-conservative (in addition to over 60 other smaller Presbyterian denominations subsequently established).[20] The largest Methodist denomination divided twice but successfully reunited, and both the Baptist and Holiness churches were pulled apart by factional disputes.

To account for the particular severity of denominational splits in Korea, a number of other explanations attempt to move beyond the Shinto issue. Samuel Moffett (1962), pointing to some general theological and historical factors particular to Korea, offers the following view:

There is no question that the horrors of the Korean War, following so closely upon the persecutions of World War II, left Korea's Christians nervously and physically exhausted, introverted spiritually by their attempts to escape compromise, and isolated intellectually from developments in church in other lands. Others say that the reasons for division are to be found in what they claim are built-in weaknesses in the fabric of Korean Christianity—legalism, over-literal biblicism, and a doctrinaire creedalism that exalts orthodoxy at the expense of ethics. (117)

Others attribute the schismatic proclivities of Korean Protestantism to the earlier regional "divide and conquer" policies of the missionaries— whereby the different mission boards partitioned Korean land among themselves for evangelical work—which engendered intense religious regionalism, another major source of conflict in Korean Christianity during the 1930s and in the period following independence (Suh 1985: 13–14; G. Han 1994: 9, 89–91). Still others blame the divisions not on the West, but on the supposed national Korean character traits of fierce regional loyalties and factionalisms that are seen to have characterized many of Korea's royal dynasties in the past (Moffett 1962: 118). Despite this infighting, churches continued to grow rapidly in this period,[21] leading many to speculate whether the schisms actually helped to facilitate growth rather than hinder it.[22] Protestant missions and societies also began to proliferate during this period.

Korean Evangelicalism since 1960

The explosive growth of Protestantism in South Korea since the 1960s, coinciding with the country's "late-late" industrialization period, has inspired much puzzlement and amazement. The decades since the 1960s, however, have not only been characterized by a rapid proliferation of churches, but also by the emergence of "mega-churches." Although the majority of churches in South Korea are still small- to middle-sized, South Korea had, by 1984, the world's largest single church, Yeoido Full Gospel church, and by the end of 1992, 23 of the 50 largest churches in the world, including the largest, and the second largest, and the seventh, ninth, and tenth largest churches. That is, five out of the top ten largest churches in the world are located in South Korea.[23] In addition to church membership, the number of mission-sending organizations and missionaries surged during this period.[24] Moreover, in the three and a half decades after the Korean War, South Korea has staged some of the largest evangelistic gatherings in the world, with millions in attendance.[25]

As scholars have noted about Latin America, students of Korean Christianity have linked the phenomenal growth of Christianity in South Korea in the post–World War II era to the conditions generated by the rapid economic development process and the accompanying massive rural-to-urban migration. Eager to play "catch up" with the West, South Korea embarked on an intensive economic development plan that eventually resulted in the so-called economic "miracle" of South Korea, transforming Korea into one of the four "Asian Tigers." However, there were enormous social costs associated with this success. Aside from the continuous political oppression by the dictatorial regime which left many in the population politically alienated, massive urbanization and the regime's "growth-at-all-costs" policy generated tremendous social and economic instability, especially as people were uprooted from their traditional family structures and communities and left to cope with the chaos of a rapidly changing society. An environment of political insecurity, caused especially by the constant threat of invasion from the communist North, also contributed to the general feeling of insecurity and instability.

In a world filled with unpredictability, Protestant churches prolifer-ated in the urban areas in particular. First of all, they were one of the few existing voluntary organizations able to provide practical aid to people while offering a sense of consolation and comfort with their religious messages (Ahn 1985; B. Kim 1985: 68–70; W. G. Lee 1994; H. Park 1985: 55). The social function of churches was crucial as well; in the anomic environment of the cities, the churches provided a family-like community, as well as a clearly defined system of morality and meaning upon which people could anchor their existence. In sum, as David Mar-tin (1990) observes, these expanding churches offered "hope, therapy, community—and a network," helping people fend off the chaos and anomie of urban living (155).

Although a comprehensive explanation for the success of Korean Protestantism is beyond the scope of this book, one more important factor played a key role in rendering South Korea a particularly hospita-ble place for Protestantism: the cooperation of the state. It is no secret that Christianity enjoyed highly cooperative and mutually reinforcing re-lationships during the 1960s and 1970s with two pro-American political regimes: those of Syngman Rhee (Yi Seungman; 1948–60) and Park Chung Hee (1961–79).[26] Through the tacit consent of these govern-ments—in fact, Rhee himself was an American-educated Methodist with an American wife—who gave the churches freedom to expand provided they did not oppose the government, the Korean churches were able to take root and flourish. Furthermore, the United States was enjoying its status as an ally that "liberated" Korea from the Japanese, and Christi-anity prospered under this identification as well as with the fierce anti-communism fanned by the state (C. Park 2003; B. Kim 1985: 64). David Martin (1990) provides some insight:

After the Korean War, Protestantism was part of the link between the U.S. government and the authoritarian regimes of Rhee and Park. That bears on the question of economic development and Protestantism. These regimes placed economic advance before due democratic process, and for that purpose relied on a combination of Protestant quietism and those long-term elements in the Korean psyche which accepted authority provided it showed some paternalistic concern and, above all, gave evidence of success. Protestant fundamentalism helped prevent the political system from blowing up. (154–55)

It is important to note, however, that Korean Protestantism was not always politically quiescent. During critical periods between the 1960s and the 1980s, a number of Christian leaders and other activists were prominently involved in movements of opposition and protest against the government. However, most of these individuals belonged to the only major, but small, liberal denomination: the Presbyterian Church in the Republic of Korea (Gijang), the denomination that was formed upon its ouster from the original Presbyterian Assembly in 1954.[27] Even when the Christian activist base and its involvement in anti-government movements expanded considerably in the 1970s and 80s, liberal Christians consisted of only about one-fifteenth of the entire Christian population (as of 1979). The positions taken by these protesters, therefore, did not represent the majority within Protestantism. The Korean Protestant establishment was, for the most part, politically aligned with the ruling regime, adroitly utilizing the pro-Christian stances of the Rhee and Park regimes in their efforts to expand the church and carry out evangelical efforts.

Finally, the Korean churches received a huge boost by the North Korean Christian refugees who flooded to South Korea after the national division to escape violent religious persecution in the North. The North Korean Christians, known particularly for their religious zealousness and fervor, felt a keen sense of frustration and alienation as outsiders in the South, and were instrumental in the erection of many new churches both in cities and rural areas.[28]

The Contemporary Picture: Beliefs, Practices, and Culture

The rapid growth and frequent schisms in the development of Korean Protestantism have resulted in an astounding number of denominations; as of 1993, there were in total at least 92 denominations in South Korea, 61 of them Presbyterian.[29] As of 1998, Presbyterianism was by far the largest denomination in South Korea, with about 72.6 percent of the Protestant population; Methodists came in a distant second, with about 11.2 percent of the Protestant population (Gallup Korea 1998: 162); Pentecostal denominations, comprising several different denominations, constitute the third largest Protestant body in South Korea, with over half of them belonging to the Assemblies of God (Martin 1990); Baptists follow at about 3.6 percent (Gallup Korea 1998); other denominations round out the list, including the Church of Christ, Seventh Day Adventist, Salvation Army, Nazarene, Anglican, and Lutheran, along with small numbers of Mormons and Quakers. The church in Korea, for the most part, has now devolved to Korean control; that is, the Protestant denominations that developed under missionary guidance prior to World War II are now controlled by Korean governing bodies, although they cannot be said to be completely free from foreign funding and influence (D. Clark 1986: 2, 18, 21).[30]

Beliefs and Practices

Korean evangelicalism, as it stands in the present day, reflects an orientation that is largely conservative theologically and culturally, intensely devotional in terms of practices, and pervaded by a current of charismatic spirit and fervor. Theologically, Korean Protestantism has generally remained staunchly conservative, even "fundamentalist," for more than a century since its introduction.[31] The reasons for this conservatism are difficult to identify precisely, but many observers see it as deriving from a combination of the orthodox legacies of the early missionaries, the influence of native Confucian traditions, and the evolution of the church relatively isolated from Western theological developments, especially liberal Christianity.

Indeed, the Protestantism propagated by the early Western missionaries in Korea was informed largely by theologically conservative Presbyterianism, especially that of Calvinistic theology, which held as its central tenets the belief in Christ's atonement, premillennialist eschatology, and the inerrancy and supernatural authority of the Bible.[32] Although the conservative churches in Korea today are by no means monolithic and lacking in variety, the majority of Protestant churches (over 90 percent by some estimations) share across denominational boundaries a common set of core fundamentalistic/conservative beliefs, especially the inerrancy of the Bible and its verbal inspiration.[33] The overwhelming majority of Korean Christians, both leaders and lay, also believe in the virgin birth of Christ, the veracity of biblical miracles, the virgin birth of Christ, the veracity of biblical miracles, the existence of an afterlife, and the resurrection of Jesus. Most of the laity and clergy also hold premillennialist views and believe in the imminence of Christ's return.[34] Studies show that on matters of politics and personal morality, Korean Protestants also hold strongly conservative views; for example, the overwhelming majority of clergy and laity believes that activities such as smoking, drinking, and premarital sex are immoral, and that government infringement on religious freedom and political involvement are undesirable.[35]

Although many churches in South Korea can be described as fundamentalist in orientation, the character of Korean Protestant churches, on the other hand, cannot be understood without its overt or underlying Pentecostal/charismatic dimension. Observers have long remarked on the undercurrent of "Pentecostal ferment" in Korean Protestantism, the fervently spiritual, ecstatic nature of Korean Protestant beliefs and practices that have always characterized Korean Protestantism to some extent and that are believed to stem from both the revivalist orientations of the early missionaries and the indigenous Korean shamanistic tradition.[36] Indeed, experts of Korean Christianity typically view Korean Protestantism to have developed along two major tracks: one, along what Martin Riesebrodt (1993) calls the "book-centered" or "rational" track, usually denoting tendencies within Korean Protestantism that can typically be described as "traditional" conservative-fundamentalist; and two, along charismatically oriented lines emphasizing the importance of the workings of the Holy Spirit and charismatic experiences, or what Riesebrodt calls "experienced-centered."[37]

Although the two strands have always existed in tension, especially given the suspicion with which the Pentecostal/charismatic movements have long been regarded by the Protestant establishment,[38] the extent and importance of this Pentecostal-charismatic tradition in Korea has nonetheless been powerful, and the surge of Christian growth in Korea, as well as the development of its character, must be viewed in light of the impetus provided by the beliefs and practices of the Pentecostal-charismatic tradition.[39] Aside from its emphasis on the Baptism of the Holy Spirit and charismatic experiences during worship, other central aspects of this charismatic orientation include the importance accorded to felt (Holy Spirit) experience in conversion and the centrality of prayer.[40] Indeed, as one pastor of an evangelical church explained it to me, although both "the Bible" and "experience" (*cheheom*) form the basis of Christianity, for him it is "experience" that takes precedence because it is only through the emotional experience of God and feeling of faith—as opposed to an intellectual understanding of Christian doctrine—that one can gain salvation. To know God or Jesus, one must experience them, not just learn from what the Bible says about them: "You see, people whose faith is based on experience can't be shaken because these can't be taken away from them. Who can refute experience, though people can try to refute the Bible? They can't deny your personal experience."[41]

One recent development that is worthy of note is that in the past few decades, we have seen a revitalization of the charismatic movement within South Korean Protestantism that has led to a more widespread acceptance of charismatic practices within the Korean churches (J. Lee 1986: 200). Although the more Pentecostal forms of charismatic expression, such as glossolalia (speaking in tongues) and exorcism, are practiced officially in a minority of churches such as the Yeoido Full Gospel Church, the Pentecostal influence can now be seen in most Korean Protestant churches in one manner or another, particularly after the 1970s (Ryu 1982; Suh 1982). Ironically, many scholars also point to the possible role of Pentecostal churches such as Yeoido in helping to spread this Pentecostal influence, especially as such churches and their leaders began to gain acceptance by the wider Christian community starting in the 1970s (Martin 1990: 146; J. Lee 1986).[42] Indeed, my observations confirm the growing acceptance of Pentecostal beliefs and practices within the Korean church. In one of the churches I studied, for example, I learned that their worship styles have been moving more in the charismatic direction over the past couple of decades; I was told that the pastor had decided at some point during the 1980s to "loosen up" worship styles, giving more liberty to the congregants to express their spiritual zeal in public. In another church, I learned that the pastor, after personally experiencing "miraculous" healing from a bout of grave illness in the early 1990s, had decided to allow greater freedom, both theologically and stylistically, becoming more accommodating to such practices as clapping, loud praying, speaking in tongues, healing, and other forms of ecstatic spiritual experiences and styles of worship.

Another notable feature of Korean Protestantism regards the general character of its religious practices, something that can be described as intensely practical and devotional (T. Lee 1996).[43] These descriptors apply to Korean evangelicals for whom dedicated observance of concrete devotional practices—whether they are Bible study, church attendance, prayer, or tithing—is often just as crucial, if not more so, to being an evangelical as are theological ideas, and that such devotional activities embody the central criteria upon which one's faith is measured and practiced. To that end, Korean evangelicalism has evolved an impressive array of innovative and devotional practices.

One of the major ways in which this devotional character is manifested in Korean evangelicalism is in the variety and frequency of its worship services. A typical Korean church, in a week, holds at least several worship services: in addition to the main Sunday service, a church commonly holds Sunday evening services, Wednesday night worship service, and Friday all-night prayer worship services. In a large church, it is not unusual to have multiple services on Sunday, as many as up to five or six. In addition, all Korean churches hold daily dawn or daybreak prayer services, which meet anywhere from 4 AM to 6 AM every day of the week. These "early dawn" gatherings, or *saebyeok gidohoe*, have their origins in the great revival of 1907 and have become a regular practice in Korean Protestantism.[44] Besides the regular devotional meetings, revival meetings, both those held in individual churches and large-scale interdenominational revival rallies, are also an important part of evangelical devotional practice.[45]

Another practice that reflects this devotional nature of Korean Protestantism is the popularity of fasting prayers and healing prayers among Korean Protestants. Fasting prayers are obviously also practiced elsewhere in the world, but much evidence suggests that Koreans are especially enthusiastic about the practice, seeing it as a special means of experiencing the divine and receiving blessings. Fasting prayers are also seen as evidence and a demonstration of the depth of one's faith. In many churches, healing prayers have also become an important feature that can be incorporated into a service or be performed separately.[46] Fasting and healing prayers are also central activities of a distinctive Korean evangelical institution known as the "Prayer House," or *gidowon*, a prayer retreat usually located in a mountainous area where believers can engage in concentrated devotion for days, weeks, or even months.[47]

Two further cornerstones of Korean devotional practice are Bible study and cell groups. Reflecting the legacy of the early missionaries, who stressed faithful reading and literal interpretation of the Bible, the study of scripture has continued down the generations as a crucial focal point of Korean evangelicalism.[48] Bible study classes are held regularly and frequently in all Korean evangelical churches, and most Korean evangelicals indicate that reading and studying the Bible are among the most important devotional activities.[49] Cell groups—small, informal gatherings of church members that usually meet weekly in the members' homes for the ostensible purpose of Bible study and fellowship—are pivotal to the organization of most Korean churches because they provide a venue to foster important face-to-face exchanges and interpersonal bonds, while functioning as evangelizing and church service units. As we will see, they are particularly crucial for larger churches that cannot easily provide the intimate family-like atmosphere of smaller churches. Indeed, the system of cell groups may be the chief reason for the success of seemingly impersonal mega-churches in Korea.[50]

Institutional Culture

A general description of contemporary Korean Protestantism would not be complete without a discussion about the organizational culture and structure of the churches, where the conservatism of Korean evangelicalism is clearly manifested. Along with their theologically conservative orientation, most Korean Protestant churches reveal strong tendencies toward cultural conservativism, much of which clearly reflects the impact of Confucian ideology and principles of social relations. Two major elements of this cultural conservatism are expressed in the following: the authoritarian and hierarchical nature of interpersonal relations within the church, epitomized by the intense leader orientation of most churches, and strict hierarchical gender relations.

A distinctive aspect of Korean Protestantism is the strong pastor-oriented, authoritarian leadership culture. Clearly reflecting the hierarchical principles of Confucian human relationships, the familistic and paternalistic structure of most Korean churches bestows upon the pastor the authority and powers associated with a family patriarch. These pastor/lay relationships are governed by the relations of "Confucian personalism" in which deference and obedience from the congregants to the pastor are exchanged for the pastor's paternalistic concern and responsibility for his flock as a "family." As one scholar puts it: "By performing multiple, secular functions, the minister actualizes the Confucian personalism, the expressive primary group relationships upon which the personal community of the church members is built" (I. Kim 1985: 234). This hierarchical nature of human relationships is also reflected in the relative status, esteem, and authority enjoyed by other leaders, such as elders and deacons, over the lay. David Martin (1990), discussing the various aspects of the "indigenization" of Christianity in Korea, offers a following description:

The further indigenization of Presbyterianism was pushed forward, perhaps all too easily, by allowing the church to approximate to the Confucian ideal of the five cardinal relations between ruler and subject, father and son, husband and wife, and so on. The result is startlingly similar to the patronal relationships reproduced inside Brazilian Presbyterianism out of the patterns which obtained in the hacienda. Pastors and elders try to stay above the laity and insist on enjoying superior privileges. Thus the universal brotherhood of Christianity is rather too successfully toned down to limited and particular relationships. (142)

This particular hierarchical and personalistic pattern of interpersonal relations has also been successfully institutionalized within Korean churches through the adoption of the Presbyterian pattern of local governance in almost all denominations (I. Kim 1985).[51] In most Korean churches, trustees, deacons, and elders who are selected by popular vote or appointed constitute the lay leadership (elders are typically appointed for life). It appears that this Presbyterian form of lay leadership has provided the Korean church with the ideal organizational structure for the maintenance of the traditional hierarchical order, as well as for the provision of status rewards.

One of the results of this strong leader orientation within Korean evangelicalism has been the autonomy and strength of the local church, in which loyalty of members to individual pastors and churches often exceeds that to their denominations. This loyalty has had ambiguous consequences; although it has encouraged church growth through inter-church competition, it has tended to weaken inter-church and denominational cooperation. As Donald Clark (1986) sums it up:

The heart of any church naturally is its membership; but many of Korea's denominational churches are actually congregational rather than denominational, focused on local concerns rather than denomination-wide projects, or issues of concern to society as a whole. . . . The results comprise a paradox. Christianity in Korea is faction-ridden over doctrinal, historical, and political issues, and depends heavily on pastoral leadership. And yet it claims many followers, displays vital forces for growth, and is capable of impressive displays of unity. (22)

Another way in which this conservative, hierarchical culture is reflected in the structure of church organization is in gender relations. To this day, Korean churches remain predominantly and unequivocally male-dominated. Despite the critical nature of women's participation in the churches and their contribution to the growth and character of Korean evangelicalism, the overall status of women within the church has not undergone a great deal of change since the early days. Although Korean Christian women, since their days as Bible women, continue to carry out more than their share of responsibilities as church workers, organizers, evangelizers, and even as lay leaders within the churches, women as a group have not been successful in transcending their secondary and subordinate status within the churches.

In terms of ordination, women are still prohibited from being ordained in the majority of Korean Protestant denominations, although three major denominations have been ordaining women for over 20 years and a number of other smaller denominations have voted only recently to ordain women. The denominations that have been ordaining women for at least two decades are the Methodist denomination (since 1931), the liberal (Gijang) wing of the Presbyterian Church, and the Korean Assemblies of God (both since the 1970s). In 1994, one of the main conservative Presbyterian denominations (Donghap) voted for female ordination. The problem, as we will see, is that due to the still-powerful cultural resistance against women as pastors, these policy changes have not led to any notable increases of women into the pastorate (P. Min 2008). And although women are granted a measure of access to certain leadership positions in the churches, especially as lower-level church officers such as deacons and cell leaders, women are, in general, excluded from the structures of decision-making and power and subordinated to male authority at every step. They continue to oc-

cupy subordinate positions in which the bulk of church service is carried out, with focus on tasks stressing individual evangelization and
other pietistic activities.[52]

Over the years, various groups, especially liberal women's Christian
groups, have worked to improve the status of women within Korean
churches. Two early examples are the subcommittee of women within
the Korean National Council of Churches (KNCC) and a group called
Korean Church Women United, which was established in 1965 to
address various women's issues as well as those related to social/
economic justice, human rights, and the environment (H. Yi 1985a).
With the emergence of various social movements for democratization
and social justice since the 1960s, numerous other liberal Christian
women's organizations have been created that have, again, concerned
themselves with the problems of women's rights in addition to general
social and political issues. Despite these efforts, and the increasing participation of Christian women in the general upswelling of social and
political protest in the 1970s and 80s, the impact of these groups on
women's issues within the church has been limited (H. Yi 1985a: 102).
Overall, the Korean Protestant church remains a place where the Confucian-patriarchal principles of female inferiority and male superiority,
sanctioned through conservative interpretations of the Bible, are firmly
institutionalized, and the secondary status and subservient roles of
women are perpetuated.

Setting and Method

The following chapters in this study will focus upon two Protestant
evangelical churches, one Presbyterian and the other Methodist, located
in Seoul, home to the largest concentration of Protestant churches in
South Korea (Gallup 1998: 165). The two churches, which I call the
North River Church (Methodist) and the South River Church (Presbyterian), are centrally located in two major areas of Seoul, one to the area
north and the other to the south of the Han River, the major water ar-
tery that bisects Seoul from east to west. The fieldwork, which was
conducted for 16 months between 1996 and 1999, consisted of intensive
participant observation of church activities and in-depth interviewing of
96 church members and leaders. Prior to my determination of these
churches as primary research sites, preliminary fieldwork was also car-

ried out in over 15 other Protestant churches of different denominations and sizes around Seoul, and insights gained from these observations also significantly inform this study.

Once the capital of the Yi dynasty, the city of Seoul has exploded in size with massive rural-urban migrations in the second half of the twentieth century. The Greater Seoul area is a sprawling metropolis home to 22.5 million people (almost half the nation's population), with 10.3 million people (about a quarter of the population) living in the city proper. The territory to the north of the Han River contains the area within the old city walls and is informally referred to as Gangbuk (literally, "river north"). In order to accommodate the swelling population, the government undertook a major urban expansion program starting in the 1970s that resulted in the development to the south of the Han of a new, wealthier area: Gangnam (literally, "river south"). Since the 1980s, Gangnam—now considered home to many middle- to upper-class families, especially the *nouveaux riches*—has come to largely displace Gangbuk as the commercial and cultural epicenter of the "new" Seoul.

The South River Church, a large, dynamic Presbyterian church of over 10,000 members, is located in the heart of the Gangnam region.[53] The church structure is a sprawling modern complex nestled amidst a dizzying array of retail enterprises and rows upon rows of identical modern apartment buildings that presently house much of the middle class in South Korea. The membership of the South River Church, although solidly middle class, reflects the relatively affluent, upward-striving demographic character of this area. The South River Church is relatively young, having been established in the late 1970s in tandem with the area's residential development, but it has thrived in a very short period under the leadership of its original charismatic founder who still presides over the church. With the rapid growth of its membership, the church complex has also expanded quickly over the years to include a prayer retreat center outside of the city. South River Church has over 60 assistant pastors and over 3,000 layworkers—mostly deacons—who oversee and lead the scores of programs and activities for which the church has become widely known.

The North River Church is a middle-class, medium-sized Methodist church of about 3,000 members that is centrally located in a bustling but somewhat more mixed-class neighborhood in the northern part of Seoul. Established in the early 1900s, the North River Church is a historic, older church that boasts an imposing gothic structure and has witnessed over the years myriad transformations of the surrounding city. Although quieter in tone, this long-standing church has also experienced steady growth in the past several decades, and it has kept up with current trends by expanding its program offerings to attract and retain its expanding membership. Supervised by several assistant pastors, this church, like South River, enjoys active involvement by its members, especially women, and is aggressively pursuing programs geared toward young members in particular. The church's deacons and other lay leaders number close to a thousand. And like South River, the leadership of the church is quite centralized, focused on the authority of its well-respected and charismatic pastor.

In any ethnographic study, the issue of sampling, or selecting which groups to study, is a serious one, and after extensive exploration and consideration of a number of churches in Seoul, I chose the two churches described above for a number of important reasons. First, the two churches belong to the largest Protestant denominations in South Korea: Presbyterian, the largest denomination, with almost two-thirds of the Protestant population, and Methodist, a distant second at about 11 percent. These churches provide, in my view, the best demographic representation of the Christian population as well as sampling along major denominational lines. Though both churches serve predominantly middle-class congregations, their respective locations in two distinct areas of the city also promised a wider range in sampling the population, although comparisons based on socio-economic categories will not be the focus of this study. The sizes of the churches were also important considerations: focusing on larger rather than smaller churches made sense because larger churches simply have more people to study, ensuring better population sampling, and they offer a greater number and diversity of activities that I could observe.

Another important consideration bearing on my selection of the churches, of course, was the issue of representativeness. In any study of this kind, achieving a perfect degree of representativeness in choosing research sites is all but impossible, and I certainly do not claim that the two churches that I selected are representative of all evangelical churches in Korea, of even the churches of their denominations. Given the large number of denominations and individually minded churches active in Korean Protestantism, it would be foolish to deny the considerable diversity that exists among the churches. Despite this heterogeneity, the majority of the churches within the Korean Protestant establishment, however, *are* united by some important common characteristics, and the two churches were chosen because I felt that they *were* fairly "typical" in many senses; that is, they were representative of certain important dimensions of the demographic characteristics that might be considered "mainstream" for evangelical churches in Korea.

The first of these dimensions is the theological and cultural conservatism of these two churches. Not only do the churches represent the two major Protestant denominations in South Korea, but their conservative leanings are representative of the general theological/cultural conservatism of the mainstream evangelical churches across denominations (D. Clark 1986: 22; T. Lee 2006; Rhee 1966; C. Lee 1966), as discussed earlier in this chapter. In fact, one scholar (T. Lee 2006: 331–35) has surmised recently that as of the 1990s, as many as 90 percent of Protestant churches are conservative-evangelical, and that both Presbyterian and Methodist churches belong squarely to what can be considered evangelical churches: "In fact, Evangelicalism so predominates the Korean church, its success or growth so influences Korean Protestantism as a whole, that Evangelicalism and Protestantism are more or less synonymous in Korea" (T. Lee 2006: 330). Although one could argue that there are some differences between Korean Presbyterianism and Methodism along the "conservative-liberal" spectrum—Methodism is regarded by some as being somewhat more "liberal" in certain respects because of its more active engagement with social justice and democratization issues—the two denominations do not display major differences in their adherence to the basic tenets of conservative evangelicalism and their general cultural conservatism.[54]

The second important demographic dimension is related to class. By certain objective indicators, the largest class group in South Korea is the "working" or "lower-middle" class (Koo 1991: 488); however, it is extremely important to note that the majority of South Koreans *identify themselves*, subjectively, as middle class.[55] On the whole, the Christian population in South Korea is more educated, urban, and of higher socio-economic status than the general population. According to a survey by Gallup Korea (1998: 11, 160, 161), Christianity has a larger proportion of college-educated individuals than either Buddhists or those with no religious affiliation, and Christians also constitute the largest group in the top third of the income bracket. Although there are a large number of non-middle-class churches in South Korea, and the North and South River Churches, to be sure, contain some working-class members and do fall on the two ends of the middle-class spectrum—the South River Church being at the upper end of the middle-class category and the North River Church at the lower end—the two churches can be considered quite "typical" in that their demographics do accord with this general "middle class" characteristic of Korean Christianity.

Despite the "typical" characteristics of the two churches with regard to the general profile of mainstream Protestantism, there are, however, some interesting differences arising from the peculiarities of each church that made for interesting comparisons. The South River Church, with its larger size and resources, has more ongoing programs and activities than the North River Church; that is, it was the "busier" church. The South River Church is, in fact, known for its innovative and successful church growth and management strategies—such as its intricately organized cell group system and extensive "disciple training" programs focused on lay leadership training—that have become a model for many other churches, including the North River Church. Furthermore, due both to its aggressive evangelization efforts and diversity of programs, the South River Church tended to have more first-time converts than the North River Church, which had a larger proportion of long-standing members. However, since these differences did not suggest widely divergent social dynamics between the two churches, especially regarding gender, this study will not focus on an explicit comparison between them.

In the end, however, accessibility was perhaps the most important consideration regarding church selection in a fieldwork site such as South Korea. Given the highly personalistic nature of contemporary South Korean society, I could not gain access to churches for the purposes of research without the personal introduction and support of figures high up in the church hierarchy. Right at the outset, this reality served as an important constraining factor in my selection process. Beyond the fact that North and South River Churches met the main selection criteria that I had initially set forth, I was able to study these two churches because I was fortunate enough to gain access through the help of two assistant pastors in each church with whom I had come to develop relationships. They provided me with the essential "stamp of approval" with which I could conduct research in the churches, and gave me the necessary introductions to church members and access to participation in various programs and meetings. Without the cooperation of these church officers, this study would not have been possible.

In both churches, I participated in as many church programs as I could. I attended all of the regular church services, including evening services, dawn prayer services, as well as revival meetings. I attended introductory seminars for new church members, and after gaining some familiarity with the churches, regularly attended cell group meetings. These meetings were particularly useful in gaining insights into the inner lives and concerns of the female members. I also attended Bible study classes as well as lay leadership training classes.

I participated regularly in special seminars held in both churches, particularly those having to do with family and gender matters, such as "family seminars," "family education seminars," "newlywed seminars," and "marriage preparation seminars." These seminars were particularly valuable in providing me with insights into gender-related issues as articulated from the perspective of the churches as well as of the women. I participated in a variety of church service groups, such as "women's missionary societies" (*yeo seongyobu*) groups and other social and community programs run by the churches to experience the various activities in which the women were engaged. And whenever I was given access, I attended officer meetings, which gave me good perspective on the dynamics of church authority relations and decision-making. Finally, to obtain a better picture of the spiritual lives of church members, I periodically attended prayer retreats outside of the city.

In sum, I tried, as a participant observer, to spend as much of my waking time as possible attending church activities and interacting with women inside and outside of the church. And my hours were not difficult to fill, since the churches almost always had something going on all day, everyday. Aside from observing and partaking in the formal rituals of the church, I spent my time talking to women, studying the Bible with them, singing with them, going out on evangelizing expeditions with them, visiting the sick and poor, and helping them with their church chores.

The in-depth interviews that form the core of my study were conducted either in the church or in the homes of the interviewees. The interviews, which included not only church members but also pastors, church officers, and outside experts of Christianity, lasted anywhere from one to three hours; some were repeated. The majority of my interviews, however, were with lay women and a handful of lay men, usually husbands of the women that I had interviewed. These interviews were obtained mainly through the "snowball" method, as random sampling in this kind of situation would have been impossible, given that no one would consent to talk to me unless I was introduced properly by someone the interviewee knew and that person could satisfactorily confirm my status and purpose. However, I did initially target my interview sample to married women between the ages of 25 to 65, and in the end, the majority of the interviewees—totaling 60—fell between the ages of 35 and 55. This was in close keeping with the age demographics of the two churches: indeed, married women in the 35-to-55 age group constitute the most numerous membership in Korean evangelical churches as a whole.[56]

This study, then, is an investigation primarily of a particular generation of women—those born between Korea's post-liberation era (post-1945) and the early 1960s, and coming of age during the 1960s, 1970s, and the early 1980s—whose experiences reflect the complex transformations of South Korea's "late-industrialization" and modernization period. For the purposes of comparison, I also conducted a number of interviews with younger, unmarried women and older married or widowed women. Furthermore, I tried to obtain sub-samples of members in different stages of conversion, based on different length of religious involvement, in order to ascertain both any differences in the significance of the church and evangelicalism in their lives and the progression in the character of church participation and its meaning for the members.

Most of the interviews, which were taped and immediately transcribed, were semi-structured, but left open-ended whenever possible in order to allow the voices and concerns of the respondents to come through. Although I had some basic questions I wanted to cover in most of the interviews, I often allowed the interviewees to dictate the course of the conversations and address whatever topics they wanted to address. This way, I was able to obtain a great deal of unexpected but valuable information and to uncover themes that had not occurred to me before, allowing me to adjust my interview questions and the themes of my research as I went along. This kind of an open-ended process has its advantages and disadvantages, of course; the main drawback being that my data may not be strictly comparable with one other since I modified my questions and uncovered new themes as my research progressed. However, the flexibility of this process allowed me to generate crucial insights and concepts as I went along and proved to be most suited to the pursuit of grasping the meanings and concerns of the participants as they existed for them.

Finally, my analysis incorporates insights acquired from an examination of a large array of church publications and literature, including church newsletters, newspapers, announcements, magazines, religious tracts, workbooks, instructional materials, and public relations materials.

A Note on Ethnography

My foremost reason for selecting the ethnographic research method, including participation-observation and in-depth interviewing, is that these methodological approaches are the best means for comprehending the ways in which the world and everyday situations are meaningful for and experienced by the participants themselves, and to gain first-hand knowledge of the ongoing life of the group studied. Throughout this study, my aim has been to take seriously the thoughts, feelings, and self-understandings of the evangelical women within the context of the world in which they live, by trying to see things as they see them, to comprehend their behavior from their own point of view, and to utilize the women's categories of thought when trying to make sense of their experiences (Glaser and Strauss 1967; Smith 1992). In other words, my aim was to be as "empathetic" as possible.[57]

The role of a participant observer, however, is a complicated one, because no matter how great one's stance of empathy, one must maintain a certain objective distance and boundary as an "objective" researcher and interpreter. Carrying out fruitful ethnographic research is dependent upon being able to negotiate these two positions both in one's interactions with the participants and in one's own cognitive stance. Although negotiating the role of a participant and an observer is a problem faced by all ethnographers, its difficulty, however, can be more intense and wide-ranging for those studying a religious community (whether as an "insider" or an "outsider"), especially if that community holds beliefs or values in conflict with those of the secular world. Other methodological issues central to the ethnographic project, such as problems of access, trust, maintenance of relations, and field-work stresses, are also magnified for a social scientist working within a "resistant" religious setting.

When I began my research, I was filled with trepidation about how I would be received in these churches, how accessible and responsive the church members would be toward me. My fears arose from concerns about the general accessibility of the Korean evangelical community to a social scientist and to my ambiguous identity as a Korean-American (albeit a Korean-born one) and as a non-evangelical person within an evangelical setting. Although I had been churchgoing as a young child in Korea and as a teenager in the United States, and thus familiar with the evangelical tradition, I had attended church only occasionally since college and currently do not consider myself to have a religious affiliation.

Surprisingly, however, my reception by church members and their responsiveness toward me were more open and congenial than I had dared to hope throughout most of my research stay. Since I had made it my policy to be upfront about my identity from the beginning—not that it would have been possible or ethical to do otherwise—everyone knew I was a researcher from abroad, but for a variety of reasons that became clear to me as I went along, many of the factors that I imagined would become potential barriers to accessibility did not become so.

I believe that the main reason for the favorable response to my involvement was the validation of my status by the pastors in the two churches, which reflects the supreme importance of authority and hierarchical relations in Korea. First of all, the pastors' support of my presence made me a legitimate presence in the churches. Secondly, since I was supported by the pastors, most church members generally assumed that I was a churchgoing evangelical, which did not hurt my ability to gain access. Even those who got to know me personally and knew that I was currently not churchgoing on a regular basis in the United

States did not hold it against me; most of them were satisfied that I had been a churchgoer in the past and assumed that I was going through a period of "lapse." And given that many of them professed themselves to be, or as having been, "nominal" Christians for a large part of their lives, they did not seem to find my status all that strange or disturbing. However, since I did not consider it ethical to present myself as more committed than I really was, at no time did I profess to being a committed evangelical when directly asked.

Another important reason for their favorable reception, to my pleasant surprise, sometimes arose from the very uniqueness of my status and identity; that is, their views of me as a kind of exotic outsider with a certain social status, as someone engaged in Ph.D. research at a well-known American institution—and as an "American" who was Korean enough for them to feel comfortable. As a result, most people I encountered did not display much discomfort or guardedness toward me. To the contrary, many of them went out of their way to try to help me, from consenting to interviews to giving me further contacts.

Interestingly enough, it also dawned on me after a while that many of my participants were actually quite eager to talk to me, and that this was due in large part to my position as an "outsider" to whom they felt they could freely reveal their thoughts and feelings without the risk of institutional repercussions. Especially after I assured them of strict confidentiality, I had the distinct impression that the church members felt quite free in talking with me; most women opened themselves up and revealed their hearts with frankness in ways I had not expected or imagined. Although I was particularly sensitive in the beginning to the possibility that the women might simply be trying to tell me what I wanted to hear, this fear was soon dispelled by the depth and direction of the conversations.

Furthermore, I believe that many women found conversations with me cathartic; talking with me often seemed to present a relatively safe opportunity to unload personal problems and feelings in ways that they normally would not—and many did so with great relish. Indeed, more than a few conversations were extremely emotional, carried out in tears. Many found me a reasonably sympathetic listener: one commented to me that she felt comfortable with me because I did not seem biased and seemed willing to "understand things." Others thanked me for giving them the chance to "unleash" their hearts and to be self-reflective. I also found that the setting for the interview was quite important in dictating the general mood of the interaction. Most women behaved in a far more relaxed manner when interviews were conducted in their homes rather than somewhere in the church. Given the advantages of a private setting, I made the effort—including long bus rides to distant parts of the city—to interview the women in the comfort of their own homes.

Another concern at the start of my fieldwork was my age and marital status. Since I was single at the time and younger than most of the women I was interviewing, I wondered if this would constrain their interaction and openness with me, especially with regard to marital issues and relationships with men. Surprisingly, again, I found that this did not seem to have a great effect; most women did not seem to feel uncomfortable about speaking to me about various aspects of their marital relationships, including sexual, and did not appear to think that I could not understand things about men and marriage just because I was not yet married. Although I, of course, do not have a good way of verifying this, I attributed this frankness to their perception of me as a kind of "worldly" person, though single, who was probably experienced in the ways of romance and thus able to comprehend such matters.

Although my interactions with church members and the lower-level lay leaders were for the most part trouble-free, the responses from some of the church officers and the higher-level leadership were a bit more guarded. Some tended to be more suspicious of my motives and what I was "taking away" from all of my research, and they took greater care to tow the official line when talking with me. Although most were extremely helpful, a few assisted me with a degree of reluctance and reservation. One assistant pastor whose marriage preparation seminar I observed at the South River Church, for example, was particularly concerned about what impact I would be having on the class members; however, he relaxed when he saw that my presence did not have too much effect. Even here, I discovered that a person was most likely to be unreservedly cooperative when the request to assist me came from above, rather than from a colleague.

That said, most leaders were quite cooperative as long as there was some form of proper personal introduction from a superior or someone they liked and knew well. Others were helpful to a fault. Many leaders not only welcomed me to their classes and groups, but spent hours talking to me with unexpected candidness, and helped me find appropriate lay members to interview. Not very surprisingly, I found that some of my interactions worked best when I was able to give something in exchange, such as editing or translating English texts for the leaders.

Cell group leaders, in particular, were most cooperative and welcoming—again, though, as long as I came with a proper introduction. For my part, however, I was concerned about the potential impact of my presence on the dynamics of such small group settings, that the members might become shy or embarrassed to open up in front of an outsider. In these settings, therefore, I decided that I was going to be as participatory as possible, doing everything that they did, as far as my personal beliefs allowed. For instance, since I always enjoyed singing hymns in church, I sang along with them, and when they asked to share my life experiences with them, I did so to the best of my ability. I prayed with them as well, as long as I could do it silently. At various times, they would invite me to pray out loud for the group, but I politely refused such requests. And when the group sometimes burst into loud, highly emotional group prayers, I obviously could not participate, although I attempted to partake as fully as possible in the moods of the group.

On the whole, I found that as long as I attempted to "blend in" as much as possible, my presence, in the end, seemed to have minimal influence on the dynamics of group interaction. When I asked the leaders if anything had changed due to my presence, they confirmed my impression by saying that they also did not perceive any great differences. On the other hand, it was also apparent that the members could not entirely forget my obvious position as an "outsider" and an "observer." Thus, while trying to include me however possible, they also treated me in these group settings with respectful distance and curiosity and as someone they were assisting, which I actually found quite comfortable. One positive consequence of this attitude was that while wanting me to join in and partake in group experiences, they did not expect me to behave exactly as they did, which made things much easier. Furthermore, to my great relief, most of them, with a few memorable exceptions, did not treat me as a potential convert to their churches since, in their minds, I was soon going to be leaving for the United

States.[58] This, however, did not stop some of them from attempting to "help" me undergo significant spiritual and revelatory religious experiences that presumably would have repercussions in the future.

Although most groups welcomed me with open arms, I did, however, feel that I had to be careful not to overstay my welcome in a couple of the groups. Although I detected little discomfort from the cell members, the leaders of these group seemed a bit guarded and a couple of them became increasingly so as time went on. I would speculate that these leaders were particularly possessive of their domains and felt that my presence interfered with their "jobs" after a certain point, an entirely understandable reaction. In such instances, I curtailed my involvement. In the majority of cases, however, I received no such discomfiting responses from the leaders.

In relation to my expectations at least, my experiences with the church members on the whole were surprisingly smooth and their offers of access enabled me to acquire many valuable insights. Despite some fundamental differences in background and beliefs between the church members and myself, we were able to engage fruitfully with one another at many levels because we shared some basic things, such as being Korean and having similar experiences of family. This, I believe, also allowed me to be genuinely empathetic—and sympathetic—with them and helped them trust me to understand them. With the women in particular, our shared gender identity and experiences reinforced this mutual feeling of empathy. Even though I was taken aback at times with some of the ways in which they reacted to their situations and dilemmas, I was nevertheless sincerely sympathetic to and comprehending of their plight and suffering, and the reasons they made the particular choices that they did.

On the other hand, I would be remiss not to admit that much of my research experience was at times quite challenging. One particularly difficult aspect was the management of interpersonal relations within a setting that was both intensely religious and patriarchal. Despite the participants' general acceptance of me, the problem of trust remained a central concern throughout my fieldwork, and I found myself expending a tremendous amount of energy at both gaining and maintaining the goodwill of a religious community whose suspicions were not difficult to arouse, and trying to remain sensitive to the various rules of interpersonal engagement particular to Korean society. In this sense, one of the dominant feelings with which I had to contend as a researcher, therefore, was one of great vulnerability, not a sense of power over my participants.

In order to sustain trust, I found self-presentation and identity management to be some of the most difficult matters to negotiate, especially given my confusing cultural and religious identity.[59] My biggest challenge was to navigate my contradictory and perhaps somewhat threatening multiple identities as a highly educated, "foreign," female, secular social scientist in ways that would not distance the participants. Although I tried as best as I could never to lie about anything, I found myself highlighting certain aspects about myself that would be deemed acceptable in the participants' eyes and de-emphasizing or even hiding other aspects: for example, aspects of my identity that might present myself as too knowledgeable, "Western," or feminist.[60]

My dealings with the male pastors represent interesting instances of the need for identity management. Since most male pastors were used to being in a position of authority, particularly in relation to women, many of them seemed comfortable placing me in the role of a relatively "innocent" unmarried young woman in need of their help. In order not to violate these perceptions of me in too egregious a manner, I found myself "playing up" to these gender norms and external expectations in various encounters, which, while generating discomfiting feelings of ethical ambivalence, also unwittingly led to my subjection to patriarchal control. Although these problems did not extend to my dealings with the lay women with whom I shared a much less hierarchical relationship, the need to negotiate some women's conflicting understandings and expectations of me, especially as they related to my ambiguous inside/outsider status, was a source of stress at times.

In sum, the most challenging aspects of "managing" my identity in order to fit in were the resulting feelings of "inauthenticity" and a sense of shame at my "opportunism." Although I do not believe that all the power in the field resides in the researcher, but that it can be exerted by the researched as well,[61] this situation nonetheless was a major source of moral discomfort. For me, however, the most difficult problem was the intense sense of inauthenticity I derived from having to engage in what felt to be a continual process of self-repression in order to fit in.

I was fortunate not to have felt too much pressure from this religious group to alter my identity, and thus was able, I believe, to balance my role as a participant and an observer more or less adequately. Attempting to be empathetic as well as "value neutral," however, required a considerable amount of suppression of my own identity and beliefs for which I was not entirely prepared.

This stance of empathy and full participation not only involved adherence to certain rules of interaction and conduct, which in itself was severely restricting and uncomfortable at times, but also required maintaining empathetic neutrality about ideas that went against my own belief system. The difficulties of carrying out research with groups whose ideology and perspectives conflict with the researcher's in fundamental ways have been addressed by a number of works.[62] I had no problems in general with empathizing and seeing things as the members did, and I did partake in and was indeed moved by their spiritual experiences; however, I did find it particularly difficult at times to deal with some of the ideological views that contradicted my own beliefs, especially those related to gender. That is, although I did not have any problems with the realities and specificities of people's religious experiences and beliefs in general, nor with individual beliefs regarding gender that were by no means uniform, I found myself having to contend with my own moral resistance to the more uncompromising aspects of the official church discourse regarding gender and family relations. In other words, I did not find it easy—in fact, it was quite stressful—to keep my thoughts to myself when confronted with beliefs that fundamentally contradicted my own.

These are problems endemic to the ethnographic project that have no easy solutions. In the face of these challenges, my aim in this work has been to make the best effort possible to portray what I have learned and observed as fairly and as accurately as possible without introducing undue biases and distortions into my interpretation and analyses. It is by now a well-accepted postmodernist and feminist wisdom that pure "objectivity" is but an ideal and that no one's perspective is free of biases.[63] I am, of course, more than cognizant of such limits to my "objectivity" and vision both in the field and in the process of interpretation and writing; that is, how my biases, assumptions, and political/ideological stances, as well as my emotional experiences and responses, may shape and condition my understandings. In these pages, therefore, I do not pretend to deny my "situated" perspectives and position. Instead, my goal has been to remain as vigilant as possible throughout the process of fieldwork and writing about how my cognitive assumptions and intellectual positioning, as well as my emotional responses, can influence my analysis. Recognizing, on the other hand, that engaging in obsessive self-reflexivity is not necessarily a solution to these dilemmas (Wasserfall 1993; Patai 1991), I resist the impulse to dwell unduly on myself, but try my best to focus on the experiences and stories of the women on their terms and hope that my portrayal of them has been rendered fairly.

TWO

Women's Conversion and the Contradictions
of Contemporary Gender and Family Relations

Ji-won is a comely married woman in her mid-40s, who resides in one of the large middle-class modern apartment complexes that dominate the residential landscape of Seoul. After having been introduced to me by another member of the South River Church as a dedicated church member, Ji-won has agreed to do an interview with me about her religious and church life and we have just sat down for coffee in her neat living room. As we begin chatting, I learn indeed that she has been an active member of the South River Church for the past ten years, serving as a cell leader and contributing her services in a variety of other capacities over the years that she has been attending the church.

Ji-won is a well-educated, middle-class woman with a husband whose salaried income from a white-collar job in the upper management of a large corporation supports her family more or less adequately. Ji-won has a carefully made-up and remarkably well-preserved look of a relatively well-to-do Seoul housewife, and her apartment, which contains all the familiar accoutrements of modern-day middle-class living in Seoul— including a large overstuffed brown faux-leather couch that dominates her modest (but large by Seoul standards) living room and the latest model large-screen television and sound system—reflects her attention to orderliness, cleanliness, and the indicators of her family's social status. Ji-won has a college degree in home economics from a well-known university but has been a housewife all of her married life. She has two sons who, though still in secondary school, are now old enough that she can divide her time mainly between housework and church work.

Ji-won busily serves me a cup of instant coffee and a plate of cookies and carefully peeled fruit while I get out my notebook and get the tape recorder ready for the interview. Although we are both a bit nervous, Ji-won seems particularly anxious and she tells me that she is concerned because she is afraid she will not have much to say. I assuage her fears by telling her that anything she might have to say would be potentially valuable, so she should not worry and hold anything back. This seems to reassure her somewhat. But as we begin the interview, it becomes quickly apparent that Ji-won does not lack for things to say. As I begin to prod her gently with a few open-ended questions, starting with how she came to be a Christian, stories come flowing out of her like water from a breached dam.

I am from a very Confucian family, very very strict, so I lived quite a restricted life when I was young. Then I got married through arranged marriage [*jungmae*] at 23. You see, right after I graduated, I worked as a secretary at a small company, and I ended up marrying the son of the president of the company. Although everyone thought I had married well, I was in for a surprise. What happened was that upon marrying, I had to live with my husband's family. See, my husband's family is former refugees from North Korea, and so even though there weren't that many of them, for years I had to take care of and serve all of them, all thirteen of them: my parents in-law, three sisters-in-law, and cousins. But you see, I didn't know it was going to be like that. The matchmaker didn't inform me about any of this. At the time, my husband had also just come out of military training and was still in his second year of college, but the matchmaker said to us that he was about to graduate.

To make things worse, my mother-in-law became seriously ill. Of course, being that my husband was the only son, everything became my sole responsibility. My mother-in-law had to get blood transfusions regularly and I had to take charge of her, bringing her to the hospital, taking care of her, and all that. And because she was sick, I had to basically take charge of the entire household. Then I had babies of course. And my babies became sick too after they were born. I lost the second child in the hospital. So as you can imagine, I spent all my time going to the hospital. When I opened my eyes in the morning until I went to bed, I had no life of my own.

But because I was so young when I got married, I thought that was how it was for everyone—I just didn't know any better. And I was really fragile in mind and in my emotions and I tried to accept everything. And I couldn't tell any of this to my parents because they'd worry, so I'd just tell them everything was okay, I was living well and so forth. And I couldn't tell my friends either because it was embarrassing—they were all waiting to see how my life would turn out since I married into a rich household, you know, the competitive thing. I couldn't tell my husband either. You see, my husband was, uh, immature. He was a good person, but he was like a kid. He was in college at first and he was busy having a good time, meeting his friends, playing pool and things. He didn't know how to show consideration to his wife, at all. And he was the only son, so was indulged, as you can imagine. But after about thirteen years of this, I went into a deep depression, couldn't eat, became totally anxious, nervous. But I couldn't tell anybody. I secretly went and saw counselors and shrinks by myself.

But then finally, all my in-laws had gotten married off and my parents-in-laws had both passed away in the meantime. So there was just the four of left alone, my two kids and us, for the first time in thirteen years. So you think that would be so great, right? But that wasn't the case. When a rubber band that has been stretched taut for so long gets released, it shakes around, right? Well, I had been like that rubber band, nervous for so long, but when I was finally released, I didn't know my direction. This sudden freedom that was given to me, I just didn't know what to do with it. So I played golf, went shopping, ate in restaurants, but there was no satisfaction. Then one day, there was a deacon of the South River Church near me and I received an invitation from her to go to church. And what struck me about her was that she was always saying that she was happy, and that she had no fear of dying. So I asked her why she believed this and she said it was because she had the assurance that she was going to heaven. At the time, I had no idea what she was saying but the statement that she had no worries intrigued me, and I started going to her cell meeting.

Conversion stories such as these, which are inevitably embedded in the larger tales about the teller's life, reveal a great deal about the lives of Korean women today. Although conversion narratives can be seen, in one sense, as a form of interpretive reconstruction of past experience based on memory,[1] a conversion narrative is also more than simply that; combined with life history narratives that reveal other aspects about the person's biography, conversion stories can play an important part in providing both the whole and intimate portrait of the life and history of the individual within which the conversion experience forms a part.

A striking feature about the conversion narratives of South Korean evangelical women that I encountered in my research was the prevalence of discourses about domestic problems and distress, which are identified by women as central motivating factors in their church participation. In story after story, the women tell wrenching tales of prolonged domestic crisis and the resulting personal suffering revolving around their marital and domestic lives that they often view as a catalyst to church involvement. As seen in the narrative above and in the stories that appear throughout the book, the women's narrative accounts depict a set of family and marriage-related conflicts—most commonly, problems of acute marital tensions, conflicts with in-laws, unmanageable domestic burdens, and frustrated personal aspirations—that appear to be a source of severe psychic injury for women and from which they struggle to seek relief.

Another narrative, this one from Hyun-mi—a member of the South River Church, aged 43, also a housewife and mother of two children—expresses her long-term struggles with a difficult married life and domestic situation, revolving especially around intense conflicts with her mother-in-law and a patriarchal husband:

From the very first, my married life was incredibly difficult. You see, when I first had a marriage interview with my husband, he struck me as really sincere and honest. He also had a good job. Since I came from a comfortable family, money wasn't so important to me as long as he had a good, stable job. I knew living with a mother-in-law would be hard, but foolishly, I thought that if I was just all good, obedient, and faithful, and I could serve them well, everything would be okay. But it didn't turn out that way.

From the beginning, my husband's family treated me very badly. From day one, my mother-in-law treated me horribly, finding all kinds of fault with me. Especially when my husband went abroad, she started treating me worse. . . . My mother-in-law has a horribly sharp tongue, that's her personality. She is the type of person who just spits things out without thinking of the consequences, how it'll hurt other people. I have the opposite personality. I tend to keep things to myself because I am afraid to talk and afraid how it'll affect other people.

My husband, he always took his parents' side from the beginning. You've got to understand; my husband is the most traditionally Confucian [*yugyojoek*] man. When we first got married, he said to me that his parents were like his limbs, irreplaceable and with him forever, but I was like clothing, disposable and interchangeable. My husband's way of thinking is that the wife is a dependent, inferior member of the family, so there is no need to respect a woman. He just did whatever he wanted. On top of it, my husband, being from a family that was not-so-well-to-do and used to fighting for things, is not generous of character. He doesn't know how to offer love, material things, whatever. And his personality—it gets more difficult to deal with the longer I stay married to him. When you are trying to harmonize two people with different personalities, characters, views, it's so hard to begin with. But I am the only one who accommodates. It's so hard for me. I still have so many scars from him, do you know what I mean? So you see, without God, I wouldn't be able to continue with my life, couldn't live. And I can't and won't get divorced either. I am determined about that. If I got divorced, it'll follow me and haunt me for the rest of my life; and I think, if I can't bear and overcome the difficulties of this marriage, how can I overcome and bear the difficulties of another marriage? So even though I have a horrible mother-in-law, I am determined not to get a divorce.

As a first step in comprehending the conversions of these middle-class women to evangelicalism, the aim of this chapter is to explore and clarify some of the major factors that lie behind such decisions to convert, and the larger social context and forces that shape these decisions. Understanding religious conversion, however, is not an easy task, because conversion for any individual occurs often as a result of a complex interaction of factors that are often difficult to reduce to a single cause. But by examining a wide range of discourses about conversion, it is nevertheless possible to identify some of the dominant themes that can offer powerful clues as to the factors and processes that lie behind the motivations of converts.

In my study, the stories of domestic hardship and personal crisis that emerged as a prominent theme in women's conversion narratives provided me with one important clue, that an important key to understanding the nature and motives behind the religious participation of evangelical women lies in their domestic experiences, especially the dilemmas related to their married lives. Although these conversion accounts are by no means uniform—in fact they are often as varied as the individual biographies—the ubiquitous theme of domestic distress that binds most of the narratives together suggests that we can begin to understand church participation as a form of response to these domestic dilemmas.

The domestic and personal dilemmas of women, however, are themselves a product of the larger social and cultural forces that determine the situation of women's lives. Understanding these problems, therefore, requires an investigation of the wider social, cultural, and economic forces that have given shape and context to the lives of middle-class women in contemporary South Korea, especially the ideological and institutional contexts within which women constitute their choices and self-understanding. In the Korean case, this analysis of middle-class women's problems must focus on some of the contradictions of culture that have marked South Korean society in the last few decades, especially those affecting family and gender.

Indeed, the turn of contemporary middle-class women to the evangelical faith, in more general terms, can be understood as part of the women's efforts to negotiate some of the difficult contradictions posed by gender and family relations in South Korea today—what I describe as the contradictions of the contemporary Korean patriarchal family. An expression of the wider cultural contradictions that have inevitably been engendered by a high-speed, "catch-up" developmental process of the last several decades, these problems of gender and family, though difficult for everyone, pose particular predicaments for women.

In the following pages, I examine the sources and the nature of this contemporary family/gender contradiction within which these stories of domestic distress, and the women's subsequent conversions to evangelicalism, can be understood, moving then to a close analysis of the dilemmas faced by these women. This situation is a complex and interesting story that has been shaped by a number of important developments affecting South Korea in the last few decades—economic, political, and social—all of which have deeply affected and helped determine the society's changing beliefs and practices about gender and family, the position of women, and the dynamics of power between the sexes. Only by understanding these developments, and the complex set of challenges resulting from them, can we comprehend the significance of the religiosity of the women described in these pages.

The Economic "Miracle" and the Quandaries of Compressed Development

The spectacular economic success attained by South Korea since its full-fledged integration into the global capitalist economy starting in the early 1960s is by now well known. After the end of Japan's occupation in 1945 and the devastation of the Korean War (1950–53) that followed, South Korea was classified as one of the poorest nations in the world, with an annual per capita income of US$82 (in 1960 dollars). Indeed, South Korea in the early 1960s was still largely a rural nation in which agriculture accounted for almost 40 percent of Gross Domestic Product (Hart-Landsberg 1993: 25–26). With the economy and the social fabric further deteriorating under the repressive, highly corrupt, U.S.-backed regime of Syngman Rhee, the first post-liberation president, the possibility appeared slim that Korea had a chance at a prosperous economic future.

In the tumultuous three decades that followed, however, South Korea achieved what seemed to be an impossible feat. Through a program of what Alice Amsden (1989) refers to as "late-industrialization" launched in the early 1960s, South Korea, in a single generation, managed to emerge from the rubble of war and the socio-economic distortions of 35 years of colonial rule to transform itself from a poor, peasant society into a dynamic, prosperous, modern nation.

This economic turnaround began under President Park Chung Hee, a high-ranking military officer who came to power in 1961 through a coup d'etat that overthrew South Korea's first fully democratic but short-lived (1960–61), ineffectual government headed by Chang Myon. Governing through an intensely authoritarian and repressive military apparatus but relying on the promise of economic growth and staunch anti-communism as the bases of his legitimacy until his assassination in 1979, Park guided South Korea's economic recovery and advancement that has made it one of the so-called economic "tigers" of East Asia.

As is widely known, the centerpiece in Park's developmental strategy was a labor-intensive, export-oriented industrialization program carried out through a series of three five-year economic plans (1962–66, 1967–71, and 1972–76). Although Park did not start with an export-oriented strategy—in fact, Park's initial goal was the establishment of a "self-reliant economy" utilizing an import-substitution strategy (ISI) aimed at expanding the domestic industrial base[2]—by the mid-1960s he had decided upon an export-oriented strategy, a decision precipitated by a combination of external and domestic factors. Externally, this included pressure from the U.S. government, which wanted to reduce its aid commitment and so pushed South Korea toward both an export-oriented policy and a normalization of relations with Japan that would turn the latter nation into a major economic sponsor.[3] Internally, the

South Korean government for its own part realized that for a country with a weak domestic market and an economy almost completely dependent upon raw material imports, an export-oriented industrialization program that would make use of its most abundant resource—its well-educated, disciplined workforce—made a great deal more sense.

By means of the five-year economic plans, Park and his government engineered South Korea's industrial development by establishing export priorities for each decade: light manufacturing in the 1960s (textiles, plywood, wigs, footwear, small appliances and the like), heavy and chemical industrialization in the 1970s (including steel, chemicals, machinery, shipbuilding, electronics, automobiles), and consumer goods and electronics in the 1980s. Throughout his administration, Park spearheaded this industrial transformation through heavy-handed state intervention, implementing the country's economic programs through highly centralized state planning and intimate involvement in all aspects of the economy. These interventionist policies included, of course, strict governmental control over finance/credit allocation as well as over key trade and investment decisions—especially in regard to which industrial sectors and companies were to be supported and developed—and protection of domestic industries.[4] These policies were aided by external conditions favorable to South Korea's export-led strategy, such as the relatively open international trade regime of the 1960s and 1970s and South Korea's geopolitical importance to the United States in East Asia.

Park's economic policies, however, were not without serious controversy and problems. Most significant of these were his highly repressive labor policies aimed at ensuring cheap wages and docile labor. During Park's rule, South Korea was wracked by numerous violent labor disputes that resulted in many lost lives, proving that many Korean workers were far from docile.[5] Another policy privileged large conglomerates (*jaebol*) at the expense of smaller businesses as key actors in industrialization, passing on much of the costs of national economic expansion to domestic consumers.[6] Despite these controversies, his policies were, at least in purely economic terms, remarkably successful. To give a brief overview of South Korea's economic performance: between 1960 and 1970, South Korea's GDP increased an average of 8.6 percent per year, and between 1970 and 1980, an average of 9.5 percent (World Bank 1982). Between 1960 and 1995, South Korea experienced a phenomenal increase in the total GNP from US$1.9 to US$451.7 billion, and an increase in per capita GNP from US$79 to US$10,076. In the same period, the primary sector, which contributed almost 40 percent of GDP in 1960, represented only 6.6 percent in 1995, while the manufacturing/mining sectors grew from 15.9 percent to 27.2 percent, and the service sector from 47.3 percent to 66.2 percent (Economic Planning Board 1996).

After Park's assassination in 1979, South Korea was not without a number of serious economic, as well as political, challenges. Politically, South Korea endured another tumultuous era of military dictatorship under Chun Doo Hwan until 1987, and subsequently underwent a painful but ultimately successful transition to democratic rule. Economically, the country experienced serious setbacks in the 1980s and 1990s that culminated in a major economic crisis requiring a financial bailout by the International Monetary Fund (IMF) in 1997.[7] Despite these setbacks, the South Korean economy, defying dire predictions, recovered to expand further, emerging as a full-fledged consumerist society by the 1980s, and was, as of 2005, the eleventh largest economy in the world with a per capita GNP of over US$16,000 (Bureau of East Asian and Pacific Affairs, U.S. Department of State 2007).

Although many scholars have analyzed this story of South Korea's economic "miracle," not as much attention, surprisingly, has been paid to the issue of the fascinating social and cultural transformations that have accompanied this rushed, high-speed development following World War II.[8] The economic transformations of the last few decades have been accompanied by unprecedented changes in the arenas of society and culture. Along with the far-reaching structural transformations that have taken place as part of and as a consequence of economic development—urbanization, alterations of class and family structure and of employment and educational patterns, etc—fundamental developments have also occurred in the spheres of belief systems, ideology, and culture, expressed not only in the changes of general social mores but also in popular culture.

Recent cultural changes in South Korea must in essence be understood as part of a story of ongoing confrontation and negotiation with Western modernity. As discussed in the last chapter, Korea began to embrace elements of Western modernity around the turn of the twentieth century as it faced catastrophic national defeat at the hands of a colonial power. This goal of appropriating Western knowledge and technology to strengthen the nation was aided by the increasing delegitimization of indigenous cultural elements, especially Confucianism, which became a scapegoat for Korea's national plight. While North Korea embraced communism and turned toward Russia, the South embraced Western modernity as it began to pursue a West-dependent path of capitalist development and modernization and came under the influence of American geopolitical and cultural power.

The sheer speed of this "catch up" development process—an attempt to accomplish in a mere few decades what took the West several centuries to achieve—has inevitably generated a number of difficult social challenges that have emerged in a number of ways. These challenges are, at base, rooted in a set of intractable societal contradictions endemic to what various observers have described as a process of "compressed" development or industrialization (K. Chang 1999; Kendall 1996). Observable across the spectrum of political, economic, and social arenas, these contradictions in turn grow out of the confrontations between the forces of hegemonic Western modernity that South Korea has been compelled so urgently to embrace, and the imperatives of native cultural practices and beliefs that have been upheld as much through a process of cultural inheritance as by political design.

It can be argued, for example, that although the state managed to achieve its transition to popular democracy in the 1980s, the South Korean political scene remains a continuing struggle between the new, popular democratic forces and what one scholar refers to as the rule and politics of an old-time "authoritarian political aristocracy" (K. Chang 1999: 35).[9] In the economic arena as well, such developmental contradictions have been reflected not only in the immense social costs associated with rapid economic transformations—including intense repression of labor, unequal distribution of wealth, and severe underdevelopment of the welfare system[10]—but also in the coexistence of a highly modern productive structure and a national corporate culture that continues to define and ground itself on "traditional" cultural principles, especially those of Confucian patriarchalism and familism.[11] It is, however, in the wider social realm, particularly in the spheres of gender and the family, that such developmental contradictions are at present most outwardly evident and most controversially played out.

In the period after World War II, Korean family and gender relations have undergone significant changes, fueled in large part by urbanization, education, and changes in both family structure and gender ideology. But as subsequent discussion will show, the realms of contemporary family and gender, despite such changes, are profoundly riven with tensions, as elements of modernity sharply confront and attempt to coexist with deeply entrenched patriarchal structures and values that still govern, if not dominate, the South Korean social and psychological life. These patriarchal principles, and the continued subordinate status of women in society, are much more than lingering cultural holdovers; more accurately, they have been reconstructed, "reinvented," and given institutional support within the contemporary context by a patriarchal-capitalist developmental regime determined to maintain stability in the face of rapid social change. In the following sections, I explicate in detail the social and structural sources of the cultural contradictions that characterize contemporary Korean family and gender and the reasons for their particularly problematic consequences for women.

The Ideology and Structure of Neo-Confucian Patriarchy

To comprehend the fundamental basis of modern Korean gender relations and the family, and the recent transformations and predicaments faced by women, it is important to begin by examining the ideology and structure of the traditional Korean family/gender system that I refer to as Neo-Confucian patriarchy. The inner workings of what we have come to view as the "traditional" Korean family system and the larger relations of gender are built upon the principles of Neo-Confucianism, a revitalization and rearticulation of the Confucian philosophy by scholars during the Song dynasty (960–1279 C.E.) in China (P. Chang 1996: 24).[12] Although it is difficult to do justice to the complexity of Confucianism, it can, in general, be viewed "both as a political ideology and an ethical and religious code developed and practiced in a patriarchal cultural context" (P. Chang 1996: 25). At the beginning of the Yi dynasty (1392–1910) in Korea, Neo-Confucianism was adopted by the ruling elites primarily as a way to consolidate the new state and to suppress Buddhism. Neo-Confucianism, which stressed a strict hierarchical order of human relationship based on age, sex, and inherited social status, was seen by the Yi dynasty literati-officials as a "compelling and well-reasoned system of thought that could be used as an ideological basis for reshaping Korean society" (Deuchler 1977: 2), and was reconfigured by the Korean ruling class into a comprehensive set of norms, laws, and customs for prescribing political rule, morality, and social relationships (K. Chang 1997: 24; S. Lee 1995). Although some fundamental conflicts were involved in introducing this social model into Korea, this project was ultimately successful and Korea became a "model" Confucian society among its East Asian neighbors.[13]

The organizational basis of Confucian society and family was a strict patrilineal and patrilocal lineage system, the solidarity of which was maintained and affirmed through the all-important practices of ancestor worship and filial piety and the continuance of which was assured through the production of male heirs. Under the leadership of the male head, the family, or the clan, was the locus of social control, welfare provision, and political integration. Within the framework of such social organization, the ideal society as conceived by Neo-Confucianists was based on two central principles of human relations: hierarchical order between the elder and the younger, and the division between male and female.[14] With age- and sex-based hierarchy at its center, this society was governed by a strict hierarchy among all groups of people, and it was believed that to adhere to and observe this hierarchical relationship was the only means of maintaining harmony within society and the universe.

Although the relationship between father and son was considered the most fundamental and paradigmatic of all relationships, the hierarchical relationship between men and women was just as pivotal. The relationship between men and women was governed by two major principles: *namyeo yubyeol* (difference between the sexes) and *namjon yeobi* (superiority of men and inferiority of women; literally, "honored men, abased women") (H. Cho 1986: 282). The principle of sex-difference served as the basis for strict gender segregation and role division, with women's "inner" sphere subordinated to men's "outer" sphere (P. Chang 1996: 25–26).[15]

For women, this rigid social system had far-reaching consequences. During the periods preceding the Yi dynasty, when Buddhism held greater sway, Korean women had traditionally enjoyed far more physical mobility, freedom, and rights. During the Unified Silla period (668–

935 C.E.) for example, women could serve as the head of the family, giving them considerable economic autonomy. In this period, three female rulers occupied the throne and queen-mothers often acted as regents for young kings, exercising tremendous political power and influence (Yu 1987: 15). During the Goryo period (935–1392 C.E.), women enjoyed a range of rights: equal inheritance, remarriage, mobility, relative freedom of association with men, and even uxorilocal marriage (Deuchler 1977: 8; Yu 1987: 15).

With the emergence of a Neo-Confucian society, however, harsh discriminatory legal measures were systematically enacted against women, along with intense government indoctrination and propaganda. In addition to solidifying the system of patrilineality founded upon primogeniture and strict lineage exogamy, new legal measures included strengthening the authority of the household head, enforcing stricter rules of sex segregation, and prohibiting remarriage of widows (P. Chang 1996). These reforms, in essence, established a stringent system of gender hierarchy and segregation seen as pivotal for an orderly society, and within this, the strict control of women's behavior, thought, and movement. The principle and practice of subjection and subordination of women to men, legitimized in cosmological terms as the subordination of *eum* (earth) to *yang* (heaven), was firmly established and the hierarchical relationship between men and women came to be seen as an essential foundation of human morality and social order (Deuchler 1977: 3).

The life of a woman in this social system was extremely difficult. Cultural training of girls was focused completely on their fulfilling the role of married women, who were viewed as the moral guardians of the family and main providers of the family's physical needs (P. Chang 1996: 27). When a woman married into the husband's family—with marriage viewed as the "bond of love between two surnames" (Deuchler 1977: 7)—she found herself in an alien environment in which she as an outsider had two primary functions: to produce sons and to provide domestic labor. Under the iron-fisted authority of the mother-in-law, the new daughter-in-law's role was often no more than that of a domestic servant, providing the most strenuous and menial domestic labor for all the extended members of her husband's household and, as the person on the lowest rung of female prestige, enduring the domination by women higher up on the ladder.

Furthermore, a woman's plight in her hew household was rendered harsher by the fact that she was cut off from her natal family when married; a woman, regarded only as a temporary member of the natal family, whose filial piety was to be transferred upon marriage to her parents-in-law, had to adjust to her new environment with almost no emotional and practical support from her natal family.[16] Her main filial duty to her own parents was to avoid any misbehavior in her husband's household that might bring dishonor and shame to her own family, and to persevere through whatever hardship that might await her there. As a way of upholding her chastity and demonstrating allegiance to her husband's family and lineage, a woman—especially from the upper classes—was also expected never to remarry. Indeed, she was expected to endure all that befell her in her husband's household until the day she died, becoming "the ghost in her husband's home"; that is, one of its ancestral spirits (P. Chang 1996: 30–31). An upper-class woman, moreover, was physically confined to the inner spheres of the house and practically cut off from the outside world—although commoner women, such as peasants, entertainers, medicine women, and slaves could, and did, out of economic necessity, move about more freely.

Although the depth of indoctrination and the level of adherence to these Confucian practices varied across classes, a woman, in her roles as dutiful daughter-in-law, obedient wife, and dedicated mother, was held to the strictest, often impossible standards of the "virtuous" woman.[17] The expectations for the ideal woman included being chaste, quiet, passive, hardworking, and self-sacrificing, and upholding these virtues was viewed as critical for guarding the honor of her family and for ensuring its success.[18] Furthermore, women's lives were governed and controlled by the principle of the three "obediences" to men (*samjong jido*)—to her father when young, to her husband when married, and to her son when old (Palley 1990: 1140; P. Chang 1996: 30)—as well as through the mores of seven arbitrary "evils" (*chilgeo jiak*), the commission of which could result in her expulsion from the household: disobedience toward parents-in-law, failure to produce a son, adultery, theft, undue jealousy, grave illness, and extreme talkativeness (Deuchler 1977: 35; Choi 1994: 191–92). In a society where a woman's social recognition and standing were gained only through marriage and through her husband, these sanctions were an effective way of keeping her obedient and submissive (Deuchler 1977: 35).[19]

A certain amount of authority was reserved for women, however, in their leadership of the "inner" sphere. Although her domestic influence, to be sure, did not extend beyond the boundary of the home, except through the influence she exerted on her husband or sons—which was, at times, considerable—this was a heavy responsibility, for as the "moral guardian" of her household, a woman was seen as being primarily responsible for domestic harmony and prosperity, and by extension, the well-being of the entire nation. Thus, as Martina Deuchler (1977) puts it: "The Confucian image of women was thus a double one; she had to be modest and submissive, but also strong and responsible. On the level of Confucian idealism, the image was considered virtuous; on the level of daily life, it often meant bondage" (4).

Another way in which a woman could acquire a measure of power in this social system was through her maternal role, more specifically, through the production and raising of sons. A Korean woman, for all intents and purposes, was considered a non-person until she produced a son, at which point, having fulfilled her primary duty, she acquired the identity, privileges, and authority of motherhood. And by becoming the mother-in-law herself later in life, a woman could finally acquire a full measure of power and status, as filial piety was extended by the son equally to the mother and to the father.

Since their future status depended completely on the position of their sons, most Korean women took to motherhood as an all-consuming preoccupation. With their greatest interest lying in producing and securing close ties to sons by nurturing their sense of filial piety, women thereby became active agents in enforcing and perpetuating the patriarchal system.[20] In speaking of institutionalized "mother power" in Korea, Haejoang Cho (1986) states:

In fact, legitimizing mother power might be the most successful way of accommodating women under the male-dominated social system. Compared with wife power, which can be found mostly in the Western countries, or sister power in Polynesian societies, mother power seems to be the most secure source of power for women under a patriarchal system. The enduring tie and strong attachment between mother and son can easily develop into the son's dependence upon his mother psychologically, culturally, and institutionally. (292)

Changes and Contradictions in Family and Gender
after World War II

In the post–World War II era, South Korea has experienced not only rapid economic transformation, but also a number of major and unprecedented changes in the social sphere that stimulated the transformation of the traditional patriarchal family/gender system. The first important shift to note in this regard is the fundamental change in the size and structure of the traditional family. Due to an immensely successful family planning program, South Korea, since the early 1960s, has experienced a steep decline in fertility rates; starting with about 6 children per family in 1960 to 1.6 in 1990, an impressive 73 percent decline, South Korea is now a "below-replacement" society, and as of 2005, the total fertility rate was 1.08 (KWDI 2007: 5). Accordingly, household size declined from 5.5 members in 1965 to 3.86 in 1988 (Economic Planning Board 1990: 278).

Along with the reduction in family size, there has also been a shift in the basic structure of the family, starting with a trend toward nuclearization. By the early 1990s, about 76 percent of all households of related members in South Korea consisted of nuclear families (K. Chang 1997: 27), up from about 66.8 percent in 1966. Another important trend has been a change in family composition: with smaller family sizes, the traditional extended family structure has become less prevalent in South Korea, although "stem families" (one set of elderly parents living with an adult couple) as well as "modified extended family" (elderly parents living with adult children but maintaining independent budget arrangements, or the coexistence of the nuclear family structure and extended family kinship ties) have become more common (K. Chang 1997: 28; D. Kim 1990: 414). Although we must evaluate with caution, as will become clear, the actual implications of changes in family size and composition, especially the phenomenon of family nuclearization, we can see in recent decades some important shifts in family demographics.

Together with these structural changes, the ideological basis of the traditional family and gender system is undergoing gradual transformation as well, especially through the spread of modern Western ideals that have come to exert considerable influence on Korean culture. In the sphere of marital and gender relations, Western models of courtship, marriage, and gender relations—for instance, the ideologies of gender

egalitarianism and of romantic love as a basis for marriage—have gained
a hold over the popular imagination, serving as an impetus for change in
individual aspirations and marital expectations, and in the dynamics of
male-female relations within the family (Kendall 1996; E. Yi 1993). Even
if reality does not yet quite match up with what people think or want,
a number of social surveys have shown a real movement away from
traditionalism in such matters as spousal selection, expectations for emotional bonding and equality in marriage, son-preference, and even beliefs
about dependence in old age (D. Lee 1986; Lee and Kim 1977: 148).

These changes in Korean family and gender relations, however, cannot be discussed without reference to the massive improvements made
in education in the post–World War II period, especially for women.
These improvements have been critically responsible for transforming
the basic conditions of women's existence and situation in the last few
decades. The modern educational system took root in Korea in the
late 1800s through the efforts both of Korean reformers and the Protestant missionaries, and then continued during the colonial period in
schools built and controlled by the Japanese (W. Han 1980; Lett 1998).
However, only a small number of Korean children, and a smaller number of girls, attended these schools, especially beyond the elementary
level, because they were established mainly for the benefit of Japanese
children.[21] Immediately after the liberation, the American occupation
provided further impetus for building up public education, especially
primary- and secondary-level vocational (non-academic) education, but
it was not until after the Korean War that a full-fledged expansion of
education was pursued at all levels, including the university level.

Reflecting the high value of—if not obsession with—education
among Koreans, the educational participation of the Korean populace
since the 1960s has been nothing short of phenomenal. By 1955, only
two years after the Korean War, primary school enrollments in South
Korea had already reached 66 percent for boys and 58 percent for girls.
Since then, South Korea has cultivated one of the most well-educated
populations in the world. With nearly all children of both sexes obtaining primary and secondary education, South Korea has a literacy rate
of almost 100 percent, and even more notably, has one of the highest
proportions of college-educated citizens in the world. As of 1990, for

Table 1
Educational Attainment in South Korea and Taiwan, 1970–1990

	1970	1975	1980	1985	1990
Secondary education, ages 12–17 (%)					
South Korea					
Male	51.4	65.9	86.1	91.0	94.3
Female	33.1	48.5	76.1	87.0	90.5
Taiwan					
Male	N/A	69.5	71.9	77.9	83.6
Female	N/A	61.7	70.0	78.6	87.4
Higher education, ages 18–21 (%)					
South Korea					
Male	13.9	13.9	25.2	51.0	50.8
Female	4.7	5.6	8.7	23.2	24.4
Taiwan					
Male	N/A	11.2	11.9	14.2	18.3
Female	N/A	8.7	10.2	13.5	19.6

SOURCE: Adapted from Brinton, Lee, and Parish (1995: 1106).

example, an astounding 50.8 percent of the male population and 24.4 percent of women were enrolled in an institution of higher education (Brinton, Lee, and Parish 1995: 1106), and more than 92 percent of all Korean parents *expected* their children to enter college (Lett 1998: 161). The degree of South Korea's educational attainment is rendered even more starkly when the educational rates are compared with those of neighboring Taiwan (see Table 1), another Asian economic "tiger": in the same year, the enrollment in higher education in Taiwan was only 18.3 percent for men and 19.6 percent for women (Brinton, Lee, and Parish 1995: 1106).

In addition to enjoying increased educational opportunities, Korean women have also been incorporated into the labor force in unprecedented numbers since the 1960s, further opening up possibilities for change. Mobilized as workers for the intensive urban-centered, export-oriented industrialization program, women have been incorporated rapidly into both the expanding manufacturing and service sectors; between 1960 and 1990, the proportion of women in the labor force has increased from 27 percent to 41.3 percent, with women actually being absorbed into the labor force at a faster rate than men (Economic

Planning Board 1960, 1990).[22] A small number of women have also made inroads into a limited range of professional positions.

Efforts toward the betterment of women's status have also been made by legal changes aimed at bringing about equality between the sexes, beginning with the guarantee of sex equality written into the Constitution of the Republic of Korea (1948). In addition to establishing that all citizens are equal before the law and prohibiting discrimination based on sex, religion, or social status, women were given full suffrage in the constitution. Furthermore, due to the efforts of various women's groups, other important legal provisions were enacted in the late 1980s, such as the Equal Employment Opportunity Act of 1987—a legal measure that stipulates equality for women in job placement, on-the-job training, promotions, retirement, and provisions for (unpaid) maternity leave (Palley 1990; S. Moon 2005: 158–59)—as well as a number of important changes in the Family Law, the part of the civil code that has been perhaps the most responsible for the disadvantaged status of South Korean women.[23]

Through such changes in family structure, systems of values, and in educational and occupational opportunities for women, real social transformations have occurred in South Korea over the last few decades that have visibly affected the basic situation of women and the traditional assumptions of family and gender relations. Although unpacking and evaluating the actual consequences of these educational advances for contemporary Korean women is a complex undertaking, we can confidently state this much: literate, well-educated, and enjoying the rewards of postwar economic affluence and the technologies of modern life, contemporary Korean women are not only the beneficiaries of living standards and freedoms of which their mothers and grandmothers dared not dream, but have also become increasingly sophisticated and informed citizens of a modern, globalizing society.

Although these changes have been real and dramatic, such developments in the social and cultural sphere have been, on the other hand, far more complex than they appear. Indeed, one of the most notable aspects of the dynamics of contemporary Korean family and gender relations is that, in the face of all of the recent changes, the underlying basis of the patriarchal system appears to remain surprisingly cohesive in many ways.[24] That is to say, in spite of all of the recent structural and ideological changes, the relational and ideological bases of the Neo-Confucian patriarchal family and gender regime continue to enjoy a surprising degree of legitimacy among the majority of Korean women and men, governing how modern families actually function, and how people relate to each other and think about themselves.

At the level of family relationships, for instance, most Korean families, despite the neo-local and nuclear structure of many, still continue to function like traditional extended families in which family members, in their clearly defined roles, are bound to one another in mutual webs of familial obligations.[25] Of the principles governing relations among family members, filial piety still remains a central value—although there may be some evidence of its attenuation among the younger generation (Lie 1998: 160)—and the relationship between parents and children, and the mutual obligations governing these relationships, continue to be cardinal. More generally, contemporary South Korea is still an overwhelmingly patriarchal and male-centered culture, where interpersonal relations continue to be hierarchical along lines of gender and age. Finally, in spite of the increasingly individualistic attitudes of the younger generation, South Korea remains an intensely family-centered society.[26] Kyung-sup Chang (1997) puts it this way:

When Korean society entered the modern industrial era after successive colonial encroachments, indigenous elites made no serious attempt to eradicate the Neo-Confucian tradition of family-centered life. In fact, Neo-Confucian values and attitudes were incorporated into public education and political discourse as a legitimate cultural heritage. In Korean society today, people are under strong moral and, sometimes, political pressure to sacrifice their individual interests for unconditional family unity, to confine familial problems within the family, and to abstain from resorting to social or governmental measures in solving familial needs. (24–25)

What, then, are some of the specific social and political mechanisms that have helped support the continuing tenacity and power of patriarchy in contemporary Korean society, and as a consequence, the nettlesome situation of women?

Partnership between Patriarchy and Capitalism

Contrary to the popular view, the tenacious survival of the ideological and functional dimensions of the Neo-Confucian patriarchal family system in the contemporary milieu is not simply a result of a "cultural lag" in a high-speed modernization process, but the very consequence of the conscious social policies of an interventionist state in pursuit of catch-up economic development. As discussed earlier, the intensive industrialization of the South Korean government in the beginning of the 1960s was a carefully planned capitalist developmental project, aimed at bringing South Korea into the ranks of industrialized nations. However, exemplifying what Heidi Hartmann (1981) has described as the "partnership between patriarchy and capitalism,"[27] this developmental program was firmly premised upon the maintenance of the patriarchal family system as the organizing unit of society, and the mobilization of unpaid female labor for domestic work and the reproduction of the workforce.

Indeed, one could say that the preservation and perpetuation of the patriarchal system of family and gender in South Korea, though reconstituted in the modern nuclear form, has been the basis upon which the stability of the postwar developmental period was largely maintained. As in the case of Japan, the cornerstone of this plan was the construction of a highly gender-segmented, patriarchal capitalist industrial structure, a system based on the family wage and designed to maintain and perpetuate the patriarchal family system by encouraging female domesticity. In South Korea, this plan was structured around a particularly rigid system of gender-based occupational segregation and pay inequality that has served successfully to keep women tied to the domestic sphere.

Women, as mentioned, were first recruited in significant numbers into the workforce for the labor-intensive export sector starting in the 1960s. This situation, unfortunately, did not signify economic advancements for women; in an economy where the workers were already exploited economically, women became the most exploited workers of all. This was achieved not only through a system of extreme wage inequality by gender, but by concentrating women mainly in the lowest-paid, least-skilled, and most labor-intensive jobs. For example, in the sphere of manufacturing, women have been concentrated in poorly paid jobs at garment/textile, toy, and electronics factories, where they earned, in 1988, approximately 45 percent of male wages (Palley 1990: 1141). Indeed, South Korea has had, and still does, one of the greatest gender-based pay disparities in the world.[28] Although labor strikes in the late 1980s helped raise all workers' wages, the gender disparity in pay was not greatly reduced; in 1990, women workers in manufacturing industries only earned 51.1 percent of men's wages in those industries (KWDI 1997: 200).

The situation has not been much better in non-manufacturing sectors. In white-collar occupations as well, such as clerical work, women have traditionally been paid similarly low wages and ghettoized into routine, auxiliary support work in offices that reproduce their domestic roles with little prospect for advancement. In many of these jobs, young women, many of them college graduates, have been expected to play the role of docile and helpful office girls, with the major functions of creating a pleasant office environment and supporting male employees through such tasks as the "three C's": making coffee, buying cigarettes, and making copies (M. Kim 1992: 160; Kim and Chun 1996; Cf. Kumazawa 1996). Professional women, also subject to great pay disparity, are still largely concentrated in traditionally "female" occupations such as nursing and teaching, and face daunting barriers with regard to professional advancement, although there has been evidence of some improvements in recent years.[29] Aside from wage inequality and barriers to entry into top positions, women have also been held back by such policies as occupational "tracking" that occurs within a company, a system whereby lower wages and work of lesser importance for women are justified by placing women in lower categories or "classes" of work (H. Cho 1986; Cf. Kumazawa 1996).

As various scholars have pointed out, such a system of workplace discrimination naturally serves to discourage and restrict the participation of women in the labor force, helping to keep them in their traditional positions. As Hartmann puts it (1976):

Job segregation by sex, I will argue, is the primary mechanism in capitalist society that maintains the superiority of men over women, because it enforces lower wages for women in the labor market. Low wages keep women dependent on men because they encourage women to marry. Married women must perform domestic chores for their husbands. Men benefit, then, from both higher wages and the domestic division of labor. This domestic division of labor, in turn, acts to weaken women's position in the labor market. Thus, the hierarchical domestic division of labor is perpetuated by the labor market, and vice versa. This process is the present outcome of the continuing interaction of two interlocking systems, capitalism and patriarchy. (139)

In South Korea, it appears that such policies have been particularly successful in deterring women's full-fledged workforce participation and hindering changes in women's situations. Faced with low pay, the lack of possibilities for professional advancement, or the gloomy prospect of a lifetime of menial work, the overwhelming majority of women in South Korea has been motivated to prefer marriage and domesticity over paid workforce participation—though it is important to point out that not all women, especially working-class women, can afford to be full-time housewives. Most poor, working-class, and even middle-class women in South Korea have been, and are, indeed engaged in a wide array of formal and informal income-generating activities. But the important point is that middle-class housewifery remains the dominant ideal for women of all classes, and when given a choice, most working-class and middle-class women would prefer homemaking to participation in the workforce.[30]

Furthermore, women in South Korea, as in Japan, have been encouraged to stay at home through so-called marriage bars—policies that implicitly or explicitly pressure women to quit work upon marrying. Indeed, marriage bars explain the distinctive pattern of post-marital exit in Korean female workforce participation and the overwhelmingly young and single character of the female workforce, whose members tend to view work not as a lifetime pursuit or a vehicle for economic independence, but as a transitional activity before marriage that contributes to the income of the natal family (Cf. Kung 1994 and Salaff 1995). In 1989, for example, 72 percent of urban female workers in South Korea were unmarried, and 85.8 percent of female workers quit their jobs within four years of employment (Ministry of Labor 1989). In 1975, urban single women between the ages of 20 and 24 were the most economically active, with a workforce participation rate of 67.9 percent; but in the same age range, workforce participation among married women was only 10.6 percent, a rate that remained severely restricted up to the age of 34 (Cho and Koo 1983: 522).[31]

The distinctive success of these policies in South Korea is evidenced mostly clearly when compared with Taiwan and Japan. Although South Korea, like its East Asian neighbors, displays low overall rates of workforce participation by women and a pattern of post-marital exit, its rates

Table 2

Employment Status Distribution by Age among Urban Married Women
in South Korea and Taiwan

Age Group	South Korea (1985)				Taiwan (1989)			
	E	S-E/E	FEW	Total FLFP	E	S-E/E	FEW	Total FLFP
25–29	8.1	12.5	6.5	27.1	36.7	13.0	5.3	54.9
30–39	13.8	17.0	8.1	38.9	29.6	18.3	10.1	58.0
40–49	19.8	15.8	11.6	47.2	30.0	19.8	7.8	57.6
All ages	13.3	15.4	8.6	37.3	30.6	18.1	8.8	57.5

NOTES: E=Employee; S-E/E=Self-Employed/Employer; FEW=Family Enterprise Worker;
FLFP=Female Labor Force Participation. All figures are percentages. Among Korean women who
reported themselves as employees, those who work in their own homes (i.e., domestic out-
workers) are reclassified as self-employed.
SOURCE: Adapted from Brinton, Lee, and Parish (1995: 1105).

of formal workforce participation by married women are the *lowest*
among the three nations.[32] Compared to Taiwan, for example, South
Korea in 1985 had lower rates of employment in every age group (see
Table 2); among married women between the ages of 25 and 29—
considered prime childbearing age—South Korean women participated
in the labor force at only one-half the rate of their Taiwanese counterparts, with 27.1 percent compared to 54.9 percent (Brinton, Lee, and
Parish 1995: 1104–5).

The nature of Korean women's labor force participation reveals another peculiar pattern, an *inverse* relationship between higher education
and employment. Contrary to standard human capital models (such as
Becker 1985) that predict higher levels of education with higher probability of employment, the relationship of education and income is the
inverse in South Korea: among married women, more education actually leads to a lower probability of formal employment (Brinton, Lee,
and Parish 1995: 1105; U. Cho 1996; M. Kim 1992; Lett 1998: 61).[33]
This situation, of course, is due to the scarcity of appropriate jobs for
college-educated, middle- or upper-class women, combined with a
strong ideology of female domesticity.[34] This again is in contrast to
Taiwan, where higher levels of female education have led uniformly
to higher levels of employment (Brinton, Lee, and Parish 1995: 1105).

The maintenance of female domesticity and patriarchal gender norms in South Korea cannot be understood without discussing how these have been effectively reinforced and actively perpetuated ideologically through the efforts of the state.[35] In tandem with a program of intensive economic marginalization that motivates female domesticity, the interventionist state in South Korea has been engaged in a conscious effort to preserve, while reshaping, the fundamental structure of the patriarchal family through cultural policies aimed at actively reinforcing and reifying the roles and subjectivities of both women and men that were normative under the patriarchal system. By means of indoctrination and socialization through educational institutions, the media, and various governmental organizations, the state worked to buttress the principles of patriarchal family and gender relations and reshape them in their contemporary form, mobilizing men as family providers and productive workers and women as biological and domestic reproducers for the project of modern nation-building.

In her recent study of post–World War II nation-building in South Korea from a gendered perspective, Seungsook Moon (2005) shows concretely how such "domesticating programs" included, from the 1960s through the 1980s, an array of classes and instructional programs for women established at workplaces, communities, and schools that were aimed at inculcating the reproductive and domestic subjectivity of mother and housewife in single women workers. Such classes not only mobilized single women as wage workers for labor-intensive industries, but also educated and prepared women for their culturally idealized role as "wise mother and good wife," teaching them basic skills for such things as household management, child rearing, fertility control, feminine etiquette, and appropriate hobbies, along with disseminating messages about patriotism, anti-communism, and the urgent necessity of economic growth. While marginalizing women economically by reinforcing their domestic identities, these programs, then, also served to depoliticize single women, manipulating "reproductive and domestic femininity to make women docile and productive for the sake of building the industrial economy" (75).[36]

In addition, Moon also demonstrates the important role of state-established women's organizations, along with state-controlled media, in organizing mothers and wives as their quasi-official instruments for disseminating state-sponsored messages. These organizations were effective, for instance, in persuading women to carry out the "patriotic duty" of fertility control, and in teaching techniques related to the "rational" management of the household (through savings and thrift, for example), a crucial part in the state's effort to "rationalize" daily life as part of its nation-building and modernization project, and more specifically, to help minimize the negative impact of dependent, rapid capitalist growth on households. As Moon (2005) puts it: "[R]eflecting the pervasive use of instrumental rationality as the core technique of ruling, the state relied on the combination of mass media and women's AMO's (administered mass organization) to generate a social atmosphere saturated with the emphasis on the role of mothers and wives in nation building" (90). She adds:

Regardless of such the actual effects of feminizing instructions on women workers, the persistence of such domesticating programs in their variations is suggestive of the extent to which the modernizing state was involved in the construction of gendered nationals in the pursuit of militarized modernity. An underlying assumption here was that whatever women might do and wherever they might be, they were ultimately reproductive and domestic beings represented in the role of wife and mother.

As a result, despite the quantitative expansion of women workers in manufacturing industries and their crucial role in the earlier phase of export-oriented economic growth, their subjectivity as full-time permanent workers was overshadowed by the normative feminine subjectivity of the nonproductive housewife. (76)

In sum, the South Korean developmental state, building upon Neo-Confucian patriarchal foundations, has been a key agent in the creation of modern gendered subjects and the reconstruction of the "traditional" patriarchal family into its contemporary patriarchal form—and in ensuring their cohesion throughout the period of economic development and nation-building following World War II. Although it is important to recognize the durability of culture and the agency of individuals and families themselves in upholding and maintaining traditional social arrangements,[37] such aspects must be seen within the context of the South Korean state's active postwar social engineering efforts that helped preserve the patriarchal social system as a foundation for a developing capitalist economy.

These developments have, then, rendered the contemporary Korean family/gender system a welter of contradictions that, in recent years, has been subject to increasing strains and instability. Though by no means losing its basic legitimacy, the Korean patriarchal family—in its reconfigured form within modern industrial capitalism—and the relations between women and men are subject to increasing tensions as conventional beliefs about what constitutes the ideal family and gender arrangements are being challenged, as are the conventional conceptions of femininity and masculinity.[38] Though difficult for everyone involved, this situation, however, has had particular implications for women. Subject to significant cultural changes that have fundamentally altered their self-understandings and beliefs regarding family and gender relations while obligated to navigate the demands of a patriarchal system, many of these women have encountered a particularly thorny set of challenges that have generated a great deal of conflicts and dilemmas.

Women's Domestic Dilemmas

To understand the fundamental conflicts of the modern middle-class Korean family and the dilemmas faced by women, one must comprehend some of the specific ways in which women's self-conceptions and subjective expectations regarding life, marriage, and family have been transformed within contemporary South Korean society. As intimated in the narratives of Ji-won and Hyun-mi in the beginning of the chapter, there is little doubt that one major consequence of recent modernizing changes in the lives of women has been a certain expansion in the horizon of life possibilities and choices, enabling women to envision possibilities beyond domestic roles. Even if the realities of the current society are hardly favorable toward women's unfettered pursuit of nondomestic goals, it has at least become possible for most women to envision life trajectories beyond the domestic sphere. For many women, then, especially for well-educated ones, a major source of personal and domestic conflicts can be seen as the restrictions of the current patriarchal family system that hinder women from rising above the path of domesticity. Unable to parlay their educational capital, talents, and energies to a wider range of goals, many women live in quiet frustration, trapped in a vague sense of dissatisfaction with their domestic roles. For others who do not necessarily aspire to professional careers, these changes have at least served to intensify the sense of restrictiveness of the current family system.

To comprehend properly the dilemmas of middle-class Korean women, however, I have found that it is necessary to look to a problem that is even more basic and immediate. Although the restrictiveness of the current patriarchal family makes it difficult for women to make full use of their abilities beyond the domestic arena, there exists another problem that is more immediately significant and relevant to the majority of middle-class women: the oppressiveness of the current patriarchal family as experienced against women's transformed expectations regarding marital and domestic life. As is reflected in the experiences of women we saw in the beginning and in others we will see throughout this book, I contend that one of the major changes brought about for Korean women by education, modern ideas, and material affluence is not simply one of heightened aspiration beyond domesticity, but of altered expectations *within* marriage and the domestic sphere. In contrast to American liberal feminist assumptions, it is a mistake to presume in the Korean context that high levels of education and modernity have encouraged all women to acquire conscious aspirations beyond familial roles, or that the major source of women's frustrations lies in their restriction to the domestic sphere. Due both to the persistence of the high cultural value ascribed to women's familial roles and the barriers against women's advancements in the labor market, the forces of modernity have generated for women not so much an impulse toward emancipation from the family as a vision for a better domestic and marital life.

At the most basic level, material improvements in domestic life in the post–World War II era have emancipated women from some of the heaviest household burdens of the past, enabling them to look forward to domestic life under circumstances far more pleasant than their mothers or grandmothers had ever hoped to experience. Along with this, modern ideas of marriage and family life have allowed women to imagine domestic and marital relations based less on patriarchal oppression and more on greater egalitarianism, as well as on bonds of mutual love, respect, and affection. Furthermore, certain redefinitions of women's domestic roles within the modern family have also been responsible for changes in women's expectations, redefinitions that have enhanced the social significance of women's domestic roles and have led to greater experiences of and expectations for autonomy, power, and independence within the domestic sphere.

As we will see throughout this book, one major transformation of Korean women's domestic tasks in the postwar period, for instance, has been an expansion of women's domestic work beyond what might typically be called "housework." This has occurred alongside a general intensification of women's family responsibilities, due both to the logic of family nuclearization and the particular demands on women's domestic labor within a patriarchal capitalist system (U. Cho 1996; Kim and Han 1996). Indeed, several observers have noted that the common perception of "housework" for contemporary South Korean women has been grossly mischaracterized (M. Kim 1992; O. Moon 1990).[39] The definition of "housework" for Korean women encompasses far more than simply fulfilling the traditional role of providing a "safe haven" for husbands and children and their physical reproduction through basic domestic and emotional work; rather, the rubric of "housework," in the context of an upwardly mobile, status-seeking, late-industrializing society, has come to include a wide range of non-traditional activities crucial to the maintenance or improvement of the family's social and economic status.

Akin to what Hanna Papanek (1979) has called "status production work," the non-traditional activities of Korean women range from an array of informal income-generating activities geared toward supplementing family income to the work of maintaining social and kin networks and overseeing their children's educations. The "invisible" non-paid income-generating activities, which involve considerable participation by women in the public domain, might include such tasks as income and property management and various forms of informal financial activity to supplement family income such as private money lending, stock and real estate investment, as well as part-time home-based work by wives, such as tutoring.[40] The work of managing social and kin relations, including gift exchange, is crucial to the maintenance and enhancement of the family's social connection and status, especially by improving access to resources and information that could be used as tools for improving the family's social standing (see also Papanek 1979).

Although these incomes may be seen as secondary and "invisible," they are of great practical importance to many contemporary middle-class families simply because the husbands' salaries are often no longer sufficient to maintain a middle-class lifestyle. Nonetheless, underscoring the vital importance of status attainment in contemporary South Korean society, the women's incomes are often earmarked for the purposes of family status production, for the acquisition of material symbols of afflu- ence and social status such as gifts, tutors for children, and high-status consumer products. Indeed, Denise Lett (1998) observes: "Because an- cestry no longer provides a legal basis for claiming high status in South Korea, concern with the production of family status in areas other than those related to ancestry, such as possession of status goods, have grown in relative importance. This is especially true among the middle class, where social mobility is most possible and most sought after" (207).

Women's domestic roles have always been accorded high value in Korean society, but such redefinitions of women's roles that have ren- dered women's tasks indispensable for family survival and mobility in the contemporary social context have further enhanced the significance and value of women's contributions. Along with these redefinitions have come expansions in the sense of autonomy, power, and indepen- dence that women experience with regard to their domestic work, en- abling them to hold a differing sense of expectations and vision of their roles. However, these transformed expectations can engender tremen- dous conflict when they clash with the realities of married life under the current family system. Although the difficulties imposed on women by the modern patriarchal family are severe in themselves, the experi- ences of contemporary women take on their particular gravity from the acute contradictions between their expectations for a better domestic life—based on the ideals of greater respect, egalitarianism, and conjugal affection—and the realities that contradict this ideal after marriage.

Again, as Ji-won and Hyun-mi's stories clearly illustrate, domestic problems for Korean women in my study pivot around conflicts with two major parties: husbands and mothers-in-law. In the marital sphere, the most fundamental source of discord appears to be the discrepancy rooted in women's expectation for a more egalitarian and companion- ate marriage and the realities of patriarchal husbands within the context of marriages that are often short on romantic love and intimacy.[41] In contrast to their expectations, the actual marital experiences of the ma- jority of women I interviewed are characterized by unceasing struggles with what are often described as inflexibly patriarchal and emotionally distant husbands whose treatment and expectations of their wives often seem no less traditional than those of their fathers.[42]

Despite some recent signs of improvement, the problem of mother-in-law/daughter-in-law conflict remains an important focus of domestic dilemmas for the women in my study. The continuing centrality of this conflict lies first of all in the fact that contemporary South Korea is a society in which the traditional ties and mutual obligations between parents and sons still remain quite strong, particularly the obligation of sons to take care of their elderly parents.[43] Given this emphasis, women are obligated to take on the major burden of these duties, especially wives of first-born sons. Indeed, wives shoulder the major burden of serving the parents-in-law as well as managing relations with husband's kin, including the day-to-day responsibilities of the physical and practical care of parents-in-law, carrying out the onerous responsibilities of ancestor worship, all with the expectation of obedience to the mother-in-law in all spheres of family matters.

Many problems arise for women when their expectations for respectful treatment—and the autonomy with which they fulfill these demanding tasks within the husband's family—conflict with the subordinate and oppressive treatment they still receive from their mothers-in-law. Furthermore, the difficulties of these situations are often compounded by the primary allegiance and loyalty of sons to their mothers rather than to the wives, and by the still-powerful moral sanctions against female defiance of parental authority.

In identifying the sources of domestic dilemma for women, we must mention one more factor that has served to magnify their domestic strains: the new, intensified demands of their current responsibilities. Although the reconstitution of women's tasks within the nuclear family has helped endow their present domestic roles with greater status and significance, these new responsibilities—particularly those related to family "status production" and intensive mothering—have also placed upon their shoulders enormous psychic and practical responsibility for family well-being and success, deepening their domestic burden and stresses. One example of this new kind of responsibility is children's education, another crucial activity for the purposes of status production. Building upon the traditional Confucian stress on learning and education, higher education in postwar South Korea, much like in Japan, has become a major avenue for social and economic advancement as well as a marker of social status; indeed, contemporary South Korean society is characterized by an unusual emphasis on education, even to the point of being described as a place of rampant credentialism and "diploma disease."[44] In a social system built upon the unspoken premise that the nurturing and upbringing of children will be dependent primarily on women's unpaid labor, it is the mothers who shoulder most of the responsibility for insuring the children's academic success, such as preparing them for fiercely competitive college entrance exams. For most of these "education mothers," such tasks are tremendous sources of psychic stress. These stresses come not only from the sheer enormity of women's responsibilities—encompassing everything from meeting the children's most basic physical and emotional needs, supervising all of their numerous academic activities including supplementary academic education, to managing relations with school authorities through contributions of voluntary services and frequent visits to schools with monetary gifts—but from the fact that so much hangs upon the children's academic success, including their own success as mothers.[45]

In addition, fulfilling these roles and tasks is made even more difficult for women by the reality of their relative urban isolation. Although contemporary Korean women are not entirely without resources from kin, their situation within the modern nuclear family deprives them of the emotional and practical support traditionally obtained from extended kinship networks. As Helen Hardacre (1993) has observed, "As the family shrinks, its ability to provide for a wide range of human needs associated with extended kinship networks decreases markedly" (137). Childcare, for example, a task that used to be shared among members in an extended family, tends to become the exclusive responsibility of the mother in the nuclear family, all while the emotional and practical attention needed for each child intensifies in a smaller family. Furthermore, caring for the sick and the aged, which also used to be shared among a large network of kin living in close proximity, has also fallen exclusively upon women, exacerbating tensions between generations.

Finally, a number of observers (Choi 1994; M. Kim 1992; Lett 1998; Rhi 1986) have noted another important factor that contributes to the intensified contradictions of contemporary middle-class women's lives:

the nature of female socialization in South Korea. Although male child preference is still strong in Korea, female children in contemporary middle-class families are quite highly valued; as youngsters, daughters receive a considerable portion of parental investment, especially in terms of education, love, and attention. In fact, it is a commonplace observation that the upbringing of daughters nowadays is characterized by a considerable degree of indulgence, with primary focus on educational activities; many middle-class daughters, for instance, are neither taught nor expected to perform housework as the mothers were, and are often coddled by the parents as much as the boys. Once married, however, girls are suddenly subject to a considerably different set of expectations for which they have been inadequately prepared, resulting in what some observers have called "marriage shock." As another clear aspect of the contradictions of the modern family/gender system, this disjunction contributes to contemporary women's difficulties by intensifying the fundamental mismatch between the expectations of women and the realities of their married lives.[46]

Conclusion

The contemporary Korean family, then, is one of the major arenas in which we can keenly observe some of the larger social contradictions of Korean society as these are concretely and palpably expressed at the familial and individual levels. The acute contradictions between the forces of "tradition" and "modernity" in a rapidly changing society are manifested most painfully in the often severe disjunctions between people's expectations and the actual reality of domestic and married life, especially for women. Although there is no doubt that cultural forces accompanying late-industrial capitalism and various aspects of modernization have delegitimized certain traditional ideas and emancipated women in key ways, the continuing imperatives of traditionalism within the very demands of the modern milieu, whether by cultural inheritance or by political design, have also created new sources of oppression for women, generating a great deal of conflict in their lives and threatening the stability of the family and the gender system.

For the generation of women investigated in this study, these conflicts revolve around their struggles to fulfill gender role expectations and achieve ideal domestic lives in the midst of a modern patriarchal family system that too often denies women basic respect, love, and equal treatment while demanding new kinds of sacrifices from them. As Kendall (1996) remarks on changing contemporary gender relations in South Korea, "Although the sum of these events [changing courtship practices] details a profound transformation in Korean gender relations, Korean women have not marched steadily in the direction of greater 'equality,' much less 'liberation'" (19). In fact, for many of these women, the very notion of the "enlightened" and "progressive" modern present may be serving to obscure some of the fundamental forms of subjections and disadvantages women still face.

Indeed, I have found that many women in this study, who suffer their problems all too painfully and unrelentingly on a daily basis, often experience these problems without a conscious sociological understanding of their larger social and structural contexts. Although they may not always be clearly aware of the larger causes for their predicaments, these women however are intensely invested in the family and in their gender identities. But because they lack the resources to significantly alter their situations or challenge the system when confronted with contradictions, their goal often remains one of creative survival within the system. In the next few chapters, then, we examine the vital role evangelicalism plays in the lives of Korean women, a role that has significant and often contradictory ramifications for women's domestic struggles and their attempts to negotiate their lives.

THREE

Search for Release, Search for Healing: Deliverance through Spiritual Practice

When one enters the darkened sanctuary of the "all-night" Friday prayer service at the South River Church, the first thing one is likely to encounter is loud, overwhelming sounds of what seem to be cries of collective lamentation. The light is dim in the sanctuary, but one can clearly make out the people gathered there; most of them, the majority of them women, are engaged in loud, emotional prayers, many in ecstatic, trance-like states with considerable bodily movements.

With raised hands and upturned faces, some shout their prayers out loud, while others, though more softly and with bowed faces, rapidly fire out their prayers as if in recitation. Some rock back and forth rhythmically in their chairs as they chant out loud, while others shake their arms and hands in the air as if possessed. Yet others pray out loud while punctuating their prayers repeatedly with loud claps, as with cymbals, and others beat their bosoms or thighs as they thump the floor with their feet. A few even lie prostrate out in the aisles, beating the ground with their fists as they cry out loud. Whatever each individual is doing, the sound that fills the sanctuary is unmistakably one of collective agony and grief, a cacophony of wails, shouts, cries, sighs, sobs, and even glossolalia. Piercing the air with wrenching cries of "Lord Jesus!" "Father!" "Save me!" many of the participants have tears streaming down their faces, their bodies and faces contorted in pain and tearful supplication.

The event described above takes place in the South River Church, and depicts what is commonly referred to as "unified" prayer (*tongseong gido*), a main form of Korean prayer practice and a central part of evangelical prayer gatherings. Unified prayer has been institutionalized in Korean Protestant churches since the beginning of missionary activity around the turn of the twentieth century; it is a distinctive form of prayer in which the gathered members pray individually, but out loud and simultaneously.[1] Unified prayer is a particularly important feature of prayer gatherings such as this one: the all-night Friday night worship service, also a long-institutionalized part of the Korean evangelical establishment.

As I mentioned in Chapter 1, prayers and prayer gatherings are pivotal parts of Korean evangelical practice. From daily daybreak prayer meetings and Friday night worship services to fasting and intercessory prayers, Korean evangelicals are distinctive in their active participation in these frequent and regularized prayer gatherings. Indeed, although praying in general is an important aspect of the revivalist tradition, the particular emphasis given to prayers in Korean evangelicalism stems from the belief that prayer is a devotional practice of singular importance, necessary for approaching and experiencing the divine— including the Holy Ghost—attaining conversion and deep faith, and maintaining an intimate connection to God.

For Korean evangelical women in particular, prayers have a highly special meaning and significance. In opening the self to God, releasing hidden pain, and pursuing God's care and blessing in everyday life, prayers are daily vehicles for experiencing healing and relief from inner suffering. Emotion-filled prayer sessions, such as the one described here, are not simply a means for expressing one's faith and achieving communion with God, but an ongoing vehicle for seeking healing from inner pain and wounds.

This chapter examines the significance and meaning of evangelicalism as a spiritual practice and experience in the lives of South Korean women. While recent studies of evangelical women around the world have been helpful in highlighting some of the practical motivations and consequences of women's evangelical beliefs, especially regarding domestic or gender relations, there has been relatively little analysis of evangelical faith and the conversion process from the perspective of spirituality, especially as an emotional and psychological resource for women.[2] My analysis is based on the premise that the fervent and devoted church participation of South Korean evangelical women cannot be understood without comprehending first the spiritual and emotional dimensions of their faith, especially as these help them deal with domestic conflicts and suffering.

Through an exploration of the central characteristics of women's religiosity, faith, and the conversion process, this chapter will investigate some of the specific ways in which the spiritual dimensions of evangelical beliefs and practices help women negotiate the challenges of their domestic lives. After examining first some of the initial pathways to conversion, I describe the role evangelicalism plays in particular as a vehicle for emancipation from and healing of domestic suffering for women. I also show that the experience of divine love, a central part of the evangelical conversion process, drives evangelical faith as a powerful source of internal empowerment and reconstitution of identity for women. This function has important implications for women not only by enhancing their capacity to overcome their emotional injuries, but also for resisting patriarchal oppression.

Pathways to Conversion

The reasons and motivations people have for joining a religious group are complex and diverse, as are their pathways to conversion. At the most general level, my sample of middle-class women in the two churches falls roughly into two groups: the first, those who began attending church as children or youths, including those born into Christian families; and the second, those who converted as adults, usually after marriage (cf. Brasher 1998: 128). Although the adult convert group, constituting about two-thirds of my sample, made up the majority of my subjects, both groups together represent two of the most typical conversion trajectories of women in Korean evangelical churches, and offer examples of the kinds of motivations that can instigate conversion.

The members in the first group typically began attending church as youngsters, either because they were born to Christian parents or because they were persuaded by friends or neighbors to visit their local church. A small minority of believers say that their initial exposure to Christianity came through attendance at missionary schools where they received religious training.

Regardless of how most individuals in this group started, it appears that their initial church attendance was not motivated by any kind of serious religious yearning, but was driven primarily by a variety of non-religious motives as well as the active proselytizing efforts of Christians near to them.[3] Almost all of them admit that as children, they attended church mainly for social reasons, to meet friends, and to have "fun" or because they liked singing in the choir or they enjoyed the food provided by the church. Although a majority of them continued to attend church throughout their years as teenagers and young adults, most say that they were still not "serious" Christians during those years, having "shallow" faith, "questioning" their religion, and often attending church only sporadically. One believer put it this way:

After going to a neighborhood church as a child, I went to a missionary college, so I received baptism when I was in my second year. And somehow, my sister ended up marrying a pastor. So I used to go to the church where my sister was. I went every Sunday, sang in the choir and stuff, but I didn't understand much. I didn't have that much faith but I carried around the Bible. I even worked as a teacher in Sunday school, but it was for me just a transmission of knowledge, not much else. So I guess at the time, you can say that my faith didn't have any roots. I received grace from time to time but nothing deep.

Although there were a few women in this group who said that they genuinely became converted in high school or in college, about 80 percent of the women in this group confessed that their "real" conversion occurred only as adults, typically after marriage. Interestingly enough, almost all of them stated that this conversion experience during their adult years was triggered by some personal trials or crises that "awakened" them to God.

For women in the adult convert group, on the other hand, initial church involvement usually constituted a more direct response to a crisis in their lives. In most cases, the crisis stemmed from some kind of serious or prolonged domestic tension that often set the women on the conscious or unconscious path of a religious "quest."[4] In the previous chapter, adult converts Ji-won and Hyun-mi revealed the role of such domestic problems in their decisions to seek religion. Another case is provided by Ok-ju, a member of the North River Church:

Why did I decide to come to church? Well there were several reasons that all kind of coincided. For one thing, my first child is a girl who recently reached puberty, and I was having some major problems with her. With this happening, I started wondering if perhaps I should not seek religion, for myself but also for her. Then last year, my husband was forced into early retirement, well, laid off basically. And with this, I became very nervous and anxious in mind [*buran hada*]. I'm sure much of this was economic, losing financial security, and on top of that, having to have my husband at home all the time, but all these things were making me anxious. I can rely on [*uiji hada*] my husband for certain things, but for all these other things I need something else to rely on, do you know what I mean? And of course, as you know, the person who stays at home [the wife] is always more nervous and anxious. And if you don't have any friends with whom to talk and share these things, you need something else to rely on. So these two things were the initial motivation. But actually, even before my husband got laid off last year, I had been thinking for a while that maybe I should try to find religion for myself. You see, I have been married for thirteen years and for a good twelve years of them, things were really, really bad. I don't like to talk about this much but my problem has been with my mother-in-law in particular. I guess other people have similar problems too, but things were so bad for so long with my marriage that I felt I really needed to do something about it.

Religious conversion must be seen as the product of a complex interaction of factors—psychological, religious, and social—the centrality of "crisis" as an important motivational element in church attendance or conversion has already been pointed out by various scholars of conversion.[5] Views vary on the substance of these "crises," but the significance of such experiences as "powerful, enduring frustration" (Bainbridge 1992: 184) that spurs conversion lies in the potential of these experiences as periods of "maximum vulnerability" for the candidate, leading her/him to be "open" or "prepared" to heed religious messages (Harding 1987: 168). Although "crisis" alone may not "explain" or "cause" conversion—that is, conversion cannot simply be reduced to crisis—an experience of great or enduring conflict and suffering can nevertheless be a key contributing factor in conversion, and for many converts, do serve directly as such a catalyst.[6] For Korean female adult converts, experiences of crises, particularly domestic, can be the key motivation for initial church attendance as well as subsequent conversion. For the group with a history of church attendance as well, crisis events, especially those that occur when they are married adults, also serve notably as a central driving force for "genuine" conversion experiences.

It is, however, noteworthy that by no means were the adult converts' paths to "true" conversion, though in many cases a direct response to crisis, any more immediate or sudden than those in the former group.[7] My data in fact suggest that many adult converts, like many of the childhood converts, spent time as "seekers," attending church for a while without experiencing conversion or going through considerable periods of "wandering" and "experimentation" before they underwent what they perceived as "real" conversion experiences.[8] Many, for instance, report trying different churches or Bible study groups where "nothing happened" or they "didn't learn anything" or were "bored." Others relate having been to "strange" sectarian churches that turned them off. Sung-ja, an ardent believer at the South River Church who had some previous exposure to Christianity by attending a Christian university, describes her "wandering" period this way:

I come from a family of Buddhists. But I went to Ewha University so I had to go to chapel and stuff like that but I wasn't very interested. Sometime after I got married, I felt that at least, I should try to learn something about the Bible since as they say, it's the biggest "bestseller." You see at the time, there was so much suffering in my marriage, mostly because of my husband. So one day in 1983, I sat down and read the whole Bible within a space of a couple of weeks. At first, I was like, what kind of a story is this? I thought it quite ridiculous. But my curiosity was piqued and I thought maybe I should find out more about it. It happened that a woman I knew was holding a Bible study session. So I went there. But I was a nightmare student for her. I confronted her about everything, asked all kinds of suspicious questions, basically fought with her for about several months. But then after a while, I lost interest so I stopped going. But strange things started to happen. When I stopped going, I started getting ill. So I thought I should try going to church, so I went to this church that the teacher went to, a small new [*gaecheok*] church. I just kept going, not knowing anything, but thinking that if I kept going, I would gain faith somehow. At the church, people were praying, crying out Father, Father! But this wouldn't come out of me. I was thinking, why should I say that? My own father's still alive! "Lord" [*junim*] came out but not "Father." But I thought since I am now going to church, I should try to have proper faith, so for the first time one day, I got down on my knees and prayed for nine hours, just asking God to give me faith. But it was so hard to believe though, so after a while, I gave up again.

In short, the centrality of "crisis" in Korean women's conversion narratives appears to suggest an obvious relationship between evangelical involvement and the efforts of women to deal with the problems and trials of life. While the nature of this relationship can take various forms, evangelical faith and conversion, as I will show, play key roles in helping women cope with the problems of domestic conflict and suffering, especially as sources of emotional and psychic healing.

Although the role of evangelical involvement as a form of response to domestic crisis appears quite clear, another key piece of evidence from my research provides support for the view that crisis experience constitutes a central factor in the women's conversion. One of the most striking aspects of the life histories and conversion narratives of middle-class Korean evangelical women to emerge from my study is the prevalence of stories involving physical breakdown or illness before their turn to faith or "genuine" conversion experiences. When I first undertook this study, I expected that I would hear stories of illnesses or physical affliction, especially as a motivation for conversion, from mostly poorer and lower-class women, who have been noted for seeking out evangelicalism as a means of addressing problems of physical affliction.[9] And indeed, the desire to cure physical illnesses as a motivation for church attendance, as well as experiences of healing miracles that provide the initial impetus for serious religious commitment, did emerge much more commonly as a theme in the conversion narratives of poorer women that I interviewed in some of the lower-class churches around Seoul.[10] What I did not expect, however, was the frequency with which the experiences of such crises would be reported by my sample of relatively affluent middle-class women in North and South River Churches. The stories related by these women typically describe an array of short-term or long-term illnesses that preceded their conversions, illnesses ranging from sudden, unexpected attacks of disease or physical breakdown to prolonged ailments of mild to debilitating severity. Although it is difficult to identify precisely the point at which the women decided to attempt a religious solution, these crisis events are described by the majority of women as significant turning points that have precipitated their church participation or conversion.

The following narrative is provided by a member of the South River Church named Su-jin, whose story is similar to those in the last chapter but demonstrates clearly how church participation was a response to the serious physical illness that she saw as resulting from her long-standing mental distress:

My parents were Christians, but as I remember it, I just went back and forth to church, didn't have much deep faith before marriage. Then after I got married I had to live with my husband's parents and his three siblings. I didn't expect this at all; my husband just up and announced a week before our wedding that we'd have to live with them. Well, when he announced it, I was surprised but accepted it, not thinking much of it, because I had no idea how hard it was going to be. I thought it'd be all right, everyone else does it. But things weren't so easy, it turned out. It was so much more difficult than I ever expected. I took care of two of his siblings for five years, then the youngest one, for eight years. Those were some of the hardest years of my life. Then when I was pregnant with my second child, I contracted bad tuberculosis. I was so sick. I was always healthy but this happened towards the end of my pregnancy. This totally shocked me. But that's when I started to really ask why. Why did I get sick like that? I realized then that it must have been from all the stress that had to do with my domestic situation. Then through counseling with a Christian, I came to realize that it was because I was a sinner. So that's when I decided to think seriously about my faith, God, and gained conviction about my salvation.

Whereas for Su-jin a case of sudden illness led her to conversion, for others such as In-hae, a well-educated 65-year-old woman who is now an exhorting deacon (*gwonsa*) at North River Church, conversion came after a bout of prolonged illness during her married life:

My husband was the first son, so he was the head of his family because his father was dead, but I married him because his economic prospects looked good, given that he had gotten a license as an accountant. But once I got married, it was so difficult for me, as the first daughter-in-law, having to do *sijip-sari*.[11] You know that in Korean society, mothers-in-law mistreat [*hakdae hada*] their daughters-in-law like something crazy, and since I was also a learned daughter-in-law, she was jealous and abused me even worse. And since I never did much household work growing up—we always had maids—it was so hard. And I was weak, my mind was fragile, and wasn't used to that kind of suffering and hardship [*gosaeng*]. So I got sick a lot.

For example, I'd go on a school field trip with my kids, and I'd just faint and lose consciousness. The burdens and stresses were too much. At first, it was so hard that I'd refuse to go to church even though my mother-in-law wanted me to. Since I worked myself to death everyday, I would have no day of rest if I went to church on Sunday. So on Sunday, I rested in secret, like I'd leave the house as if I was going to church but would just wander around the market or the neighborhood mindlessly before going back home. Also, I came to hate God—why did he make me marry into this wretched household and make me suffer this way?

But one summer, I got so sick that my mouth finally "turned."[12] And this is when Jesus appeared to me, robed in all white, when I was half-conscious. This is when I came to the North River Church. And while there, I received enormous grace [*eunhae*] from a revivalist pastor, realizing for the first time the truth about salvation. I was 45. From that day on, I became so "hot" that I could not stop evangelizing everybody I met. On my way home that day, I was evangelizing everyone on the street. They all thought I was crazy. Then I was on the phone for hours for days on end, evangelizing to everyone I could. I couldn't help it. I had received the evangelization "fire" [*yeol*].

Although for a small minority of middle-class women, the turn to religion may have been an effort to deal directly with the emotional or physical consequences of their illnesses or injuries, for an overwhelming majority of the women I interviewed, the significance of their physical illnesses did not lie so much in themselves, but in the women's understanding that these ailments represented the symptoms of their domestic anguish and suffering. Thus, unlike many lower-class women, these middle-class women typically turned to God in times of physical suffering less in an attempt to *cure* their sicknesses per se than as an effort to find a way to cope with the psychological and emotional distress of which they understood their illnesses to be the palpable symptoms.

Thus, it is no accident that for many women, the physical illnesses they suffer are also often psychosomatic, the so-called diseases with "no name." Although a small number of the women I interviewed suffered from recognizable illnesses such as tuberculosis or ulcers, in over two-thirds of the cases the women suffered from a range of apparently stress-related ailments that the doctors were often unable to diagnose. In-hae described her suffering from some kind of undiagnosed neurological or nervous disorder prior to her conversion. Young-Shin, a member of the North River Church, relates the following story of her illness:

I started to develop these illnesses, but they said it was a stress-related nervous disorder [*shingyeong seong*]. I was in so much pain that I was unable to sleep. At one point, I was awake for four days straight. I was unable to blink after that, and had massive headaches. At Severance Hospital, I had myself examined head to foot. But they said it was psychosomatic. So they told me to go see a psychiatrist. The psychiatrist gave me these drugs for six months that basically turned out to be sleeping pills. So when I didn't get better, I started to think carefully after a while. I went to the hospital so many times, took all these drugs, and nothing was helping! So I thought since I tried everything and that didn't work, I should try to hang onto God only.[13]

In the case of Ji-seon, another college-educated housewife from the South River Church, her road to conversion began one day while she was at the market with her baby daughter; while walking, she was suddenly "struck" on her lower back like a "ton of bricks," causing her to collapse and lose consciousness for 20 minutes. After she was brought home, she became paralyzed for days, immovable and in immeasurable pain, but the doctors could find nothing wrong with her. She was only able to overcome her incapacity after days of intense prayers by a deacon from a well-known charismatic church who lived in her building, during which she realized her true nature as an "evil sinner" and began tearfully and genuinely to repent for the first time.

The reason for her "evilness," as she related to me in confidence, was that she had secretly hated and despised her husband for years because of his and his family's "deceit" in not giving her the kind of future she had been promised when she got married, including her plans to continue her education and become a professor. Another woman, also a college-educated housewife at the South River Church, told me how her recurring and debilitating health problems—including migraine headaches, dizziness, cold sweats, stomach ailments, and claustrophobia—that she developed in the midst of a severe crisis at home with a sick child and difficult in-laws could not be diagnosed by doctors, who only told her that "there was nothing particularly wrong" with her. Her only recourse was to turn to a cell leader who prayed hard for her and told her, "you just have to do what the church tells you to and you will be all right."

Another significant point suggested by these stories is that for many women, the origin of their debilitating ailments and distress seems to lie as much in the women's intense *suppression* of negative emotions—such as anger, resentment, and bitterness—as in the nature of their problems (see also S. Park 1993: 135). Paralleling what has been presented in the previous chapter, a major source of such problems for women here are conflictual relations with husbands and mothers-in-law, the two figures who most dominate and define the lives of women. A 43-year-old woman from the South River Church explains her pre-conversion domestic situation in the following way:

You see, the reason I was in such a bad mental shape was that I was very unhappy, stressed, and depressed at home. My married life hadn't been easy. My in-laws ran a cake-making business, which required a lot of work, a lot of which I ended up doing. And I had to do all the housework too. See, I was the last child in my family, and didn't know how to work like that. So getting married and living with parents-in-law was a shock. My mother-in-law wasn't a bad person but the work was too hard. I felt like she was making me do everything and I was bad at refusing. I used to go home to my mother and cry all the time. And I fought with my husband a lot about it. It was really really hard for me, mentally, physically, so I came to gradually hate and resent my husband.

On top of it, it was unbearable because they didn't treat me with respect. You see, my husband's family is very conservative. Their attitude was, you don't have any right to speak—they totally ran over and ignored [*muksal hada*] me. It was maddening and unbearable. So I was thinking, why do I have to live with this kind of disregard [*mushi*]? I wasn't treated this way at home. But if I didn't obey, I felt I was insulting my own mother and father, that my in-laws would think they hadn't raised me properly. So I couldn't rebel. But it wasn't real obedience [*sunjong*] as far as I was concerned; it was just enduring, on the outside, just not to give my parents a bad name.

And my husband, I suppose that he thinks I am this inside person who doesn't know anything about life so he doesn't bother discussing anything with me. If I talk about politics and stuff, he says things like, what do you know about it. He does watch out for me but that's just because he's afraid I would be "tainted" by the world. So he sees me as this totally ignorant-of-the-world woman of the house, not knowing anything, just raising kids and doing housework. He still does that. He's always telling me not to do this or that, but I'm over 40! He was two-faced, too, I felt. He went around and did all these bad things and told me and the kids not to do this and that. He just wants to imprison me at home. At first, I was so angry that I had to put up with this kind of a person and I told God I won't put up with it. I said it was unfair that he can do whatever he wants and I have to be this good, pious, Christian woman. I wanted to live a worldly existence, too, a little. It felt really unjust, that as a Christian, I had to put up with this kind of existence. I felt such hatred for my husband. When his business started failing, he started to go wayward.

He drank, he gambled, played instead of trying to save the business because he was despondent. . . . With all this hatred for him, I would refuse to pray for him. I just watched him, to see what he would do. That's probably why his business failed in the end. But God helped me be patient. If He hadn't, I don't know what would have happened by now.

It needs to be mentioned that a term commonly used by many women to refer to the source of their psychic ailments is *han*, a Korean concept that, while difficult to define, can be described as a kind of pent-up and repressed set of emotions stemming from accumulated anger, resentment, and bitterness rooted in years of suffering and victimization by injustice and oppression; the term also connotes feelings of resigned sadness, sorrow, and regret that are a result of these bitter feelings and various unfulfilled desires. Relatedly, another common descriptor used by women in this study to describe their ailments, especially psychosomatic ones, is the term *hwabyeong* (or *hwatbyeong*), literally meaning "fire disease," which according to one dictionary definition means "an ailment supposedly caused by one's pent-up resentment (or animosity, grudge) and mental depression." According to my findings and other studies of this phenomenon (S. Min 1989; S. Park 1993), commonly recognized symptoms of this disease include unbearable tightness and pain in the chest (often described as a "lump" in the chest), shortness of breath, headaches, as well as a hot sensation throughout the body.[14]

Typically, after many years, such feelings of anger turn into deep bitterness, which then turns into despair and helplessness as the women find themselves unable to alter and transform their situations for the better. As is evident in the preceding narratives, the deepest source of bitterness for many is typically their husbands, not only because of their patriarchal behavior, but also because of what the women see as the husbands' inhuman insensitivity to their plight and their practice of taking the side of their mothers rather than their wives.

In accounting for the pervasive problem of self-repression found among women in this study, there is, however, another factor that contributes to and exacerbates women's difficulties: the lack of outside channels or outlets for articulating their problems. In South Korea, there are relatively few legitimate channels to which women can turn and seek help with their personal problems. I have found that women, first of all, have difficulty attaining outside help because there is still great stigma attached to mental illness and to discussing personal problems with individuals outside of the family. However, even among the women who did seek psychiatric help to treat their depression and other emotional problems, none of them seemed to find it very helpful in the long run. One woman who did finally consult a psychiatrist said that it did not work for her because she found it difficult to talk to a man about her personal domestic problems and confessed to me that she had not told him half the things that she was telling me.

Such relative unavailability of social channels, or other types of emotional or psychic "outlets" for women's problems and grievances cannot be overemphasized in the South Korean setting.[15] As one woman put it: "Things were so piled up inside me that if anyone even touched me, I would just break into a river of tears. There was no one to console me, no one to talk to." Such a lack leads to prolonged repression of destructive emotions, which often appear to be primarily responsible for the women's eventual psychic and physical ailments.

Self-repression, however, appears to stem from another source: the women themselves. Many women in my study expressed great frustration and helplessness with their own inability to be assertive in expressing their needs and interests, defying authority, or fighting back. Although the sufferings endured by these women and the accomplishments they are able to attain suggest enormous strength, fortitude, and assertiveness, an overwhelming number of women saw *themselves* as having "meek" or "gentle" personalities, being the "obedient types" who were not very good at expressing themselves or their feelings. Many confessed to having spent years keeping their frustrations to themselves, and it was clear that this constant, sustained repression of anger and other negative feelings, particularly in their efforts to live up to the dutiful, self-sacrificing gender ideal of the virtuous woman, appears to play a large role in deepening their psychic distress.

Whatever the source of their anguish, Korean evangelical women in this study seem to seek in their religious experience ways of coping with and finding relief from domestic suffering and pain. As one female elder at the North River Church put it, "I don't know, for most of the women, maybe church is an escape from the domestic situation. I certainly see it as a resting place for the mind." By examining some of the major dimensions of the conversion process, the following section describes the role of women's evangelical faith and spiritual practices in fostering emotional and psychic healing.

"Opening Up" the Self

In general, conversion is understood as a transformation or a turn-around that implies a radical change in the nature of the person undergoing religious conversion (Bainbridge 1992: 187). At the most basic level, it is a fundamental change in self-identity (Mol 1976), of a worldview, and even of an entire emotional world. In evangelical terms, conversion means self-transformation as it occurs through "rebirth" and salvation in Jesus Christ. Conversion, however, is not necessarily a uniform, predictably patterned process; even within the same religious tradition, conversion can be meaningful to different individuals in different ways and be experienced uniquely by different groups of people. Within the Korean evangelical tradition, and particularly for women, the significance and meaning of evangelical conversion and faith starts with the "opening up" of the inner self, especially as a means of releasing inner pain and suffering, and of acquiring solace and consolation through the forging of an intimate, direct, individual relationship with God (see also Westley 1977).

Prayer, as one of the central elements of Korean evangelical practice, is seen as an important means of communicating with the divine and of deepening one's faith; as such, church members are not only expected to partake in the array of formal prayer gatherings in church, but they are also urged to pray constantly, anywhere and anytime, whether in church, at home, or in other public places. According to a pastor from the North River Church:

God's church is, first and foremost, a church that prays. You must pray without rest, pray without rest, as God commanded. Repent. You will feel cold in your heart if you don't fervently pray. Accepting God into yourselves is not just calling out "Jesus" when you need help. You must always be ready, spiritually, to meet him, through constant prayer. You must realize that when your spirit is clean through constant prayer, things will go well in your life. If your spirit isn't cleansed through prayer, things will not go well. When you get on your knees and pray, God will send you blessings. You must pray at dawn, pray before meetings, pray all the time. You must pray whether there are others around or not. You will experience the Holy Ghost through prayer. Other things you do in the church are important too, but prayer is the most important. The other day, as I was leaving after the dawn prayer, I saw this one member leaving the church singing and praising God. That really moved me. This person, who comes to dawn prayer when it's cold and everyone else is sleeping, that person has pure faith. Pray in the mountains, pray alone in your room, pray when others are sleeping. Pray until the very end, pray unceasingly, pray all the time. Pray with faith, without doubt. You must have that kind of spiritual strength, and there must be at least one person in your home who prays like this. Some people, when they pray, words pour out like silk; we need that kind of spiritual prayer. It only comes out of deep faith, from receiving God and the Holy Spirit. There is nothing outside prayer. It's the most important thing and the thing that'll make our church grow.

This statement suggests that while prayer is a means to experience God and to develop and even demonstrate the strength of one's faith, it also has the important purpose and function of fostering in believers a particularly intense, experiential faith, as well as a powerfully close, emotional connection to the divine that leads to a relationship of great mutual intimacy and dependency. Above all, for Korean believers, such a relationship to God, maintained through daily, fervent prayer, is highly significant in one particular way: it provides an important channel of self-revelation on the part of the believer to God that has central implications for her attempts to attain healing. Indeed, watching and listening to the fervent, emotional, and spiritual prayers of Korean evangelical women, one appreciates the crucial role prayers play in enabling women to open up their inner selves, especially to express their deepest feelings and sense of pain, and to ask God for help in alleviating their suffering. As one woman confessed: "Before, I didn't have anyone to tell my problems to. Now, when I have pain in my heart, I just pray to God and he takes my worries away. God comforts me, consoles me, and makes everything better."

For Korean evangelical women, many of whom are handicapped by the lack of outside channels through which to reveal and discuss their domestic troubles, such a medium of release appears critical to helping them acquire a measure of relief from their suffering and to attain solace. Regardless of whether a follower has yet experienced any profound transformation of herself or her life—that is, regardless of where she is on the conversion path—for women struggling alone to cope with domestic pain and conflict, this direct, intimate relationship with God, maintained through constant and repeated prayer, seems to become vital in their efforts to deal with the problems of life.

Praying, then, whether alone or in groups, is usually a highly emotional affair, involving lavish heartfelt confessions and intimate self-expression. It is a vehicle through which one reveals one's deepest dilemmas and agonies, and through which one implores (*gan/gu hada*) the divine to forgive and intercede. Regardless of what specific solutions women might seek, be they the understanding and forgiveness of a loving God, the exorcism of the Devil, or the granting of blessings and miracles, such a process of self-revelation seems to generate for most women an enormous sense of release and freedom from their daily troubles. As one woman poignantly put it: "I found a God who responds to all my cries, however small, a God that watches over me, a God that consoles me when things are difficult and painful. I was always so oppressed [*nullida*], and had no means to express [*pyohyeon hada*] myself, but now I can, because I know I am a child of God."

"Opening up," however, is not just an individualistic process limited to the arena of prayer, but can also occur within a collective context, such as through fellowships in small group settings, most notably, cell meetings. Previous studies have explored the importance of social interaction and group processes for fostering the act of conversion.[16] According to these views, intensive group processes in which the members—through repeated interactions and mutual sharing—adopt new worldviews, interpretive schemes, behavior, and language of the community can serve, in addition to crisis-related motives, as a key factor in facilitating conversion.[17] In the Korean evangelical context, gatherings such as cell meetings, as venues *par excellence* for promoting such intense collective interactions, not only promote faith and conversion, but provide crucial opportunities for openness and release for the participants.

In settings such as the South River Church, cell groups are elaborately institutionalized vehicles consciously designed to foster such openness and sharing among members. Although directed ultimately to deepening faith, openness, and commitment to God—indeed, the Korean evangelical establishment is more than aware of the benefits of intensive group interactions for fostering faith and greatly stresses the importance of collective participation—such settings also provide the intimate environment for the members to share their lives and problems with one another, enabling emotional release. These meetings serve as crucial sites for women to obtain relief and consolation from their domestic troubles, often functioning as the first step in the conversion process. As one woman put it: "When I went to a cell meeting for the first time, I experienced an indescribably peaceful feeling. What I realized there was that other people were not different from me, in their lives, problems, and feelings. Until then, I thought my life was peculiar, but that was not the case. And I received consolation from that, before anything else."

As soon as a new member registers with the South River Church, that member is hooked up with a cell group in her or his residential area. As in many other churches, cell groups are organized not only regionally but also along gender lines (though not always), and are held on a rotating basis at the members' homes.[18] Although the main purpose of these weekly meetings is Bible study, the members devote more time on the fellowship that follows the study session. The Bible study, usually structured around topics from workbooks put together by the pastor and led by competent and well-trained lay leaders, is itself designed to promote discussion of personal lives and thoughts. As such, these meetings offer a fascinating window into the personal concerns, problems, and conflicts of the members.

The meetings, which for female groups usually take place in the mornings, typically last anywhere from two to five hours, and begin with Bible study. However, the study session, though taken seriously, usually does not last more than an hour or an hour and a half. The fellowship period that follows commonly takes up twice as much time, and the members usually appear to enjoy themselves greatly during these hours, especially the luncheon period that immediately follows Bible study. The lunch is provided by the hostess, and is usually a bountiful meal. Around the food, a great deal of interesting and intimate conversation flows that is usually a continuation of topics started during the Bible study.

However, whatever the topic under discussion in the Bible study on a given day, whether it be the issue of sin or of Christ's redemption, the themes of discussion invariably center around the problems of women's domestic lives. Since the typical method of the leader during the discussion is to ask the members to relate the topic on hand to concrete events and happenings in their lives, women are led to volunteer stories and problems of their lives, facilitating intimate sharing. As women share stories of domestic problems and dilemmas that are, by any standard, intense, these discussion are often quite emotional and wrenching.

Although the specifics of each tale differ, the stories that emerge, not surprisingly, are typically those revolving around severe difficulties involving husbands, mothers-in-law, and children. Many deal with financial matters and the women's struggles to cope with them. However, regardless of the different kinds of stories that surface, these discussions share a level of commonality in the kinds of problems that emerge and reflect the women's deep mutual identification with and understanding of one another's dilemmas and sufferings. In sum, these tales are expressive of valiant efforts by the women to remain sane and to hold their marriages and families together in the face of great domestic difficulties, as well as of deep, often subconscious, ambivalence and conflict about their domestic roles and responsibilities.

Despite what appears to be cathartic and therapeutic solace offered by such group sharing, the meetings offered by the South River Church are, in the end, also unmistakably designed to deepen spirituality and openness to God, with the aim of encouraging the conversion process. Thus the role of the leader is not only to guide the members in reinterpreting their situations and problems in the context of the evangelical interpretive schema, but also to aid them in developing spiritual openness by encouraging the practice of prayer during the meetings. Although the level of spirituality of the group, according to my experience, varied with the proclivities of the individual leader, this goal was generally accomplished through the liberal use of vocal prayers in which the members were encouraged to express themselves openly. Aside from fostering spirituality, these vocal prayers are also an opportunity for members to learn *how* to pray, as well as to learn what it means to be an evangelical by opening their thoughts and feelings to the group for redefinition.[19]

The Power of Surrender

As cell groups open up, share, learn the gospel, and pray, the convert experiences a gradual reconstruction of his or her worldview and identity according to the perspective of the church, a reinterpretation of life with new metaphors, images, and stories, along with a reorganization of biography (Rambo 1992: 173). Testimonies, for example, are rituals that express this process of biographical reconstruction encapsulated in a dramatic form, a creative linking of the convert's personal story to the group's story (Rambo 1992: 173). By placing the problems and situations of the members in a new framework of religious interpretation and context, this process of reality reconstruction offers not only new, compelling explanations for the way things are, but also dramatic implications for how the members cope with their earthly dilemmas and conflicts.

For Korean evangelical women, this cognitive reconstruction begins with an understanding of the concept of sin, an important first step in a process that is to culminate in conversion and salvation. Korean evangelicals comprehend the concept of sin in two very contrasting ways: one, as something caused by an external force, namely, Satan; and two, a result of individual human moral transgressions and failings. Either way, the notion of sin is crucial to an overall reconstruction of the convert's worldview and identity as a Christian because she must first realize and admit her state of utter helplessness as a sinner before being able to invite God into her life to be helped and saved. As a leader in a South River Church cell meeting stated one afternoon: "As a sick person seeks a hospital, only those who truly realize the nature of the depth of their sinfulness and depravity can truly seek God and hold on to the cross."

As many members will point out, however, learning of sinfulness is not sufficient in itself to lead to conversion, to truly "meeting" Jesus. Achieving conversion, most people agree, requires the next essential step, that of surrender. Indeed, in general discussions of evangelical conversion, many observers point to "surrender" as the most important turning point in the conversion process, a step that is a prelude to genuine commitment in which a person, after admitting that she is a lost sinner, delivers herself up to Christ as savior, becoming "born again." In the Korean evangelical view as well, an act of complete surrender to God is seen as the most important step that enables a person to truly accept God as a savior.

What, then, is the exact meaning of surrender for Korean evangelical women? Only by understanding what surrender means for them in concrete terms can we fully comprehend the significance of evangelical

faith in their lives. Let us begin, then, by examining a narrative on surrender and salvation offered to me by a church member one day:

The key to salvation and peace in your life is completely surrendering yourself
to God. It is not possible for us to live by our own wills and intellect. We must
entrust everything to Jesus. To be "reborn" in Jesus like a newborn baby is to
admit and accept the need to rely on Jesus for everything and to stop trying to
figure things out on our own. And once you really accept Jesus this way, you
will go to heaven and receive peace.

Quite typical of Korean evangelical rhetoric on salvation, this statement presents surrender as the act of giving up oneself and control
over one's life to God. Not unlike the ideas of surrender described in
various charismatic or sect-like groups in America (see Gordon 1984;
Westley 1977), the notion of surrender presented above is far more than
simply an act of commitment to faith and a promise to live a new kind
of life; rather, it is centered on the act and notion of total and complete
relinquishment of control—over oneself, one's life, and even more importantly, one's will—to God. Since we, as helpless and inadequate sinners, are incapable of effecting any changes in our lives through our
own ability and will, we can only achieve any kind of improvement in
our situations by relying completely on the workings of God. Only by
letting God take control over our lives will we be able to gain peace,
happiness, and freedom from the suffering and pain that plague us daily
and be able to "go to heaven." As one pastor put it: "Believe in Jesus,
surrender everything to God, simply do and obey as he wills, and be
free from all your worries and pain."

This concept of surrender in Korean evangelicalism is central to the
religiosity of evangelical women. For those who are burdened by an
overwhelming sense of domestic responsibility and tormented by conflicts that they feel helpless to solve or to control, the act of surrendering is an important means by which individuals can obtain a sense of
relief and emancipation from their psychic burdens, a process that
Galanter (1978) has called the "relief effect." For example, one woman
talked about her efforts to cope with her child's sickness: "In the beginning, I used to be so scared for him, so scared that when I went to
the hospital, I couldn't even pray. But this was because I was hoping
for everything by my own strength, to make things better by my own
actions. This is why I was always afraid. I didn't entrust in and rely on

God to make everything all right and take care of everything. Now I know that I can only survive through my faith and reliance on God."

Indeed, I would argue that the notion of surrender in the Korean evangelical context has come to take on a distinctive, further intensified meaning: that of "entrusting" (*matgi da*). Going beyond the recognition of God's power in one's life and the relinquishment of one's desires and self-control to the higher power, the notion of "entrusting" intensifies the idea of surrender through an emphasis on the *totality* of the act, in which everyday, earthly responsibilities and decisions are turned over to God. Such a notion, reflecting also a belief in the childlike dependence of human beings on God, encourages reliance on God to solve all day-to-day problems, and seeing the will of God in all basic decisions. One woman who seemed on her way to becoming converted described this state of mind: "I think I am beginning to see why people seek God. I am beginning to understand the feeling of, ok, forget it, I'll just trust in God to watch over me and take care of everything, you know, the feeling of being a child throwing a tantrum at God to take care of things. I am beginning to feel like that."

Among the women in both the North and South River Churches, such attitudes of total, practical dependence on God prevail. Many women say that they live their lives by "hanging onto" God, and, believing themselves to be completely helpless and powerless, turn over every life decision to God, trusting God to "take care of everything." Whether or not the women are actually so powerless in real life, the point here is that they *believe* themselves to be so, and that God has complete control over their destinies. One woman, after relating to me some of the heart-wrenching stories of her hard life, said that after she found God, she was able to make peace with her life and its hardships:

Things only happen through God. Since I can't do anything on my own, I always trust that God will solve things somehow. So when I pray, God seems to make things happen for me. Even if bad things happen, I think it's God's intent, and I just try to be thankful. If things get twisted from human perspective, I try to think that God must be doing this to give me something better. So if I think this way, my mind is peaceful.

By delivering women from the weight of their anxieties and burdens, such beliefs and acts of entrusting seem, then, to be pivotal in helping women better cope and transcend their hardships, setting them on the road to healing.

In the Korean context, however, surrendering and entrusting also imply another important meaning: an attitude of dutiful obedience to God, in which salvation can be attained only by totally following what one thinks is God's will.[20] Given this attitude, it is not surprising that the dominant evangelical view of the relationship between human beings and God is that of little children to an all-knowing, caretaking father who will take care of all of the children's problems in return for obedience. It is also difficult to ignore the extent to which the concept of the God-Father in Korean evangelicalism reflects the image of the ideal Confucian father figure: a moral, stern, distant father who will be just, caring, and even loving, but who also demands utter obedience and submission in return. As the mirror opposite, human beings are seen as little children, not simply in the sense of being innocent and trusting, but also highly dependent and helpless, and like infants, petulant, even immature (see also S. Park 1993: 40–41).[21]

The act of surrendering, however, facilitates the healing process in ways other than by providing relief and liberation from psychic burdens and pain; it also serves, ironically, as an important source of empowerment for the "helpless" believer, both by cleansing her of destructive emotions and by enabling her to gain a sense of renewed strength in God. Not only does surrender release an individual from the burden of pain and worries, but in the very act of surrendering, she is moved to feel less helpless, gaining strength from the belief that God has taken charge of her life and that she can accomplish things with "God's strength." Although Korean evangelicals, in my experience, are not likely to articulate this experience as a process of "regaining" self-control as some other studies of evangelical conversion have found (see Gordon 1984), they do, on a practical level, attain a large measure of freedom from the former sense of helplessness, and a sense of renewed strength in themselves by allowing God to take control. As one woman stated: "Faith really helps with the difficult times. It becomes something to lean on. I used to be egotistical before, trying to have my way in everything. Got mad at everything. Now, I depend on God. When I am about to do something, I just think whether what I do will make God happy or not. Now somehow, I feel more self-sufficient." Viewed from another perspective, surrender is also an act that helps the believer regain the ability to cope with life by allowing her to become rejuvenated, by helping her to re-direct energies that have been used to maintain previous struggles and harbor destructive emotions. That is, it is precisely at the point of sur-render and relinquishment of herself and problems that the believer's previously misdirected energies, ironically, can be re-channeled into a new life (Rambo 1992: 175).

Most Korean evangelicals expect surrender to be a powerful process experienced particularly through prayer, and ideally, through the ex-perience of the Holy Spirit. The Holy Spirit is also important to this process because surrendering cannot simply be an intellectual act; it is only by letting the Holy Spirit enter and take total control that the follower experiences true "giving up." Indeed, when women recall a moment or moments when they have consciously "surrendered" them-selves to God, they remember these events as occurring usually during fervent prayer; for most of them, these events are described as being significant "experiential" events in their religious lives in which they were able to finally "meet" God and "accept" him into their newly "God-centered" lives.

The intense, experiential nature of these divine encounters are such that although they are felt no doubt as intense spiritual experiences, they are also described, for many women, in physical terms, such as feeling "hot," having something enter their bodies, and even speaking in tongues. For some, moments of surrender have even been occasions for experiencing bodily healing. One believer describes her moment of conversion: "During the prayer, I felt something 'descend' on me, and I felt something in my waist and back, like discs that were misaligned realigning suddenly. And I cried like crazy the whole time. I had cried so much, it was embarrassing to step outside. But when I arose after the prayers, I felt so light. From that time on, I have been receiving grace continually and I have been 'hot' ever since."[22]

Love, Forgiveness, and Empowerment

As a major personal transformation, evangelical conversion entails a gradual reconstitution of the self and identity. This ongoing process is commonly termed "rebirth," in which the believer establishes a new identity in life by "shedding" undesirable aspects of her previous self and adopts new, more positive qualities, outlooks, and patterns of behavior consonant with her new belief system. One basis of the conversion process for Korean evangelical women lies in the acquisition of a new self-conception as the recipient of divine love, an aspect that has dramatic ramifications for internal healing and empowerment.

Despite the conventional image of God as a stern, distant, and all-powerful figure, there is a contrasting view within the churches of God as loving and forgiving. According to this view, believers are not simply delivered from their burdens by giving up control to an omnipotent God, but emancipated from suffering by surrendering to the bosom of a loving God, who will forgive, understand, guide, and protect, as a kind father does for a child. As one pastor in the South River Church assured the members: "We are terrible sinners, but it is not us that God hates, but our sins. He, on the other hand, absolutely loves human beings, so much so that he killed his own son for us."

In the South River Church, where the institutional emphasis on divine love seemed particularly strong, the theme of God's love dominates the rhetoric of surrender and conversion among women. According to almost all the women I interviewed, surrender is not simply described as an act of psychic unburdening, but a powerful experience of God's overwhelming love. And for most women, the importance of divine love appears to stem not just from an intellectual understanding of a God who loves, forgives, and cares, but from an ongoing emotional experience that profoundly transforms their sense of selves. One woman described such an experience at a revival meeting:

Before the meeting, I guess I had some experiences, but they came little by little, like the knowledge that God was living and among us. But this meeting really confirmed all of this. . . . I learned to pray a lot there and the experiences started to come. That was the definitive turning point for me. I never cried so much in my life. And it was there that I realized what kind of being God really was. I realized really for the first time that Jesus was my savior and that God loves me. Until then, I didn't feel or know that God was love, how much he loves me. There, I felt all of this in my bones, both spiritually and bodily. I was literally shaking, shuddering, and crying because I was so moved by this experience. I felt for the first time the vastness of God's love and I was suddenly just filled with thanks and gratitude for everything. At that point, I felt that I wanted to spend the rest of my life in the service of God. I am constantly overwhelmed by these feelings now.

For most of the women in this study, it is clear, then, that the idea and experience of God's love occupy central positions in the development of their identities as evangelical Christians. As one woman declared: "Before, I didn't know who I was. I would look into a mirror and I didn't know who was looking at me. But now, I know who I am. I am the person God created and the one God loves." For these women, however, their new identities and experiences as divinely loved beings have another important implication: they serve as a source of profound emotional healing and empowerment—especially for those suffering wounds sustained through a lack of love and self-worth—that help them reconstitute and transform their self-conceptions in fundamental ways.

Whether they are due to conjugal conflicts or tensions with in-laws, domestic conflicts of various kinds, as we have seen, constitute the main sources of daily emotional suffering for Korean women. Underlying these conflicts, however, seems to be one significant origin of emotional pain for many Korean women: a deep sense of deprivation in regard to marital love and affection, stemming particularly from situations of loveless marriages or relations with husbands who may be unaffectionate or disrespectful. Many women also describe feeling highly unappreciated and taken for granted in their married and family lives despite all that they do, which leads them to feel greatly unloved and unvalued. For other women, such sense of emotional deprivation in marriage is compounded by their experiences within their own natal families, that is, of not feeling sufficiently loved by their parents.

For women suffering from these kinds of problems, the experience and knowledge of divine love has particular ramifications in their lives. For many of them, the experience of divine love serves to make up for the love that is glaringly missing in their lives. A mother of three, in reference both to her husband and her own parents, explained: "I never felt like I received much love from anyone, but all this was compensated for by God. For the first time, I felt loved, blessed, special."

In addition to enabling women to overcome the wounds of emotional neglect and deprivation, the belief in God's love also empowers women by providing them with a greater sense of self-worth and esteem, giving them the strength to better cope with life's difficulties. Another woman remarked: "Things were so bad in my marriage, I felt I really needed to find something for myself, someone. I was so lonely and there were so many conflicts and problems. But I found love through God, and understood that he loved me and he was close to me, and with that, I felt I could overcome anything. Looking back now, I feel like my life had been directed to that moment."

Such a sense of empowerment can help women better negotiate relations with those whom they see as their "tormentors." For example, the new sense of inner strength that comes from confidence in God's love can offer women a kind of sense of inner autonomy, giving them an emotional armor with which to deflect pain inflicted by others. A woman in the North River Church described the changes brought to her relationship with her husband: "Before, when my husband would say hurtful things to me, I would get really hurt, but with my faith, it doesn't hurt me anymore. So I say to my husband, you can try all you want to torment me, but I won't get mad, and I am not tormented. If you want to know why, I wish you could experience for yourself what I have been experiencing." Ironically, the sense of confidence and self-worth gained through God's love not only helps to protect women against emotional injuries but can also be used as a means to resist male authority. Such a sense of empowerment can even serve as a "weapon," as we will see, in challenging and subverting the husband's authority.

Forgiveness is another way in which the understanding of God's love can help women promote internal healing and better cope with their situations. Feeling empowered, loved, and forgiven by God means that an individual gains the capacity to forgive and love others, acts seen as central to healing and achieving emancipation from bitterness. According to one pastor, the reason there is so much *hwabyeong* among Korean women is because they do not forgive; for him, forgiveness was the only "cure" for *hwabyeong*. Indeed, one woman, speaking of her seething hatred for a sister-in-law who treated her with enormous "inhumanity" and disrespect throughout her married life, tells of how she was finally able to free herself from hatred by such an act of forgiveness:

During one worship service, the pastor told us to put our hand on our hearts and pray to forgive anybody who gave us *han*. And at that moment, I thought of my sister-in-law. Until then, the only way I dealt with her was through self-repression. But I conversed with God about it, and asked how I can forgive her for all the sins she committed to me. But you know how the Bible says that if someone hurts you 7 times, to forgive that person 70 times for each [instance of hurt]: that's 490 forgivenesses for seven hurts. Well, that basically amounts to saying forget about these sins, doesn't it? I thought about this and realized, there is no sinner in the world one cannot forgive! Then I just cried. Then all of a sudden, I felt something calming down inside my heart and everything became real quiet around me although there were so many people praying and shouting loudly. Then I felt my strength ebb away and felt this indescribable peace. And I realized this was God's response. And so from then on, I stopped hating my sister-in-law. And when I did that, my body was cured and these feelings of hatred ceased inside of me, all at the same time.

Forgiveness is accomplished not only through the strength to love others, but also through the new interpretive framework gained through the understanding of sin. By recognizing that other people's hurtful behavior results as much from sin as from their own choices, one obtains the capacity to see others through a new transcendent, forgiving lens. In seeing others as *victims* of sin rather than as the cause of suffering, a person can begin to feel pity for others rather than hatred, letting go of negative and bitter feelings. One member of the South River Church relates how she was able to transform her view of her ill father-in-law, whom she disliked immensely but had to take care of: "Accepting God made my home situation easier to deal with. It was still hard the first time. But I could finally deal with my situation with a 'happy mind.' I could finally see my father-in-law in a different light: instead of being resentful of him and disliking him, I started to see him as a person to be pitied." Furthermore, acknowledging sinfulness helps a person to forgive others by refraining from placing all the blame on other people.

Indeed, the virtue of forgiveness is stressed for women as a major strategy for dealing with their domestic conflicts and destructive emotions; women are exhorted to love and forgive in all circumstances, emulating the forgiving and self-sacrificing Jesus. Condemning hatred and bitterness as sin, as something caused by evil forces aiming to make everyone miserable and create conflict in people's lives, women are urged to fight these impulses and let go of negative feelings through love and forgiveness, no matter the sins of others.

Not surprisingly, however, these blanket exhortations to forgive and love sometimes become additional sources of internal conflict and hardship for many women as they struggle to put these injunctions into practice. Although love and forgiveness may offer women a certain sense of temporary liberation and peace, these injunctions—as means by which women are called to draw upon their virtues of endurance and docile acceptance befitting the ideal of a patient, self-sacrificing mother and wife—can be felt as calls for extreme self-repression and denial.

Conclusion

By taking evangelicalism seriously as a *religion*, that is, as a spiritual, religious, and emotional experience, this chapter has illustrated the roles of evangelical faith and conversion in helping Korean women negotiate their domestic dilemmas and transcend patriarchal oppression. Particularly through processes of emotional release, self-revelation, and surrender to divine love and control—all rendered possible through the development of a direct, intimate, and individual relationship to God—evangelical faith enables women to overcome and heal their pain as well as empower themselves, allowing them to better deal with their domestic conflicts, reconstitute their self-conceptions, and even resist patriarchal domination.

For Korean evangelical women, the church offers opportunities for improved domestic coping, even patriarchal resistance, not just spiritually but institutionally as well, through its program of church work and activities. Despite the unquestionably subordinate status of women within the church hierarchy and authority structure, their church participation provides them with important emancipatory possibilities by offering them a means of attaining social/psychic autonomy and empowerment, especially as they appropriate the church as a space for autonomous female interaction and for exercising non-domestic talents and abilities. The next chapter explores these aspects of women's church participation, as well as some of the problematic and contradictory dimensions implied in women's evangelical church involvement and conversion.

FOUR

Negotiating Women's Space:
Community, Autonomy, and Empowerment

Yoon-bin is a deacon at the North River Church, and a mother of two in her early 40s. She is also the owner of a small business in the neighborhood, a modest shop selling custom-tailored clothing a few blocks from the church. Yoon-bin is one of a handful of women in the church who are self-employed on a full-time basis, and as would be expected of someone running her own business, she keeps extraordinarily long working hours. Yet, she is also one of the most ardent and enthusiastic members of the North River Church, with a life that seems to revolve essentially around two things: work and church.

Yoon-bin converted in her early 30s after experiencing what she describes as an earth-shattering spiritual and physical healing experience in which she was cured of long-standing stress-related ailments arising from the difficulties of her marital and domestic life. Like many of the other women, Yoon-bin lived through many years of difficult marital problems that she says resulted in a variety of psychosomatic illnesses, ranging from insomnia to stomach ulcers. She began to attend the North River Church industriously as a "last straw" after all medical treatments had failed, and after praying fervently for six months and receiving a laying of hands from a revivalist preacher, she was "miraculously" cured of her illnesses.

Closing her store when necessary, Yoon-bin spends as much time as she can in the church, participating in almost every activity and event, usually going in every day. She is a member of a women's missionary society (*seongyo bu*), sings in three different choirs, attends all services including the daily dawn prayer meetings, and participates in all the church's special events. She is also recognized especially for her evangelizing zeal and abilities, including the successful evangelization and transformation of her husband, who for years had vigorously opposed her church attendance and had been abusive. Indeed, she tries to use her place of business to evangelize, seeing it as an "important opportunity" for proselytization, even at the risk of turning off her customers. Yoon-bin describes the meaning of and reasons for her dedicated church involvement:

After I got cured of my ailments through God, I realized I simply didn't have any place to "rely on" besides God, to tell you the truth. So I started my real life of faith then, and have been fervent [*yeolsim hada*] ever since. Even though I am so busy, I am in three different choirs, I am in the intercessory prayer group, I never miss a cell meeting, and I evangelized a lot of people and pray for them a lot. I evangelize really hard. I sing, too, whenever I can, not only in church but anywhere, when I'm working, whatever. Although I am not very good at singing, I receive so much grace during singing. I listen to the Christian radio all the time, it's like my best friend. I go to the dawn prayers as much as I can, it feels so good! . . . I also do the missionary society. Since I love God so much, I do as much as I possibly can. And I evangelize so hard because if I don't share what I know, I feel pent up. I feel real sorry for all those who don't know God.

Yes, friends tell me I'm 'hanging' too much onto God and religion, that I should pay more attention to my business. They ask me, what is the point of going to church so much? But it's not that way for me! And my husband now knows that too. . . . Before he became converted, he used to get very upset at my going to church but now, he knows that if I don't go to church like I do, I'd be sick person! So he says to me, for you, work is not what's most important. What's the point if you have money but get sick so we have to pay the hospital bills? My husband knows this, so going to church is one thing he now doesn't say anything about. Like today, I had lunch with a woman at church, spent a couple of hours gabbing and didn't come home until two in the afternoon. So you know what my husband says? 'I hope you had fun gabbing!' . . . For me, church comes before everything else. Even if I'm with non-church friends, if a church matter comes up, I cancel and go to church. But my friends know what God's meant for me, how I've changed, and that I can't live without Him. So it's a happy life.

Among the women in both churches, the kind of fierce dedication as expressed by Yoon-bin is not atypical. Indeed, many of these evangelical women display an unusual level of intensity in institutional dedication and enthusiasm, and upon their conversions, church participation comes to take a central place in their lives. There is no doubt, though, that for women such as Yoon-bin, devoted church participation must be taken seriously, before anything else, as an expression of their sincere faith in and love of God. Clearly, the motivations behind Yoon-bin's frequent church attendance are religious and spiritual; it is a means for acquiring the experiences of God's power and healing central to her daily existence. Yoon-bin's narrative also alerts us to something else, however: that for women such as her, church involvement may also have a far wider significance than what is deemed purely "spiritual" and "religious." That is, for many members, the church may also possess great meaningfulness in their lives as an *institution*. Indeed, our understanding of Korean women's powerful attraction to evangelicalism hinges on comprehending what the church and church life mean for women institutionally as well as spiritually.

From "Helpmate" to "Kitchen Herd"

To understand clearly the meaningfulness of evangelical women's church participation, it is useful first to examine closely women's place within the institution of the church and the character of their church activities. In relation to women's status, Christianity in Korea has historically been given a certain amount of recognition for its "emancipatory" effects. Protestant missionaries, along with Korean reformers and the Japanese, were among the first to introduce modern forms of schooling to Korea.[1] The missionaries, however, are noted for their distinctive contribution to women's education; although the first modern schools established by the Koreans and the Japanese occupiers systematically excluded girls, the Protestant missionaries worked to open up educational opportunities for girls and women, starting with the establishment of the first modern girls' school by Methodist missionaries, Ewha Hakdang, which later grew into Ewha Womans University in Seoul, the premier women's university in South Korea today. In addition to educational efforts carried out through Bible schools and classes, 25 mission schools were founded between 1886 and 1908, of which about half were schools for girls (Yu 1987). Although the ultimate goal of the missionaries, to be sure, was to promote evangelization through education, the genuine impulse to help improve the lot of women seems to have been present, and Christianity, by helping to pioneer women's education in Korea in the first half of the twentieth century, can be given credit for having a lasting impact on the status of women in Korea.

The influence of Christianity notwithstanding, the Korean Protestant church has evolved over the years as an unquestionably male-dominated institution, reflecting not only the legacies of the male-centered institutional tradition in Christianity itself but also its syncretic blending with the elements of the Confucian-patriarchal cultural tradition (Kang 1996). Despite the enormous centrality of women's work to church maintenance and expansion, there is little question within the Korean evangelical establishment about where women stand as a group. Hewing to a literal interpretation of the Biblical injunctions regarding the secondary place of women in society and in the home, women as a whole occupy an unequivocally subordinate status and role within the church organization and hierarchy.

As mentioned in Chapter 1, women have not yet been granted the right to ordination in many of the denominations despite the efforts of various Christian women's groups to alter this situation over the years. But even in the denominations that have historically allowed female ordination, such as the Methodist Church, the difficulties and obstacles for women pursuing the pastoring vocation are such that very few dare attempt it.[2] It is difficult for ordained women to find jobs because large and prestigious churches rarely hire women as assistant pastors, but only as *jeondosa* (ministerial interns or nonordained pastors). In conversations with a number of female Methodist pastors, I discovered that for women to find pastoring work, they must typically start or "pioneer" their own churches, typically in undesirable locations (for instance, in non-urban areas), under very difficult conditions, and for very low pay. The day-to-day difficulties stemming from the congregants' resistance to and negative perceptions of female pastors also pose formidable challenges and stresses. For these reasons, there are only a small number of ordained women who actually practice.[3]

Although at present women are appointed in small numbers to eldership in those denominations that allow female ordination, such as the

Methodists, the highest official position to which most women can real-
istically aspire is called *gwonsa*, a term that can be roughly translated as
"exhorting deacon" (I. Kim 1985: 235). Ranked higher than a deacon but
lower than an elder, the *gwonsa* is a position of lay leadership that one
pastor described to me as a kind of "glorified deaconship," having been
invented mainly to "accommodate and reward women for long years of
service."[4] Indeed, women, as well as men, are appointed *gwonsa* in recognition of their many years of dedication to the church, usually as deacons. At the North River Church, for example, a member becomes eligi-
ble to become a *gwonsa* after serving three years as a deacon.[5] Although
in most churches the position of *gwonsa* is for men a stepping stone to
becoming an elder, for women it is often a terminal position that ac-
knowledges spiritual leadership but holds little decision-making power.

The most common lay leadership position offered to women is that
of deacon (*jipsa*). Although the terms of eligibility vary among churches,
the requirement for being appointed a deacon is typically baptism and
at least six months to a year of church attendance. Like the position of
gwonsa, a person is tapped or appointed as deacon in recognition of dedicated church attendance and service.[6] The standard criteria for judging
such dedication are regular attendance in church and cell groups, including dawn and other prayer meetings, regular tithing, and willingness to
take on the variety of tasks that the church might ask of a person. Other
types of outward evidence of personal devotion, such as spiritual zeal,
also help.

Despite the subordinate place of women within the church organization, their activities and work are hardly limited in their range and constitute an important foundation for institutional maintenance. Organized
into various forms, the work of women, as both lay members and leaders, spans every area. In fact, one might say that the significance of lay
leadership positions, such as female deaconships, lies precisely in their
role as instruments for organizing and channeling women's labor power.

For many women, appointment as a deacon is often a double-edged
sword. Although most women appreciate, and even seek, such recognition, they also realize that as lay leaders in the church, they will be expected to undertake many responsibilities and become more proactive
in church affairs. These responsibilities may range from leading or participating in various types of volunteer service, working in the kitchen,

to training to become cell leaders. Whatever the responsibility, deacons are expected to form the core of the church volunteer workforce and lay leadership and devote a considerable amount of their time to church service. Indeed, most of the women with whom I spoke seemed to enjoy their status as deacons, but many also expressed considerable ambivalence, saying that the work demanded of them is sometimes too much, that they are constantly asked to do more, and that they find these requests almost impossible to refuse as "good" Christians. In many cases, the demands require women to be at the church almost every day of the week.

Consistently, women also express a great deal of frustration about the often menial and supporting nature of their work; many women, though obediently accepting their tasks, are more than aware that they are the ones responsible for the back-breaking and unpaid day-to-day labor without which the church would not function. As one woman put it, "we are but the church's army of laborers after all." The women were especially unhappy that they, as opposed to the male deacons, were responsible for all of the "dirty" work of the church, such as cleaning and cooking.

Another common way of mobilizing female labor is to organize church volunteers into groups called "women's missionary societies" (*yeoseongyobu*). Composed both of deacons and lay members, these groups carry out a large portion of the practical work of the church. Typically, the women's missionary societies are organized by age—for example, one group for 21- to 30-year-olds, another for 31- to 40-year-olds, etc.—and each of these age-based missionary societies has an annual budget to spend on its activities as well as a formal organizational and leadership structure. With a chief "director" and other officers (such as secretary and manager) at the helm, each society is typically broken into various "divisions," such as planning, education, culture, research, service, finance, and social work, with each division headed by "assistant directors."

As the names of the various divisions suggest, these activities encompass almost all forms of service necessary to the operation of the church: evangelizing, home visits, organizing and running of special events, sponsoring special prayer sessions and retreats, and carrying out community service. Each society's "service division" is responsible for the "dirty work" mentioned above, such as cleaning latrines and carrying out "kitchen duty," which encompasses everything from lunch preparation and clean-up for the entire congregation after the Sunday worship service to any other type of food preparation required for special events. As one deacon complained, "I come to church to get away from home, and what do I have to do here? Same things I do at home. You know, we are really just a herd of kitchen workers [*bueok ttegi*]."

Responsible for crucial church tasks while subordinated to male authority at every level of the institutional hierarchy, women within the church have been designated two dominant roles: "service workers" (*bongsaja*), as one female church leader termed it, and "helpmates" (*bojoja/doeum baepil*). The formal and informal control over women's status are buttressed ideologically by traditional Confucian-Christian views, especially those stressing silent obedience and submissiveness, that place enormous pressure on women to conform to the ideal image of the virtuous and deferential female.[7] According to one female *gwonsa* in the North River Church, the dominant expectation of women within the church can be summed up as, "to be quiet, obey, do what one is expected to do, and sit tight." Although she observes that many churches nowadays make efforts not to be so rigid, she sees that this kind of attitude, "after so many years of female oppression," is "hard to cast off" on the part of both the church leadership and the women themselves, making change difficult. She notes further: "Most churches think that women are there to serve (*bongsa*), without saying much. They see this as faithful behavior. Women who don't do this are seen as somehow being 'crazy.'"

Despite the indispensability of their services to the church, the general position and status of women within the Korean evangelical church, it is clear, are subordinate and secondary, defined at every level by their gender status and largely reflecting and reproducing their gender roles within the family and society. Although there are opportunities for women to exercise leadership, especially through such positions as cell group leaders and Sunday school teachers, the primary function of women within the church is to provide reliable volunteer labor, ingeniously mobilized through a system of status and rewards issued by the church. Given their awareness of the limitations and the obvious gender "injustices" of their positions, though, what are some of the reasons behind the enthusiasm of so many women for church work and participation? What motivates such a large number of them to dedicate their time, labor, and hearts to the church, willingly submitting to the church's myriad demands?

Women's Space, Women's Community

Despite the obvious limitations of women's roles within the institution of the Korean evangelical church, their involvement in church affairs must be seen as a mix of constraints and opportunities. Although at first glance it may be easier for us to fixate on these limitations and constraints, we must focus closer attention on some of these opportunities, as they are perceived and experienced by women, if we are to understand the meaningfulness of church participation in their lives.

For many of the dedicated church members with whom I have spoken, church involvement, at its most important level, is not seen as something requiring any special explanation; as mentioned earlier, church work is to many women a natural extension of their deep religious commitment and love of God, an act of carrying out "God's work." However, upon speaking to a wide range of members of varying levels of religious commitment and observing their institutional lives within the church, I can sketch a broader picture in which women's church involvement is driven by a mix of motivations and incentives far more complex than those that can be termed purely "religious."

The story of Yoon-bin is a good place to begin. Her earlier passionate narrative suggests that Yoon-bin views her church work as an expression of her fervent religious commitment and her love of God. Ever since her powerful conversion experience, Yoon-bin's life has shifted focus from the things of the world to those of God, and the church has become an important center of her existence. In performing church work, she sees herself as glorifying God by carrying out his bidding. Her narrative, however, also clearly suggests something else. For her, the church functions as something more than simply a space in which to worship and perform Christian duties; rather, it is for her an arena for frequent extra-domestic social interaction in a legitimate space away from home. Having established to her family and husband, who were initially anti-Christian, the absolute necessity of her religion and church life—that she would be a "sick person" without God—

Yoon-bin considers the church not only a place of spiritual succor but an important extra-domestic social arena. I contend, then, that the role of the church as a sphere of extra-domestic social interaction and female community is, in many significant ways, a major source of attraction for Korean evangelical women. Although inseparable from its spiritual and religious significance, the church is nevertheless enormously meaningful for women as an institution, especially as a focus of women's social activities.

The importance of the social dimensions of the Korean church for its female members becomes evident to any observer after attending a church in Seoul for any length of time, not only in the abundance of women's groups and activities of various types, but also in the amount of time that women such as Yoon-bin spend at the church during a given week. Whether the women are there for primarily social or spiritual reasons, it is clear that for many of them, the church serves as a major hub of non-domestic activity and community.

Regardless of the type of activity in which a member becomes involved, this participation in collective church activities—especially in the form of small, gender-specific groups—draws women into an appealing social community that provides them with a means of regular social interaction and engagement outside of the home. Other studies of Korean Christianity have not failed to notice the importance of churches as spaces providing intimate face-to-face-interaction for members in the midst of urban anomie (see I. Kim 1985). Although this may be a valid observation at the general level, the phenomenon of women's church participation has an additional dimension: beyond its function as a sphere of family-like interaction that counteracts the anomic conditions of urban, modern living, the church is especially meaningful as an extra-domestic "refuge" from the confines of family life—one that may have important subversive implications. We can observe these dynamics with particular clarity in the cell groups, which function as focal points for small, intimate, family-like social interchange among members. In larger churches such as South River, which rely heavily on elaborate cell systems for the organization and monitoring of its members,[8] cell groups are indeed seen as the "family within family," a focus of social life and a setting that provides most of the "primary" personal relationships for members within the church.

For many evangelical women, cell groups often do serve as the center of their social lives, and as a locus for the formation of their closest friendships and non-familial bonds. By functioning as venues for frequent social interchange and for the intimate sharing of lives and problems on a regular basis, cell groups come to serve as compelling settings in which to forge intimate bonds with others and to develop long-lasting friendships. Many women call the cell groups their "second family" and claim over time that the cell group associations have become progressively more central to their lives. One woman active in a cell group remarked:

As time went on, my social relationships with people outside of the church began to appear meaningless. I had no interest in doing the things I used to like to do, going shopping, playing tennis, whatever. Slowly, I found myself losing interest in these mundane things and becoming distant from friends I used to have outside of the church. Now, aside from a couple of long-time childhood friends, most of my friends are from the church, especially from the cell group. We do everything together and since we have the most important thing in common, God, and have the same values; it is truly fun.

Another woman from the South River Church said of her group:

What I realized through my group was how wonderful interaction [*gyojae*] with other members is. That was the biggest realization. First of all, you study together, and through that, you all become one through Jesus Christ. The members meet together first because they are told to but then realize that they all really need each other. And to realize this, and that you can pray for other people's difficulties together as one mind, that is a wonderful thing—to feel frustrations, torment, sadness, pain, and happiness together and to pray for one another together. It is the kind of interaction you cannot experience out in the world.

In most churches, the cell groups are not only settings for social gatherings but also organizational hubs for various church activities, which further group and interpersonal bonding. At the South River Church, cell groups are one of the primary vehicles through which the members are mobilized as a group to participate in various types of church work. In the cell group with which I was involved at the South River Church, for example, one of our many volunteer activities included making regular visits to a social service center run by the church in a poor area of Seoul in order to cook and serve lunch for the elderly and the indigent in the neighborhood. While there, the cell group also made home visits to the handicapped and the infirm, holding private worship services for them and bringing food and other necessities. The cell group also made regular visits to the prayer retreat center and participated as a group in various other church functions.

In addition to its role as a locus of emotional and psychological support, the cell group also provides practical services to its members as a kind of "mutual-aid" society. For instance, members can come together to help one another in times of financial crisis—which can be quite frequent even for those who are middle class—and the cell group serves as a valuable clearinghouse for exchanging and sharing practical information that helps the members with the business of day-to-day-living and enhances their domestic and family well-being.

Other small group settings that facilitate interpersonal bonding might also include women's missionary societies and Bible classes. Much more than vehicles for carrying out their stated activities or tasks, these groups also serve as important arenas for extra-domestic socializing, where women can form friendships, seek temporary relief from their domestic existence, and partake in non-domestic activities. One woman from the North River Church described her experience in her missionary society:

When I came to this church, I got myself plugged into the missionary society because even if I stayed home, it's not like I would be meeting my friends or doing anything useful. And socializing with those of my age here, it's fun and provides the motivation to be even more enthusiastic about the church. These members feel even closer to me than my relatives, and with them, I talk about everything, because we see each other so often. So because it's so much fun, it made me get involved and work even harder.

Particularly for first-time churchgoers, the social attractions of the church can often serve as important incentives for continued church attendance, with cell groups often providing the initial attraction. However, even if a member does not come to church for social reasons, it is clear that once a person becomes involved, church life often begins to take on important social significance. And for most, the social environment and interaction has the vital effect of reinforcing or facilitating the growth of faith, underscoring again the observed importance of group interaction for fostering conversion. The following is a comment from another member of the North River Church regarding her experiences in a series of Bible-study classes:

You know, the Disciple Training course was important for me in realizing a lot about my faith, but the social interaction [*gyojae*] aspect of it was, for me, as important as the messages we received in class. The group that you study with becomes an everlasting link, a relationship that you cannot sever. And as you interact with them, learn with them, your faith and commitment to religion and church grows because you reinforce one another. When you see others growing in faith and serving the church, you want to do so also.

Regardless of a member's progress on the path to conversion, the centrality and importance of Korean churches as social institutions providing female-centered community and extra-domestic space cannot be overlooked in understanding its significance for evangelical women. As an aside, a testament to the importance of this social dimension is the less-than-positive reputation of evangelical women in South Korea as a "noisy horde of socializers" who mill about busily in groups. Although socializing is not necessarily the only reason for women to participate in church activities, it is for those women who have few legitimate social outlets away from home, an undeniable draw as an important locus of non-domestic social and emotional support that can help women cope with some of the conflicts and restrictions of their home lives.

In Quest of Recognition: God's Work and Status Rewards

As complex, self-sustaining organizations, the churches are more than places of religious worship and social gathering. They are elaborately organized hierarchical structures with a complex division of labor in which each individual contributes to the overall functioning of the institution through specific tasks. As such, the churches provide for their members varied opportunities for contribution, goal accomplishment, and leadership. As members become involved and participate in various church activities, the church, then, becomes more than simply an arena for social interaction, but also an important performative space with its own system of rewards and recognition. Aside from the church's significance as a social community, what does the performative dimension of the church further reveal about the dynamics of women's church involvement?

Church involvement is so heavily stressed in most Korean churches that the performance of various services is seen as part and parcel of one's faith—and as evidence of one's religiosity. Indeed, as one woman explained, "We are basically told to believe, do church service, and then go to heaven." Although some people look upon these demands critically and do not find such pressures entirely comfortable, many women, regardless of their level of dedication, come to view church involvement as an important source of social recognition and approval; it therefore comes to constitute, in many cases, a subtle or powerful incentive for active church participation.

Most women, of course, do not begin participating in church activities with the conscious goal of seeking recognition from the church or other church members. As the members become progressively more involved, however, many of them come to find the various implicit and explicit forms of social recognition and approval both rewarding and seductive. A deacon of the North River Church describes this feeling:

Sometimes it can be too much, since I do so many different things; I can even neglect house responsibilities. The good thing, though, is that in doing church work, I can gain a lot of knowledge, and whatever work I do, I get recognized [*injeong batda*]. That is so, so good and rewarding for me. Oh, it's not so much that other people are saying that I am such an industrious person, but since I am doing God's work, I *can* raise my head about it and feel proud. That helps a lot.

The word *injeong*, translatable as "recognition," or "acknowledgment," is a word that appears ubiquitously in the narratives of women when they discuss their institutional involvement. In whatever form, recognition from those in the church community for one's dedication or a job well done seems to be something of key importance to women as they participate in church activities. What does this, then, suggest to us about the meaning and importance of social recognition in the lives of women?

The institutional recognition women receive within the church becomes crucial for many of them as a form of approval and recognition that lies outside of the domestic arena. For many women, the only source of societal recognition and reward lies in what they do in the domestic sphere, so recognition derived from church involvement, as a form of approval rooted in a larger social field, can help in significant ways to affirm and enhance their general sense of self-worth and self-esteem. The domestic roles and work performed by women are by no means unvalued in contemporary Korean society, but involvement in church activities provides a key opportunity to gain significant recognition for non-domestic activities and talents, especially meaningful for those who feel underappreciated for what they do at home.

An important source of recognition for women within the church is the pastor. Although women may tell themselves that they are performing church work for God, many admit to the fact that "recognition" from the pastor is an extremely important source of reward and satisfaction, a factor that can motivate them to get involved and work hard. One vivid illustration for this comes from a story told by Ji-sun, a member of the South River Church, who in the following narrative explains that the particular attraction of smaller churches—the kind she used to attend before coming to the South River Church—lies precisely in the satisfaction derived from being recognized by the pastor:

It's kind of embarrassing to think about now, but one of the reasons I was so dedicated at that church is that I got all this recognition from the pastor, as well as from other people. In that church, I was very close to the pastor because I was so conspicuous with all my church service. In a small church, even if you do some small thing, the church leaders and other people know right away, so you get recognition. It's a stupid thing, looking for recognition from other people and not God, but there is a lot of that. There are a lot of great things about the South River Church, but one thing is that in such a big church as this, the head pastor doesn't really know you as well. Of course, you are known by the assistant pastors and other leaders, but still, despite all the good training and grace I receive here, I feel like there is something lacking here sometimes, like there isn't the kind of recognition I wish for. I know this is stupid, and this is all because of my ego, but I can't say that I don't miss that somehow.

For many others, recognition, approval, and acceptance by their peers are just as important. One woman from the North River Church explained:

When people think you are sincere and dedicated and recognize that you come to church and do a lot and do it enthusiastically, although I believe that only God can really say who is really devoted and it's much more important what *He* thinks, people recognize that and pray for you. And this makes me really happy and proud. There are many here who telephone my family, help us with time and money, especially when things are difficult.

Despite the existence of obvious gender inequalities that limit the status mobility of women within the church and the often stressful demands made upon female members, the church can provide, through its formal and informal systems of rewards and recognition, compelling incentives for church involvement. Beginning initially with verbal and informal recognition and encouragement, rewards are soon distributed in the form of formal status positions that take on great importance to the development of enhanced self-conceptions of individuals.

It is important to point out, however, that the church is not simply an arena in which women act out the role of passive recipients of social or status rewards. Reflecting perhaps the powerful drive for recognition characteristic of those belonging to a socially excluded group, the church is also an institutional sphere in which women actively seek and compete for recognition and rewards, a place where women, as one observer put it, seek to "display" something of themselves. As one female *gwonsa* of the North River Church observed:

I like to think people are mostly enthusiastic for spiritual reasons and they do church work enthusiastically because it's God's work. But, if I must be honest, I must also admit that there may be other motivations, that women, as women, are doing it because they are trying to develop something of themselves, and that they are not necessarily doing it for God's glory but to show off something of themselves. This is self-centered, but they are trying to achieve something for themselves, perhaps subconsciously. But I don't believe that you can sustain deep commitment with these reasons only.

As another member commented, "I think in a lot of cases, doing church service is for self-fulfillment, satisfaction of ego (*jasin chungman*). It's not for Jesus, to pay him back for what he's done for us. It's to receive recognition from others, for others to think you are good (*chak hada*). That's a good feeling, so you try even harder, to look good to other people." As remarked by yet another member, "Well, I think once you come to church, after a while, everyone wants to become a deacon."

The power of this drive for recognition and status that seems to underlie the zealous church involvement of women emerges again in the experiences of Ji-sun, who admits that she initially chose to attend the small, "pioneer" church rather than a large, well-established one before coming to the South River Church precisely because she wanted to "stand out" and count for something in the church through her contributions. Although she did see her actions also as a consequence of her spiritual zeal, she was more than cognizant about her other more "worldly" motivations, of which she was not particularly proud:

Of course, I really wanted to serve the church, do something for it, help it grow, through my contributions. But the truth was that I kind of liked being recognized, admired, and being looked up to, so performing church service and going to that church was to show myself off and because I was intoxicated with myself. And you know, because that church was in a working-class kind of neighborhood, with not many well-educated people, we stood out! And we lived in this big house at the time, so people thought we were really well-off and well-educated. And we also made many large tithes, which also made us very important in the church. Come to think of it now, I think that was most of it! It's really kind of embarrassing.[9]

As important as the system of interpersonal rewards and recognition seems to be for helping to promote dedication to church service among members, there is, however, an undeniable sense that rewards, particularly formal rewards, are not distributed equitably among all. The unequal distribution of rewards between the sexes, the most obvious form of inequality, has been discussed earlier. Because the church leadership perceives status rewards as being especially important in motivating the loyalty of male members, the church pays particular attention to quickly rewarding deserving men with positions of status and leadership, such as deaconships and elderships, despite the greater devotion and dedication often displayed by their wives.

Although most wives, since they desire to involve their men in the church, rarely object to this kind of gender-based inequality, women are more likely to voice disapproval and dissatisfaction when the unequal distribution occurs within their own gender and along class lines. For example, there was a sense among various members in the North River Church that despite their hard work, those women from lower socio-economic and educational backgrounds tended to be "slighted" or "overlooked" in terms of rewards or recognition, causing these women great "sorrow." The perception is often that the members are recognized and rewarded not on the basis of faith but on "materialistic consideration," such as how much and how often they tithe—a consideration, of course, that favors the well-off. Sometimes those who have particularly stellar educational credentials are subtly (or not so subtly) cultivated or groomed by the church leadership for positions, an attempt at favoritism that becomes quickly obvious to the whole congregation. For instance, one young married woman who was recently made a deacon at the North River Church described her surprise at how "suddenly" and quickly she was made a deacon, in contrast to some others who spent years waiting to be one, and could only attribute it to the prestige of the university she attended.

At the South River Church as well, those rare cell leaders with only high school educations are more than aware that they are in the minority, and must often battle continuously with their sense of inferiority. This unfortunate situation is summed up well by a deacon at the North River Church who has come recently to experience this situation ever more acutely because of a sudden downturn in her financial situation:

I have come to feel increasingly frustrated with the church since my family's bankruptcy. It made me realize how advantageous it is to be better off in this church. It's just like the wider society. You know, there is a lot of invisible work to be done, like in the kitchen, but we all want to shine in those areas where others can see us. But I know so many who do invisible work without recognition and are sad because of it. Because of the large number of well-off people in this church, the poorer tend to be ignored. There are many who feel that they are not getting important positions because of rich/poor distinctions. I experience that now because I am in difficult financial straits myself.

Despite obvious inequities and problems, the system of rewards and recognition offered by the church seems nevertheless to provide a structure of incentives for women's church involvement, attesting to the enormous psychic importance of and need for social approval and recognition for women.

Confidence and Fearlessness: Toward Internal Transformation

Church participation does not simply lead women to an enhanced sense of self-esteem and self-worth derived from external validation and approval, but it often results in a deeper, internal transformation of self and identity. In the course of partaking in various types of church activities, many women, in spite of the limitations of their subordinate status, profess to gradual experiences of enhancement in self-confidence and personal power that transform their sense of identity and self-conception.

While carrying out "God's work," many experience this transformation of the self, first of all, as a notable increase in self-confidence that arises from having demonstrated to themselves and to others their extra-domestic talents and abilities. Through the chance to accomplish and tackle things they did not previously think possible, the women experience a considerable sense of empowerment that appears to have a profound impact upon their sense of self. Mi-kyung, an established deacon at the North River Church and a housewife and mother of three in her late 30s, illustrates in the following story a typical process by which this can occur within the church:

When I was little, I had a lot of greed/desires [*yoksim*]. There were so many things I wanted to do and be. In church, one of the things I had always wanted to be was a Sunday school teacher and here, I secretly wanted to do it for a long time. But for a long time, no one was asking me. But *gwonsa* Yi asked me one day that I should teach, telling me that I'd probably be very good. But at first, I refused him, saying that oh, no, I couldn't, I am not qualified! But he kept urging me. A few months later, there was training for Sunday school teachers and they asked me to try the summer Sunday school because they were short of teachers. I said, how can I since I am so inadequate, but he said to me that if I prayed hard and prepared, I could do it. So after receiving this training, I went to dawn prayers everyday. I memorized all the kids' names and prayed for them everyday. After this summer, I became so close to the kids and saw that kids really liked me and followed me. So I kept doing it and I am still doing it, for five years now.

Young-shil, another deacon at the North River Church and mother of a teenage daughter, is considered one of the most active and enthusiastic members of the church. Her situation provides a particularly poignant demonstration of the kinds of radical internal transformation and self-reconstitution that women can experience through their involvement in the church.

More than others, Young-shil, for a long time, had been suffering from an acute sense of low self-esteem and worthlessness. In addition to her lack of college education, the biggest source of this has been her marital situation; though not yet divorced, Young-shil had more or less been abandoned by a husband who, after years of marital conflict, went abroad to work and refuses to return home. Blaming much of this on herself, Young-shil sees herself as a colossal failure as a woman and a wife, a "marginal" female, and carries around a sense of great shame and embarrassment.

So deep was her shame that she was at first afraid to come to church. But at the insistence of a close friend, she began attending the North River Church several years ago, keeping the truth of her marital situation vague, if not secret, from others. After experiencing a profound conversion experience shortly thereafter, however, Young-shil subsequently became an ardent churchgoer, joining various activities and fervently evangelizing and, according to her friend, "praying her heart out everyday to be made a deacon because she wanted to be one so badly." Her wish was soon fulfilled; Young-shil, in recognition of her devoted service to the church, was quickly made a deacon a few years later. Eventually, Young-shil became so fervent in her faith that she decided to enter a seminary part time, and by the time I got to know her, she was in her second year at a Methodist seminary, planning to devote the rest of her life to God's work.

Despite her initial hesitation, Young-shil discovered in the church a place that gave her a new sense of self as a "child loved by God" who "need not be afraid of anything." Church activities gave her expression, visibility, and support through which she was able to develop and demonstrate the power of her newly emerging self both to herself and to others. And through these activities, she was able to overcome her previous sense of severe diffidence, which kept her from pursuing things she deeply desired and from demonstrating her true abilities:

Before, I never imagined that I would be able to do any of these things, that I could be a deacon, be in charge of these various things. In all my life, I never had confidence about anything. But I feel now that God always has my back, so I pray and read the Bible before I go anywhere or do anything, and I become confident. So through church, God would help me overcome my lack of confidence, make my mind peaceful, and make my anxieties and depressions go away.

She was able to gain more confidence by overcoming her previous shyness and highly self-conscious and introverted personality, which resulted in her fear of interaction with other people. Evangelizing, in particular, helped her overcome this fear because as she put it, "In order to witness Jesus, I had to get to know people! I had to try to understand them so I could find the right way of getting through to them." In church, she was especially self-conscious of what other people thought of her because of her marital situation and her humble financial circumstances, but by repeatedly reminding herself that she was doing God's work, she was able to overcome these anxieties. For example, she did not think she was fit to be a cell leader because of her less-than-model home life, and when some members failed to show up to some of the meetings, she would take it personally and become "indescribably upset." She was, however, eventually able to overcome this insecurity by persuading herself that she was serving as "God's vessel." The ultimate mark of her growing self-confidence and self-transformation, of course, was her enrollment in the Methodist seminary, an experience that gave her even greater self-assurance about her abilities.

For both Young-shil and Mi-kyung, their sense of empowerment is, of course, also experienced as deriving spiritually from God. As they tell it, they gained strength through God and their faith in Him to see them through critical times. Such a sense of spiritual empowerment notwithstanding, the women just as importantly experienced and attained personal transformation through the institutional context of the church, which provided a crucial venue outside of the women's domestic sphere in which to demonstrate their unutilized abilities and achieve their untapped potential, allowing them to enhance their sense of self-worth and alter their sense of identity in tangible ways. Furthermore, it is difficult to ignore the sense of the many unspoken thwarted aspirations of the two women's lives, such as Mi-Kyung's allusion to her many youthful ambitions. Mi-kyung's desire to be a Sunday school teacher seems to have remained as one of the few attainable non-domestic goals after most of her other life options had been closed off. For Young-shil as well, the "burning desire" to become a deacon seems to be an expression of her deeply hidden aspiration for some form of personal achievement and public recognition. The intensive church involvement of these women, then, can be seen as an important means of pursuing individual self-fulfillment, something that had largely been denied to them but has now resulted in a deep sense of personal achievement and a more empowered, reconstituted self-identity.

This process of self-fulfillment, empowerment, and transformation of self-identity can be seen clearly in the experiences of cell leaders. In many Korean churches, cell groups serve as an arena in which a selected number of women can serve in pivotal leadership roles. In the South River Church in particular, cell leaders, after undergoing intensive systematic training, perform enormously important functions as teachers, counselors, and "shepherds" of church members, making cell leaders, in effect, unpaid "lay pastors."

In the course of their duties, all of the cell leaders, to differing degrees, describe undergoing a profound process of self-empowerment as they learn to exercise their leadership abilities and discover the talents they never thought they had in teaching and spiritual pastoring. Although differing in the extent to which they consciously articulate this change, their work as cell leaders seems to have acquired enormous significance as a source of self-esteem, confidence, and fulfillment. As one cell leader describes it:

By being a cell leader, I have gained great self confidence and I have learned that I had hidden talents and abilities, like leadership ability. And being a cell leader is a source of enormous satisfaction as I watch the members pray together and grow, watch their lives change with the cell meetings, and watch some of them become cell leaders themselves. Watching them grow and make an effort to become better persons and Christians, that's the best.

Throughout the various narratives dealing with the process of self-transformation and self-reconstitution, the theme of personality transformation is also one that emerges over and over again, in which meek and passive creatures transform into confident, bolder, outspoken individuals who can tackle various tasks of life with greater fearlessness. Many women contrast their shy and introverted "original" personalities with their more assertive selves, which they say were gained through faith and church participation. One such woman reflected:

By going to church, my personality changed 180 degrees. In one corner of my mind, I hated being left behind and being left in the background of things, but I didn't have the courage to take the front line in anything. But through going to church and believing in Jesus, these impulses in my insides became expressed outwardly, and I became so outgoing, a person who can speak out anywhere, can talk well and a lot. From being this demure and introverted person, I became this outgoing, bright, and cheerful person.

For some women, the apparent "confidence" and "extroversion" that they saw Christians possess was a catalyst in their desire to become involved in the church and to pursue church work in the first place. According to one woman at the North River Church:

When I was a teenager in school, we had to perform in front of others, like singing and so on. I was always so shy, passive, and easily embarrassed. But I noticed that the friends who went to church were so good at it. They seemed to do everything well. And when you see Jesus believers, I always felt that they were strong in leadership and, how shall I say, wherever they were, they always seemed to stand out. So I thought, if I believed in Jesus and went to church, can I become like that? So that's why I first went to church.

Echoing my earlier observation about the self-repressive tendencies of many of the women I had gotten to know, a large number of women, interestingly enough, would say that alongside their introverted and passive personalities, they also always had a hidden, unexpressed, or re-pressed side that was "active" and "passionate." Although this tension reflects clearly the ongoing struggle of Korean women to meet the normative expectations of the ideal female, the experiences of conver-sion and church participation seem to have become, for many of the women, a means to release or liberate the assertive aspects of their per-sonalities in ways that are legitimate, that is, in the name of God and God's work.

Self-Cultivation and Learning

In addition to its role as a place for pursuing self-achievement, the evangelical church is also perceived by women as a venue of learning and self-development. In a society deficient in the institutional struc-tures, opportunities, and societal validation for adult learning, especially for married women, the church and its activities seem to represent for many members a chance to acquire knowledge and expand mental ca-pacities outside of the home, to "learn things of the outside world."

According to many members, the church, as a social institution, is first and foremost an arena that provides opportunities for women who might otherwise be confined to their homes to develop valuable social and interpersonal skills and to expand their intellectual and spiritual ho-rizons. One woman at the North River Church described her experi-ence and feelings:

Besides recognizing me for the things that I do, what church gives me is the chance to gain a lot of knowledge, information, learn a lot about human relations, how to deal with certain people, how to interact with people. Because I learn these things, my views change a great deal. I find that my perspectives, which were kind of rooted down before, are challenged and transformed. I also find that I can learn a lot from the female leaders in this church. There are so many things I don't know, but through church life, I learn about all these things, human relations, how to deal with situations.

The church is perceived as a learning environment by many members as a place for a kind of intellectual development, for acquiring new knowledge about a wide range of things and for the opportunity to "use one's brain." One college-educated woman made this observation: "Ever since I got married, I never had a chance to use my brain. Over the years, I felt my brain rot away. But by participating in all these great classes at the church, I started to learn again, to use my brain again. I study the Bible assiduously several times a day and I spend time on the assignments like I used to in school. I have become a model student again."

As this woman suggests, many women find the Bible classes and various seminars offered by the churches on religious or family topics especially helpful as means of intellectual stimulation and self-improvement. To attend classes regularly and to carry out homework assignments serve as opportunities for concentrated study that many women find valuable to their mental well-being. One woman from the South River Church confessed, "I take advantage of every class or seminar offered at the church. I go to everything. Since I know I am inadequate [*bujok hada*], whenever I get the chance, I try very hard to learn." For those with few other ways of pursuing intellectual development, these types of learning opportunities offered by the church, then, provide chances for women to become intellectually active again. In the South River Church, the training process for becoming a cell leader is perceived as a particularly satisfying vehicle for systematic learning and intellectual development. Given that the training to become cell leaders is quite intensive—involving three years of coursework—undergoing this program gives participants the chance to experience a great sense of accomplishment, as well as the feeling of being engaged in a highly meaningful pursuit outside of the home.

Conclusion

In many ways, the evangelical church is a complex, multifaceted social institution that provides its members with a range of opportunities, rewards, and sources of fulfillment that might not necessarily be considered spiritual. For many evangelical women, the church undeniably serves as an as an extra-domestic sphere in which to relieve and cope with the tensions and conflicts of everyday life; for those with few other culturally approved means of social or intellectual engagement, the church functions as one of the few legitimate public arenas within which to pursue social interaction and experience non-domestic fulfillment.

Reinforcing their experience of spiritual empowerment, evangelical women find in church participation a source of empowerment that can lead to internal self-transformation. Running parallel to personal growth in the spiritual realm, achievements through church work can result in experiences of new forms of personal power and alterations in self-conception and identity that can have considerable ramifications for the ways women negotiate their environment and interpersonal relations.

By providing women with the means for self-empowerment and psychic/social autonomy that allows them to transcend the limitations and restrictions of the patriarchal family system, church participation, along with spirituality, is also a means of gender resistance for Korean women. As in the aforementioned case of Yoon bin, church attendance becomes for many women a subversive means for carving out their own social and psychic space, and in the process, for countervailing the powers of male authority and the demands of the family system. When women pursue church involvement against the wishes of their husbands or other members of their households—such as when women become so "Jesus-crazy" that they completely "abandon" their households to do nothing else but church work and prayer—this act can serve as an act of outright rebellion.[10]

For many Korean evangelical women, however, such emancipatory struggles through religion are not without profound contradictions. Although religious participation serves a vital role in women's efforts to cope with and resist patriarchal oppression, the potential for full-fledged self-empowerment can be, at the same time, undercut by effective self-redomestication and a re-disciplining process that can circumscribe their potential powers. As noted in the Introduction, much of the existing scholarship on women's participation in conservative religions has focused on the meaning and impact of the "paradoxical" accommodation by women to the ideology of "submission." In many of these recent studies, there has been a clear effort to bring out some of the more unexpectedly "liberating" facets of submission, especially as hidden or "subversive" instruments of gender negotiation and even of critique and transformation of patriarchal relations.

The next two chapters examine the complex meaning and dynamics of evangelical women's engagement with the ideologies and practices of religious patriarchy as they play out within the South Korean setting and their contradictory consequences on women's religiosity and lives. Focusing in particular on women's responses to the religiously supported ideologies of submission, obedience, and female gender identity, I show that women's accommodation to submission in the Korean evangelical context is a highly contradictory process—involving women's "subversive" efforts at negotiation and resistance as much as their profound acquiescence to patriarchy—that results in intensely oppressive as well as liberating consequences.

FIVE

Bargaining with Patriarchy:

The Politics of Submission and Gender

Despite their prominent role in the struggle of Korean women for liberation from patriarchal oppression and control, the evangelical churches in this study are first and foremost vehicles for propagating the traditionalist ideologies of patriarchy aimed at maintaining and restoring the cohesion of the existing family structure. Whereas many women successfully appropriate evangelical religion in various ways for the purposes of resisting and coping with the injuries and restrictions of the patriarchal system, they are also, within the churches, confronted with a powerful set of religiously sanctioned views on gender and family that are geared toward reinforcing the traditionalist conceptions of women's roles and gender identity.

Focusing on the meaning and politics of female submission, I examine the complex dynamics and nature of women's engagement with evangelical patriarchy as they play out in the Korean evangelical context. Beginning with a brief discussion of the central dimensions of the churches' ideological programs on gender and family, I explore the complex responses of women to the churches' ideological efforts, particularly as these relate to women's attempts to negotiate their domestic situations. The engagement of evangelical women with religious patriarchy involves a complex interplay of negotiation, resistance, *and* serious normative consent, and must be understood as a highly contradictory process both in terms of women's responses to the churches' efforts to redomesticate them—through their redefinition of women's gender identity and discipline of their powers—and of women's own attempts to negotiate their place within the patriarchal system.

Domesticating Willful Women:
The Evangelical Ideology of Family and Gender

The views on gender and family encountered in many Korean evangelical churches have one main goal: the stabilization of contemporary family relations through the transformation of female behavior and consciousness. The churches do, to be sure, attempt to "reform" men as well, but there is no mistaking the fact that the bulk of attention is focused on fostering female accommodation to the church-sanctioned order of family and gender as a means of ensuring family stability. In other words, the churches provide women with an array of important channels or "outlets" through which to cope with the problems and conflicts of the patriarchal family while seeking ultimately to bring about the resolution of these conflicts by securing women's commitment to the principles of patriarchal gender relations. In the course of my fieldwork, I observed these endeavors and processes in such settings as family seminars and cell meetings, both venues in which the church vigorously pursued its efforts to reform women.

"Smarty" Women: A Diagnosis of the Contemporary
Family Dilemma

According to the official discourse espoused by the North and South River Churches, as well as a number of other evangelical churches, one of the most vexing issues in contemporary Korean society is the problem of the family. Along with the larger social problems of perennial concern to South Koreans, such as national division, political repression, economic insecurities, and governmental corruption, the problem of the modern family is, as manifested by increasing levels of marital conflicts and youth problems, a serious expression of the crisis facing Korean society today.

These family problems, according to the churches, are a reflection and manifestation of the general degradation of the wider social and moral order, a decline in traditional values and a turn away from the fundamental principles of human relationships as defined by the Confucian system, in particular the hierarchically governed relationships based on gender and age, the violation of which spawns conflicts between women and men, young and old. In the realm of the family, the problem is attributed to the deviations of individuals from the all-important principles of gender hierarchy and roles that are the bedrock of family order but have been undermined by the influence of modern individualism and egalitarianism.

The rhetoric of church leaders within family seminars and cell meetings, however, suggests a more specific diagnosis of the problem: although the leaders generally attribute the problems of the family to deviations by both men *and* women from the proper principles of gender, men and women are not seen as being equally responsible for the problems. For them, the source of the current family crisis lies primarily in the actions of women, in female violations of the gender order.[1] According to Ms. Cho, an esteemed teacher and leader of the South River Church family seminar, the problems of the family stem from this gender situation:

Many Korean women don't know why they have so many conflicts at home. They think they are doing all right, but after taking my seminar, one thing they realize that they all have in common is that they have all been too "smarty" [*jallancheok hada*] in front of their husbands.[2] They have tried to possess too much power, leadership in the family. Only when women change these things do husbands become truly family-oriented. . . . The purpose of my seminar is first of all to strengthen the basis of faith in the members, and to teach the women the position and duties of a wife, and how to raise children. Most Korean women these days just meet someone, get married, and just live. They don't really know how to maintain a family life. I try to teach them the importance of family life, how important the role of the wife is to the husband and to the family. I try to instill in them the proper faith and Christian values through which they can influence the family as proper mothers and wives. The point is to transform their basic ways of thinking.

Ms. Cho suggests that women's violations of the family order can be reduced to two major transgressions: their attempts to rise above their proper positions and their "forgetting" of the importance of their family roles. However, given that this view of women's attempts to overstep their proper stations, to be too "powerful," is not unique to the Korean setting (see Rose 1987), what do these concepts mean in the Korean context? In particular, what does being "smarty," or self-important, denote?

At the most basic level, being "smarty" signifies women's violation of the fundamental principle of gender hierarchy and order by stepping out of their prescribed role and authority boundaries.[3] In the Korean context, however, the application of such a term suggests a more encompassing critique of the fundamental deviations of contemporary women from all of the basic principles of "virtuous" Confucian femininity and womanhood, the decline of which are seen as the real causes of the modern family crisis and the unhappiness and suffering of women themselves.

To comprehend what the churches understand as the nature of these female deviations and how it sees them as adversely affecting the modern family, it is helpful to consider how the churches define the major behavioral transgressions or "wrongdoings" of contemporary women. I observed in several family seminars and cell meetings that the contemporary behavioral transgressions most frequently identified as being committed by women can be grouped under three major categories of "sin": egoism, haughtiness, and impatience.

The term "egoism" (*igi ju-ui*, which can also be translated as "self-centeredness" or "selfishness") denotes all forms of behavior deemed to reflect self-centeredness in women, behaviors that directly violate the self-denying and submissive qualities of the ideal Korean female. Within the church discourse, all those actions considered to be egoistic refer in particular to women's assertions of their own desires and wants within the family, to "have one's way in everything." Although this term in the Korean context does not so much signify selfishness in terms of pursuing one's own personal desires as much as those regarding the welfare of the family—although the former does apply in some cases—such an assertive orientation on the part of women is perceived to be responsible for the greater part of the domestic conflict. As one woman was led to confess: "Before my faith, I used to be so egotistical, trying to have my way in everything. I got mad at everything. Now, I depend on God. When I'm about to do something I just think whether it will make God happy or not by what I do." Another woman elaborated on this attitude:

Before taking the family seminar, I was so self-centered. Got mad so often. When my husband said or did anything insensitive or hurtful, I couldn't endure it. I always had to say something confrontational, objecting. That is not in keeping with a life of faith. Even with the kids, it was centered on me, not on them. I drove them to do this or that so they would not lose out to other kids because of my own desires and ambitions, not theirs. But I didn't realize how it hurt them, all the things I said, did. It killed their self-esteem.

The above passage demonstrates how the charge of "egoism" is not only a critique of female assertiveness, but of something even more basic: the very existence of many and varied desires themselves, especially those that lead women to have "unreasonable" expectations of others, particularly of husbands and children. Such desires and the inability of women to keep them under control, then, become responsible for everyday discord and conflicts within the family.

According to the church, the primary area that is adversely affected by women's egoistic behavior is the sphere of marital relations. First of all, women's attempts to perpetually "have their way" in everything instead of deferring to the wishes of their husbands result not only in day-to-day marital discord but in aberrant behavior of husbands and eventually in their alienation. More specifically however, serious conflicts are seen often to arise from the wives' attempts to assert their desires or wants toward their husbands, especially those related to the husbands' earning capacity or general conduct, because when wives are disappointed in these matters, which is often the case, resentments build, with grave consequences for the husbands.

For example, the inability of women to control their desires in this sphere results in such unproductive behaviors as constant "stir-frying" or "nagging" of husbands, which not only anger, but ultimately emasculate them. For instance, one woman, speaking of her "greed" for money, admitted that she would not let her husband quit a job in which he was acutely miserable because she was afraid of financial implications for the family, subsequently driving her husband to drink and estrangement.

Mothers also project their desires or wants upon their children as destructive ambitiousness. Confessions abound by women of their unbridled "greed" toward their children; one women, for instance, admitted how pushing her children "to the limits" in school because she was so concerned about the "face" of her family to the outside world resulted in the children's permanent "mental paralysis."

Another female transgression commonly identified in the churches is feminine "haughtiness" (*gyoman*) or pride, a trait closely related to egoism. Haughtiness in the Korean evangelical women's context refers to the attitude that a woman thinks she is better or knows more than others, especially her husband.[4] Commonly, women confess to the sins of haughtiness when they see themselves as having behaved without the restraint of proper feminine modesty and humility, another characteristic of the ideal "virtuous" woman. In the words of one woman: "I really try to work on my personality, but it's hard to change. By nature, I'm quite hot-blooded you see. I have a lot of desire, greed. I have not been very good since my youth, I think. I was always really haughty. And you know, I had a good education too, so that made me even more arrogant, I guess. It's really hard to change these things." As another woman described her behavior:

I used to be so full of myself when I was in college. I used to not think much of boys, I used to think I was better than they were. So the thought of obeying men, that was very alien to me. So I caused a lot of trouble with my older brother too. I wouldn't even bring him a glass of water when he asked. So when my husband and I first got married, he used to tell me to turn on the TV and stuff and I used to think, you do it, and I wouldn't. But then, this kind of thing just caused a lot of trouble and made me irritable and unhappy. I realized it would actually be easier just to do it for him but I would still object all the time. So this caused so much trouble. But then I thought, if I really loved him, wouldn't I want to do everything for him? Do I really love him? But I still didn't think I should do it.

Aside from being a major source of marital conflict, "bad" attitudes such as haughtiness and egoism lead to other negative consequences: for example, when things do not go their way, women are led to destructive emotions such as frustration, anger, and resentment that intensify family conflict. In cell meetings, members seize upon violent outbursts of "ill temper" and emotion as particularly "sinful" behaviors demanding correction, because these are seen to have highly adverse effects on other family members. As one woman divulged: "One of the things I'm trying to so hard to change is my temper. I think I have the tendency to just act on my emotions. I am so irritable, get angry whenever things get bad, especially at my kids. If they don't do schoolwork or something, I'm always yelling at them. I know that this has a very bad influence on my kids but sometimes I just can't help it. So I repent about the same thing every week."

The groups also consider negative and critical attitudes toward others as being particularly detrimental to domestic relationships. Frustrated in a variety of ways at home, women are seen to develop all too often the nasty habit of criticizing and cutting others down, particularly their husbands. As one woman at a cell meeting disclosed: "What is my habitual sin? I find that my most egregious and habitual sin is toward my husband. I say things to hurt him all the time. I repent every week and pray that I may uphold him humbly and courteously but this resolve doesn't last me a week."

Finally, many contemporary women are seen to be guilty of another "sin": impatience (*mot chamda*), a lack of forbearance toward difficult situations and the shortcomings of others. As a cell leader noted in one of her sessions, things may have gotten much easier for women in the modern age, but being a woman is still an extremely difficult matter in South Korean society, and women will not be able to keep their families together—and preserve their sanity—if they lose the ability to endure. After all, marriages stayed intact in previous generations despite the unspeakable difficulties of women because they were able to endure any kind of suffering. Nowadays, to the contrary, women have become weak, spoiled, and selfish, with a sense of entitlement not conducive to enduring the difficulties of domestic life:

These days, families are faced with unspeakable conflicts. High school kids beating up their fathers, couples beating each other up. We seem to have arrived at an age where people can't endure things. Until now, we obeyed and submitted to our parents. But now, the attitude is that people are born perfect so that they can do whatever they want. What kind of principles [*wolli*] are we using to raise our children? Things are this way because of us [women]. We only focus on the negative things, the bad times, can't endure them, and forget the good times. But what kind of effects do these negative emotions [*gamjeong*] have on our children?

Despite its official view of women as essentially weak and dependent, the church invests tremendous energy in attempting to reshape women's gender subjectivities. This emphasis suggests that the church's efforts are a response to the dangers and threats posed by what it perceives as the innate powerfulness and willfulness that reside deep in the Korean female psyche that manifest themselves as strength in the domestic sphere, but that have become increasingly unruly and undisciplined in the modern age.

Indeed, as we can see, many of the narratives shared by group members do not suggest images of "weak" women, but to the contrary, those of tough, aggressive women filled with an array of tremendous ambitions and desires that become sources of frustration because they cannot easily be fulfilled within the constraints of Korean society. These ambitions may not be for the purposes of personal self-fulfillment but rather directed toward their families, but women's single-minded pursuit of them nevertheless suggests not passivity but a high degree of aggression, and their interactions with their family members often suggest concerted efforts at dominance rather than submission. This observation, again, reflects the reality that the image of Korean women has always been double and contradictory: submissive and subordinate on the one hand, but as "pillars" of the household, strong and "tough" (*eokseda/gang hada*), even aggressive, on the other, especially in the realm of domestic affairs (see also Deuchler 1977).

In many ways, this view of Korean women's character is expressed in the often contradictory and confused self-perceptions held by the women themselves. That is, despite the tendency for many women to see themselves as essentially "meek," "gentle," and "inconfident," these women simultaneously see themselves as tough and aggressive, particularly when it comes to ensuring the survival and well-being of their families. But regardless of whether these self-perceptions arise from an experience of their actual powers within the domestic realm or from an exaggerated sense of their aggressiveness juxtaposed to the ideals of submissive womanhood, many women, although subscribing to the necessity of toughness, also harbor a great deal of ambivalence and guilt about their "strength," which they come to believe is antithetical to the harmony of their families and to their own happiness so must thus be controlled with the help of God. As one cell member admitted: "I always had such a strong personality that God had to work really hard to manage me. I had so much suffering in my life but my strong personality made it worse. I have always seen that those women with gentle characters tend to lead relatively peaceful lives."[5] This belief reflects a piece of common, oft-repeated wisdom: that women with "gentler" (more pliable or accommodating) personalities are destined for happier, or at least less conflict-ridden, lives in the Korean society than those with more assertive personalities.

There is irony inherent in the gender ideology and structure of the Confucian family system: although the family provides a highly legitimate space for the expression and exercise of women's powers within the domestic sphere through its strict division between the "inside" and "outside" and the tremendous value it places on women's domestic roles, it must also address the constant danger posed by the possibility that these "powers" will break out of their bounds by vigilantly and relentlessly containing them, particularly through a close control over women's gender subjectivities.

The Path to Family Harmony: Endurance and Docile Obedience

Given such a situation, what solution does the church recommend for resolving family conflicts and restoring domestic harmony? To be more precise, what are the best and most efficacious methods for enabling women to resecure proper gendered self-conceptions, to embrace correct gender roles and standards of conduct? In this effort, the church counsels two major behavioral injunctions as strategy: "docile" obedience (*sunjong hada*) and endurance (*chamda*).

According to the churches, family conflicts which are caused first and foremost by women's willfulness, egoism, arrogance, and violations of the proper codes of conduct, can be remedied first of all through docile obedience. Obedience by women is crucial because it is the essential behavioral principle necessary to helping reestablish gender hierarchy, especially as a means to discipline women's willful impulses. Although the churches do advise that the husband should love the wife in return, they stress that the only way to attain real family harmony and reestablish family order is for the wife to begin to obey the husband in a heartfelt and unconditional manner that sincerely recognizes his superior position and authority. The following remark by a South River Church cell leader reflects this understanding:

I really believe that for any woman, obedience is something she has to deal with and accept. Without the wife obeying the husband, God will not use that home. We think the husband has to treat the wife well for the wife to obey but that's not the case. A wife has to obey first, unconditionally. So I counsel obedience first before anything else; it's the first thing I advise. A wife obeying, raising her husband continuously and making him the leader—that is the most essential aspect of marriage, the most important part to which everything else will follow.

In their relationships with their husbands, wives are first of all exhorted to practice total obedience because not only is such obedience the supreme and "fundamental responsibility" of the wife as commanded by God, but also because it is the only means to ensuring the happiness of her husband and children, as well as of the wife herself. Qualifying that obedience does not necessarily signify that women are "slaves," many leaders nevertheless teach emphatically that obedience is a "responsibility," not a "choice," and that the wife "must obey the husband like she obeys Jesus Christ," or disharmony will result. To be sure, the degree of emphasis placed on the "absoluteness" of female obedience varies somewhat among the leaders, but this injunction, in my observation, is tempered more by the idea that there needs to be mutuality of consideration between husbands and wives than by qualifying the need for the wife's obligation to obey.[6]

Realizing the absolute centrality of obedience, however, is not enough because most people do not know how to obey properly. And since obedience is, even for those with the best of intentions, not easy to carry out, it is something that requires much effort and practice. A major purpose of family life seminars, such as the ones held in the South River Church, is therefore to provide women with the specific methods and practical strategies with which to carry out submission in a proper manner and transform their behavior in a more productive way.

Many of the methods for helping women achieve "true" obedience are based first of all on the principle of preventing domestic conflict by diffusing the individual will and desires of the wife and making those of the husband the center of the relationship.[7] As taught in the seminars, some of the important principles women must observe in carrying out proper obedience, for example, included "studying up industriously on all the ways to make the husband happy," "avoiding living for oneself," and "avoiding doing anything that the husband does not like." A wife must also observe absolutely the husband's superior position and never go against the husband's will or decision. In being properly obedient, wives are exhorted to cease being aggressive, arrogant, and assertive, no matter how unjust the situation may seem; according to one cell leader: "Wives, obey not only husbands who are good, but husbands who are not so good, who are evil to you. Husbands change when wives obey."

To achieve the difficult goal of proper obedience, the women learned a technique in which they go home and, while imagining that they were talking to their husbands, practice telling themselves over and over again: "Yes, you are right. Everything you say is correct. I'll do everything you say." Another technique was an assignment in which women were told to wash the feet of their husbands every night, as Jesus had done for his disciples. The seminars also taught that obedience, if possible, should also extend to the bedroom. Speaking from her own example, one cell leader related to me: "Well, to be honest, my husband's always been a bit of a romantic. I, on the other hand, was always like a block of wood. Like when my husband would try to be tender in bed, I would just shove him off and stuff. Nowadays, even when my body's really tired from working all day, I obey, though inside, I wish he would not touch me."

Becoming obedient in the Korean context, however, not only means that women develop the desire and capacity to submit to men, but, reflecting the Confucian cultural emphasis on obedience as a supreme virtue, that they also reconstitute themselves as obedient individuals in general. This means that obedience and submission are encouraged in individuals to all kinds of authority, from the religious authority of the pastor and the secular authority of the President, to the authority of one's parents and elders. One seminar leader, in discussing matters of child-raising, made the following point to the women about the supreme necessity of developing an obedient character:

What should be the proper disposition of children? Make sure the children are obedient! That is first and foremost. The Bible teaches this. You must foster a disposition where they know how to obey other people. We mustn't become a country like America where children call their parents by name! Disrespect of authority—this is the biggest problem in the United States. But, in order to teach your children this, you yourself have become an example by obeying and submitting to those higher than you. It is your responsibility to uphold and maintain family order [*jilseo*]. And we should begin by not doing things like cursing out the President. We can maybe criticize him, but don't curse him out. This is not Biblical. Teach the kids to respect teachers! Teach them always to greet and bow to teachers properly. Say good things about the teachers in front of your kids. The teachers are teachers because they are somehow superior to you. . . . What is stupidity? Disobedience. Not obeying God, not obeying those above you. Look at those demonstrating college students. If you revolt against society, against your superiors, who will perish? You. Our social system is given by God. Don't try to spar with it. Obedience is a good thing.

Besides obedience, endurance is another virtue women must arduously cultivate in order to avert family conflict and disharmony. As church leaders noted, a reason for the instability and conflict in modern marriages is that women have lost the ability to "endure." The first step to cultivating the capacity to endure is to recognize that life for women, though better nowadays, is still full of pain and suffering, and that they should not expect things to be so easy. Describing life as that which "uses us and spits us out," one leader, for instance, observed that life's difficulties can only be overcome with the wife's patient endurance and "tears." Reflecting on her own experience, she told the members:

My husband, too, though he's a devoted Christian now, it took a lot of work and persuasion to turn him around. Even if your husband's from a Christian family, it takes a lot of tears from the wife. . . . There were so many difficult things in my life with him. But then I took this attitude and started praying hard. When I did that, I felt this peace. God has a path for you. You just don't know it, that's all. You must just endure [*chamda*] and wait [*gidarida*]. . . . In this difficult world, God is the only real love and strength. If you just look to reality when you encounter difficulties, it's too difficult. Only God can give us the strength to go through all this. Pray to God. He'll change your thinking, although the reality may not change.

Like obedience, enduring patiently the shortcomings of others, regardless of how difficult, is the key to family harmony and women's own long-term happiness because it is through such exemplary behavior that others will be inspired to change. Indeed, one seminar leader at the South River Church, in a discussion on how to deal with mothers-in-law, asserted plainly that love is the "ability to endure." She said, "I know it's really hard to consider your mother-in-law like a blood relative, but try. Try to get rid of your prejudices against the word 'in-law.' Celebrate her; she has given birth to your husband and raised him. And don't expect to get from her as much as you give. Always apologize first, listen first. Love is not a feeling, but the ability to endure patiently and infinitely."

Developing the capacity to forgive after the example of Jesus, of course, is necessary to cultivate endurance, as are pious self-sacrifice, unselfish love, and patient "waiting." To a cell member who confessed her unbridled hatred for an insolent, irresponsible, and disrespectful younger sister-in-law, the cell leader advised, "Be filled with love first and forgive her. Then she will change. . . . We get disappointed in others because we expect too much from them. . . . And pray as hard as you can. If you sin by hating so much, you are the only one who loses out, so if you pray for whoever is in front of you, you are able to have the strength to endure and overcome any hatred toward them. Don't be enslaved to sin." She also reminded her members of the rewards of spiritual authority and power that await those who patiently and without question "wait" under any circumstance, trusting in God's plans and power to take care of everything.

In teaching the capacity to endure, the leaders stress the important technique of cultivating positive attitudes toward life's situations, a strategy that requires both the acceptance of any given structural situation and the ability to cope through attitudinal changes. According to this view, we can neither prevent life's adversities nor change our given circumstances. Given this fact, we can only cope with life by changing the way we think about and deal with our situations. One way to do this is to develop a "happy" day-to-day outlook and to restrain oneself from complaining about one's situation or about other people. In counseling marital relationships, one seminar leader asked:

What kind of a person are you to your husband? Do you complain everyday or are you happy? It's all up to you, your attitude, how you think about things. Your environment isn't always going to be or become whatever you want it to. So it's all in how you deal with it. This is what I had to do in order to deal with my mother-in-law, whom I had to serve for thirty years. . . . There are many things you think you can't bear, I know. But you can deal with them. Try to be happy everyday, think of your husband, that he's alive and around, and of your kids who give you laughs. Find happiness today and in everything.

Reminding women that they are responsible for the "atmosphere" of the household—that is, the happiness of others—the leaders frequently focus on developing a positive attitude toward husbands in particular. This includes not only becoming less disgruntled about husbands but actively pursuing various ways to make them happier in order to improve

148   *Bargaining with Patriarchy*

marital and domestic relations. One male seminar leader disclosed to me in private his view regarding the romantic/sexual dimension of this issue:

You know, the trouble with Korean women is that they don't know how to express affection and love properly. Once they get married, their attitude is, well, now I've given you everything, including my body, so what else do you want? So they become frumpy housewives, live in the kitchen, and nag their husbands. They don't know how to give affection, express love. They have to work on that more. See, men really enjoy that kind of stuff.[8]

Aside from obedience, another way to make happier husbands, then, is for women to seek out as many other ways of becoming as pleasing as possible to their husbands, including improving their general demeanor, appearance, and ways of relating to the husbands. According to this leader, this might encompass making an effort to be more "sexy" at night and pursuing studies in order to be able to "converse" with the husband like a "friend" or developing an interest in his hobbies. Another seminar leader advised that women look in the mirror for at least half an hour everyday and practice putting on varied facial expressions, to make sure that their faces do not become "stiff" and ossified in expression from perpetual resentment and unhappiness. She also advised women to get in the habit of hugging husbands when they get home, and "lock" eyes with them at least for five minutes to "convey love."

The Paradox of Submission

Not surprisingly, the responses of women to the churches' efforts in reshaping their gender identities are quite complex. Despite the tremendous weight of religious sanction behind the views on gender/ family relations advocated by the churches, the reaction of many evangelical women to the churches' views and efforts, especially in the initial stage of church participation, is one of considerable questioning and ambivalence. Far from being "duped" into false consciousness, numerous evangelical women display a strong sense of injustice regarding the churches' doctrines on gender, especially the categorical views of women's inferiority and their strict injunctions for absolute obedience and submission. One woman described to me her first reactions to the messages conveyed at the South River Church family seminars conducted by Ms. Cho: "Yes, well, in the beginning, I thought, gee, is she trying to turn us into slaves? How can she do that, with feminism and all nowadays? Why should the wife obey the husband only?" Another woman remarked, "Yes, we are taught to obey our husbands as if he were Christ. We are taught things like, women are really the stronger ones so we should be the ones who should endure, obey, and so on. But you know, this is not an easy thing to do."

Yet, despite their struggles with the churches' views, many women express, and come to develop, a surprising degree of support for the churches' perspectives. Although many members, at one point or another, do recognize and even wrestle with the fundamental unfairness of the churches' interpretations of gender/family relations, their conversions to the evangelical worldview accompany a serious acceptance of the churches' interpretation on gender and family and involves deep commitments to the churches' position.

By examining the puzzle and meaning of women's accommodation to the ideology of submission, the following pages will shed deeper light into the complex nature of Korean evangelical women's religiosity. Women's engagement with submission, though on the surface paradoxical, is itself a highly complex and contradictory process within which are inscribed women's efforts to negotiate, resist, as well as accommodate to the patriarchal system. Such contradictory dynamics of submission can best be understood by seeing this phenomenon first of all as an instrument in the strategic efforts by women, within the constraints of their circumstances, to address their domestic situations, a process that is shot through with attempts at gender negotiation and contestation. At the same time, submission for many evangelical women in this study is not something that can simply be explained away in terms of "resistance" but is a process involving serious ideological acquiescence, reflecting both the churches' success at reforming or "redomesticating" women's gender consciousness and agency.

Negotiating Patriarchy: Bargaining for Love and Respect

Despite the ideological force inherent in the doctrine of female submission, the practice of submission acquires its multivalent effects and meanings because many women choose to embrace it first of all as a strategy, a strategy for negotiating their domestic situations. Rarely did

I encounter in my fieldwork anyone who at one time or another did not question the wisdom or legitimacy of the church's call for perfect female obedience and endurance; but even those who eventually become highly committed ideologically to the church's views embraced submission because it is perceived and experienced by women at one level as a necessary instrument in their attempts to deal with domestic problems.

One superficial explanation for the appeal of submission as an instrument for dealing with their domestic situations might be that by giving in, submission is simply a way to relieve, avert, and prevent domestic conflict for women with very few options in life. After talking with and observing the actions of many women, however, I found that the act of submission is rarely approached or experienced by women only as passive capitulation to male power, but also as a strategy for bringing about changes in the domestic arena, that is, as an instrument of negotiation for improved domestic and marital relations.

According to Deniz Kandiyoti (1988), any given society is characterized by a distinctive form of patriarchy that she calls "patriarchal bargain," a set of concrete rules and constraints within which women must strategize to survive. Different forms of patriarchy present women with distinct "rules of the game," calling for different strategies to maximize security and life options, with "varying potential for active or passive resistance in the face of oppression" (274). And when a given patriarchal system is subject to dramatic social transformations, this situation may give rise to opportunities to reshape this bargain, opening up new areas of struggle and renegotiation of relations between the sexes.

Drawing on Kandiyoti's framework, we can analyze the accommodation of Korean evangelical women to the ideology of submission as a means by which contemporary women attempt to cope with and renegotiate the relations of gender in the domestic arena. Within the current set of social and cultural constraints in which women are placed, the strategy of submission, powerfully buttressed by religious sanction, may be seen by church members as the most logical and effective way of renegotiating domestic situations. In the Korean case, submission may be viewed as a means to renegotiate or alter the terms of the "classic" Confucian-patriarchal bargain in ways that would be more favorable for women within the changing contemporary family context.[9]

Many women see this renewed commitment to the principles of submission and traditional gender roles as a tool, first of all, for effecting changes in the behavior of other family members, especially their husbands. For many women, the belief is that through their own perfect adherence to the rules of virtuous conduct as endorsed by the church, they can inspire their husbands to reform their behavior. More specifically, the hope is that by observing the wives' sincere and heart-felt willingness to change *their* ways and become more obedient, the husbands will become "moved" to change. As one woman said to me, properly learning her position as a wife enabled her to treat her husband so well that that he became entirely turned around, becoming "devoted" and "honest" (*seongshil*), and seeing "little by little that God was alive."

What, then, are some of the specific changes in men that women, through sincere obedience, can expect to inspire and that can lead to domestic and marital improvements? Here, several key themes emerged. One of the most frequently mentioned was that domestic situation improves when wives can successfully inspire their husbands to treat them better, especially by making the husbands more respectful and loving. A typical description of such a change in demeanor features husbands who are transformed from being insensitive, disregarding, and gruff-mannered to being more "tender" and "softened up" toward their wives. In other words, moved by the wife's own behavior of greater tenderness, softness, and her attitude of self-sacrifice toward him, the husband, in turn, comes to behave in a more tender, considerate, and respectful manner toward her. A few women related the following stories of successful spousal behavioral changes:

Before, my husband always tried to have his way in everything. He made all the decisions on his own, although he would go through the motions of asking my opinion. He didn't really listen. Now, when I say something, he really tries to listen to me. He listens to my opinions and he follows me a lot more. He used to have a real bad temper too. But he's also gotten much better with that. Our purpose in life is to make God happy, and he really tries to live up to that.

Before the family seminar, I used to get so mad whenever we fought, but after what I learned at the family seminar, I tried to stop getting so mad, but to listen to my husband, to endure, and when I did that, he was taken so aback and moved that he started being "careful" [*josim hada*] with me too. So we started being more careful together and things got better.

You see, my husband is extremely traditional, he just wanted a real traditional wife. He used to give no respect to me, because I'm just a woman and a wife, but now, he thinks he must give women respect, too. He never used to listen to me or my opinions, didn't give me the time of day. But now, he listens; if anything, I have more to say now. Of course, my husband still has his traditional aspects. He doesn't like for women to be forward, or to be progressive. Like when I praise with my hands raised in church, he doesn't like that.

Many women also reported that as their husbands grew more considerate, they also came to better express their affections, surprising them with such unheard-of practices as bringing flowers and gifts. Indeed, fostering greater "expressiveness" and "affection" in husbands, especially because so many Korean men of the middle-aged and older generation are seen as congenitally incapable of such displays, is viewed as one of the major ways women can "improve" husbands.

Another way in which a wife may get her husband to change is by helping him become more communicative. Many women reported that when they became more submissive, soft, gentle, and less assertive, especially by talking and nagging less, their husbands began to "open up."[10] As one woman said, "The thing I try to do most is to talk less. Being less reproaching, nagging. And as they told me at the seminar, I try not to do things he doesn't like. Before, I used to nag him because I hated him but now I try not to get on his nerves. When I stopped talking so much, he started to open up, started to talk about his hopes and thoughts." According to another woman:

My husband is a man of very few words, he hates to talk, and he never complimented me on anything, never showed any gratitude for anything I did for him. He's from Gyeongsangdo,[11] you know. This drove me crazy. We would go to bed, and I would want to talk about this or that, and he would just turn his back to me and say that he's tired and wants to go to sleep. It was infuriating because he would give me no response. And I wanted to talk about everything. We had no conversations. So I was constantly nagging him about this and that. But one of the things I learned from the family seminar was that for ten years, I was trying to change my husband, and that I needed to see my own shortcomings. And when I started doing that, and stopped going after my husband so much, he just softened up.

These improvements on the part of their husbands are sometimes accompanied by what many women see as more lasting, long-term character changes: from one who was selfish and domineering, for example, to one less self-centered, more considerate, and more understanding, or as one woman put it, with a "bigger mind." Contrasting the "natural character" of men and women, one woman suggested: "You know men, their love is not comparable to the love of a woman— all they think about are their own bodies, their own hardship." With God, men may not become quite as loving as women, but at least they can become more understanding, as related in the following accounts:

Well, I'm not sure how much of his character changed, but one thing's for sure. Before, he always thought of himself more, he was egoistic. But now, he tries to be more understanding of me. Especially since the church made him an exhorting deacon [*gwonsa*], he realized one has to be a bigger, more understanding person. Of course, there's still much more to change in him, but he's becoming a bigger person, little by little.

My husband was very self-centered and dictatorial. He would never admit this to himself. I felt that early in my marriage, I had to follow him in every way, accommodate to him all the time. So after several years, I got very resentful. But through the church, I realized that I should look to my own faults first. I realized that I was always asking *him* to change and control my situation all by myself. This didn't work. What I learned most of all through the church was that the woman was the "helpmate" and I learned to see how I should help *him*, not how he should help *me*. The most memorable assignment was that one where I had to go home and say yes to everything he said. He really liked that. Now my husband does things without my asking him. When I showed recognition of my own shortcomings, admitted them to him, apologized to him, he just softened up. Now when I am apologetic to him about something, saying I'm sorry I'm so bad at this or I can't do that very well, he just pats me and says, don't worry.

An important clue to how the ideology of submission/obedience may be viewed as an instrument of gender negotiation by women appears in the ways the church actually presents this ideology to its female members. The church makes it unquestionably clear that women must follow the commands to obey and submit because these injunctions are inherently "right" as ordained by God; however, these ideas are frequently and undeniably presented to women not simply as injunctions, but as strategies to be employed by "clever" women to improve their domestic situations. In other words, reflecting the evangelical establishment's tacit recognition that such ideas would be more compelling to contemporary women if made persuasive in terms other than their status as Biblical truths, evangelical leaders frequently present them in ways designed to appeal to women both as inherently legitimate as the Word of God *and* as beneficial to their "self-interest," whatever this may be. The following passage, from a lecture by a family seminar leader, shows one manner in which this is done:

Wives, the first reason you should obey your husband is for your own happiness's sake. The Bible says your husband should be the head; what does it say about the wife? That she should be the neck. See, when my wife acts unyielding or stiff [*ppeotppeot hada*], I find myself being even more so. When my wife approaches me gently, I become even more gentle. So that's when I realized, ah ha, this is why women must obey. It's because God made men this way that he asked women to obey. Women are men's neck. When women are unyielding/stiff, men get stiffer, and when this goes on, men break in half. So among men, there are many who are lacking in spirit [*gi*]. Why? It's because wives are stubborn and unyielding. So you must become soft. So, you don't obey because you are stupid, but because you are smart. . . . Wives, but you must also obey for your husband's sake. Even those men who rule the world—if they are not cherished at home, they become tragic figures. Accolades from the world aren't real happiness; real happiness resides in the home. . . . What kind of an animal is a man? According to a famous psychologist, a man is an animal who is happiest when he feels he is admired. And who can make him this way? The wife. . . . If you make your husband king, what do you become? A queen! So why wouldn't you do it? If the wife does not obey, the husband loses desire/will [*uiyok*]. Only when the wife obeys gently, can the man become more manly.[12]

One of the first aspects to note about the above passage is that on one level, women's interests are presented negatively; that is, the speaker suggests that it is in women's interests to obey because not to do so would entail that they suffer great pain inflicted by disgruntled and unhappy husbands. With this view, the leader implicitly recognizes the reality of the constraints and limitations placed on women in South Korea. In other words, women must obey because of the way men and women are biologically constituted, as well as because of the way in which the society is set up. As one woman confided to me: "You know, with unreasonable Korean husbands, you can't contradict/fight them. It doesn't work. Korean men's ways and ideas about women are so restrictive. So a woman has to use her brain."

On the other hand, this conveys an equally powerful message: that women should see obedience and submission not simply as capitulation, but as a practical strategy for bringing about positive domestic changes by dealing wisely with unruly but in a sense fragile men whose physical and psychological well-being depends enormously on the way women treat them. That is, despite the obvious disparity inherent in the structural position of women that causes their happiness to be dependent upon their husbands' good will in the first place, submission and obedience, nevertheless, are presented not simply as acquiescence to male power but as a vehicle for the exercise of women's own power and influence through their ability to shape male behavior. In this sense, then, obedience and submission are portrayed in light of positive and enlightened "self-interest" by which women can improve their domestic situations through their ability to influence male behavior and well-being. Indeed, along with promoting the view of the innate male "weakness" in need of feminine strength and assistance, it is not surprising that the leader would also try to render the prospect of obedience even more palatable by telling women literally that it is a means of "controlling" their husbands: "Wives, please obey your husbands. This is not that difficult to do, you know. If you obey, you can control your husband any way you want."

Aside from inspiring better treatment of the wife, a second major motive for effecting male transformation is to render the husbands more "domestic" and "family-oriented." The women I talked to in the two churches were rarely victims of outright male abandonment or financial negligence; however, they were often troubled by problems of infidelity, physical or emotional abuse, and general alienation as a result of marital stress and conflict. According to the women, however, one change they can generate at home through self-reform is to motivate men to "come back" to the domestic fold. As one woman described it: "Well, things just became more comfortable [*pyeon hada*] at home. And my husband, he used to stay out a lot, like going drinking late and stuff, but as our home became more comfortable, he started coming home. And on Saturdays, I would make an effort to make special foods and we would spend Saturdays together over these special foods."

Although infrequent, the husbands' turn toward "domestic" and "family-oriented" behavior signifies that the husbands will become so inspired to behave better that they would actually begin to participate in domestic chores, such as helping out in the kitchen. In such cases, the husbands are described as having become more "modern." Interestingly enough however, getting husbands to quit smoking and drinking—one behavioral transformation often cited in studies of evangelical conversion in other cultural contexts as a major index of women's success in reforming men—does not appear to be so easily accomplished in South Korea. Although some men may cease excessive drinking as part of their efforts at self-improvement, men on the whole rarely quit smoking and drinking entirely unless they become deeply converted themselves.[13]

Finally, becoming more "domestic" or "family-oriented" also implies for many women that the husband has learned properly to function as the family's "head." Fulfilling the obligations of the proper family "head" is a core aspect of the evangelical male family role, generally denoting the responsibility of the husband as the spiritual leader of the family. And although Korean evangelical women often complain that their husbands do not know how to properly "lead" the family in this manner, they also intend something more specific by the notion of "leading" the family: namely, that a husband takes the responsibility for everything that happens at home.

For these women, "taking responsibility" means that the husband serves not only as the spiritual leader in the home, but that he holds himself strictly accountable for everything that occurs in the home, including all that occurs in the domestic arena. To put it another way, as husbands "lead" and guide the family, they must learn to take sincere responsibility for all the good things as well as the bad related to the home, rather than hold the wife responsible for everything. The following comment by one woman about her husband's transformation best explains this view:

One of the ways my husband changed through the church is that he used to blame me for everything, but he stopped doing that and started taking responsibility for everything himself. He saw himself as my helper, to take that seriously. Before, when the kids were bad, he used to just hit them out of anger; now he repents for all those things he used to blame me for, and for pushing all the responsibility on me. And when I look at his church workbook, I see dried tears on the pages. So what he learned in church is what a husband and a father is supposed to be within Jesus Christ.

By "lifting up" the men and making them the "leaders," women manage to transfer a part of the domestic moral burdens to their husbands, renegotiating conjugal responsibility and redefining the boundaries of gender roles. And although women are asked to criticize themselves and attempt to improve the family situation through the sacrifice of submission, men are, in the end, also moved to become repentant, self-critical, and reflective about their responsibilities for what happens in the domestic arena. In South Korea, the transformation of men to become more family-oriented is more than increasing their attentiveness to the home, but a form of female gender bargaining in which women shift a major portion of their moral responsibilities in the domestic sphere to the husbands—burdens that are seen by society as solely belonging to women and are one of the major sources of their domestic stress.

However, the strategy of submission does not always guarantee the desired outcome; to the contrary, women's very actions can generate consequences that ultimately countervail their emancipatory efforts. On a basic level, efforts at reforming others do not always generate positive results, if at all. More significantly, the practice of submission can have important ramifications for the disciplining of women's own powers and behavior; for instance, despite the success some women may enjoy in effecting real domestic improvements, their attempts to reform male behavior through submission can implicate them in a process of their own behavioral transformation, intensifying their traditional role adherence and helping to maintain the existing relations of power. That is, insofar as the reformation of their own actions and attitudes is what women must offer in exchange for the husbands' behavioral improvement, the integrity of the existing gender relations is maintained.

Nevertheless, the accommodation of women to the ideology of submission and to traditional gender roles does represent a strategy to deal with domestic dilemmas and actively negotiate gender relations. Submission is far from being simply a defensive stance to avert domestic conflict, but a conscious tactic for resolving family conflicts and even renegotiating the terms of marital relations. Through their efforts to reform the husband in particular, these Korean evangelical women assume the submissive position in an effort to bring about better treatment and more respect for themselves within the family, enhancing their status as well as marital intimacy and peace. For many women, submission is also a means of redrawing public/domestic boundaries at home by deepening male involvement, morally and practically, in domestic affairs.

Obeying with a Vengeance: Resistance in Accommodation

At the same time that submission serves as a tool for domestic bargaining, especially as a way of inspiring transformations in others, it is also used and deployed by women as an act of passive resistance. Submission, then, for many women, is a compelling weapon of gender negotiation that operates through various forms of non-overt resistance.

Despite the enormous difficulty attributed to submission, many of the women in my study pursued the church-endorsed program of obedience with intense dedication. While this attitude was puzzling enough when espoused by those who professed belief in the church's teachings, it was even more perplexing to find such behavior in those who claimed to be highly ambivalent about such teachings. The following is a confession by Sung-ja, of the South River Church, who wrestled for a long time with the doctrine of submission advocated by her church:

When I first heard at the seminar to obey absolutely, I couldn't believe it. It was ridiculous to me. I was so sad. How can I? Do they know what I had been through? That I was practically dying inside? But I guess what God was saying to me was, no matter what your husband is like, obedience comes out of your relationship with me, so obey your husband for me. So I said to God, then give me one good reason why I should, if you do, then I will obey, even through tears. Then, what God came back to me with was, well, where did the money come from for the food that went into your mouth? From your husband, no? You didn't earn the money! But I thought, gee, it's not like I got married for this. If I had stayed with my parents, I could eat anything I want, live affluently. But then I thought to God, you are right, I do *not* make the money. So even though it seems unbearable and unjust that I should bow my head to him and obey, I said to God that I will do it from now on, because you have given me this reason. I said to God, I will bow to my husband when I receive his salary every month. But when I tried to do this, it was intolerable. I did say thanks to him as I was receiving the salary envelope, but I had my head turned the other way and my eyes were red from crying because I couldn't stand that I should have to say this to him. It was so unjust. It was so intolerable. I just wanted to die rather than do this. Why would I have said such a thing to a man who had tormented me and betrayed me for so many years? Well, it took me six months just to be able to look him in the eye as I said thanks to him. It took me three years from that to obeying him in other ways. But let me tell you, I was "dead" for those three years. It was so hard to do. I was a river of tears all the time because it was so hard. But I was resolved that no matter *what* he did, I would not reproach him, and to obey absolutely. But can you imagine how I was boiling inside? I thought of killing myself many times during this time if it weren't for God telling me over and over again to "wait."

Given the intensity with which Sung-ja obviously struggled with this doctrine and its practice, we can infer that her attempts at submission over the years were probably accompanied by a considerable sense of capitulation, even of oppression. Despite what appears to be her basic acceptance of the economic basis of male authority, her account indeed presents a strong sense of injustice and anger, even rejection, regarding the view of the "natural" necessity of female obedience. Yet, this passage also clearly shows us something else: her simultaneous and dogged determination to carry out the injunction of obedience to the letter. Although such acts may seem puzzling on their surface, it is, however, precisely in such extreme acts of self-denial and acquiescence that we can discover women's efforts at resistance against male domination. That is, supreme acts of submission, or what I call "obedience with a vengeance," may often serve as a subversive weapon for both pursuing gender negotiation and resisting a sense of powerlessness.

One way that such acts of submission can serve as "subversive" instruments of gender bargaining for women is by enforcing upon others the obligations of long-term gratitude (see Anyon 1983). In this particular economy of gratitude (Hochschild 1990), attempts to pursue perfect fulfillment of virtuous conduct—such as Sung-ja, who was "resolved" to "absolutely" obey her husband and not reproach him "no matter *what* he did"—are not only a means of transforming others by inspiring admiration but also represent a kind of moral compulsion and pressure to oblige others to respond in kind sooner or later. One woman commented:

You know, if I didn't obey, and just ran off like I wanted to, would my husband have the gratitude that he has now for me for what I had endured in the past? I think if I didn't obey, we would have gotten divorced by now. And believe me, I wanted to, and just live peacefully. But I prayed like crazy, just 'hanging onto God,' asking him to please show me the right path. When I did that, my husband came back to the right place.

The following narrative offers a powerful illustration of the psychology behind such an approach toward submission. The family seminar leader Ms. Cho exhorts her audience to deal with and effect changes in their domestic situations through a strategy of radical subservience—by thinking of themselves as "missionaries" and "slaves/servants":

I want to tell you about my own experiences. You see, I was the last daughter-in-law in our family. This meant that for years, I had to stand on my legs and do all the kitchen work from morning to night while others played. At first I was, of course, very resentful. But then I started to pretend that I came to this house as a missionary. What this meant for me was that I was to think of myself as a slave/servant [*jong*] to these people.[14] And when I did this, everything became easy and all of a sudden, all the physical work became a joy. So every morning when I woke up, I prayed to Jesus, please help me think of myself as a missionary. And this made everything happy. I thought of what I could do for them, not what they could do for me. Then one day, my mother-in-law came to me and said, how can you do everything without complaining? At that moment, I took her aside and whispered to her, it's because I believe in Jesus. And that's how I got her to church.

Ms. Cho presents this approach of extreme subservience and self-sacrifice not only as an important coping mechanism to deal with the intense trials of domestic life, but also as a long-term strategy for effecting change in others by inspiring gratitude and admiration.

Strict adherence to feminine virtues and submission, particularly in emulation of Jesus Christ, also becomes a way to influence others: by presenting themselves as beyond reproach through virtuous behavior, women can acquire a certain moral authority within the family that enables them to compel others to hold up their end of the "bargain." Indeed, observing the proper gender roles and demands of femininity grants women the legitimacy to exercise greater power within the domestic sphere, resembling the situation within the original "patriarchal bargain" of the Korean family system. Submission and adherence to traditional gender roles, then, are a means by which women negotiate for greater domestic power, authority, and status that is sometimes unavailable to them by more direct methods.

For Korean evangelical women, the sense of moral and spiritual authority gained through acts of supreme submission and self-sacrifice, however, serves not only as a means of gender negotiation but also as an important form of internal resistance and contestation against experiences of gender oppression. Victor Turner (1974) talks about the way the oppressed are able to challenge authority structures by exalting their "positions of structural inferiority." Exalting their own self-sacrifice and submissiveness as morally superior and their suffering as Jesus-like helps many women in this study to acquire a sense of moral and spiritual authority over their husbands and other "tormenters." This sense of spiritual authority also allows women to "resist" internally and transcend, to a degree, the injuries and degradations of patriarchal oppression.

Women are able to achieve internal resistance and contestation against male authority not only through inversion of gender status but also through "displacement" of male authority. Although they may abide by the injunctions of obedience to men, many women see this as an act of submission to the commands and authority of God, not to their husbands, a reasoning that displaces the earthly authority of men. As one woman remarked: "Enduring and holding myself back were truly tormenting. But I could tell myself, I'm not doing this, God is doing it. Endurance is not something I do but which is God's doing." In fact, for many women, in South Korea and elsewhere, God/Jesus often comes to replace the husband as the supreme authority and object of worship in life, a kind of a "spiritual third" (Burdick 1993).

Indeed, God is often seen by many women not just as a Father, but also as a husband or a lover, one who can perfectly fulfill the needs of women in ways that no husband can. In response to the question of how much her marital troubles were related to her gaining faith, one woman confessed: "Yes, God has taken the role of my husband in a lot of ways. . . . I used to wonder pitifully about why I don't have any husband 'fortune,' begrudging myself and God, but I have come to stop doing that. I have realized that I shouldn't expect things of other people, like my husband, but just walk toward God. This is what God has taught me, so I am filled with gratitude." One cell leader even told her cell members: "You know, sometimes reading the Bible can be boring. But when this happens, pretend you are dating God, that you are having a love affair with him. Pretend that the Bible is a love letter he's written to you."

Submission as Acquiescence:
Resecuring Feminine Identity and Consent

For women in South Korea and elsewhere, the practice of submission is not simply an instrument of interpersonal manipulation but something that can imply a deep assent in its ideological validity. Recent studies of women and traditionalist religions in other cultural settings have tended to focus on the strategic or instrumental nature of women's involvements in these religions. In his study of Pentecostal women in Brazil, for example, John Burdick (1993) describes the ways in which Brazilian women's choice to submit is constituted for the most part by rational and strategic motives for improving their domestic situations. Accordingly, Burdick suggests that *crente* women do not necessarily possess a deep belief in the legitimacy of submission, regarding their decision to subordinate as an act of obedience to God, not to men, and seeing obedience as "just a law they have to obey" (111).

Other studies, such as Elizabeth Brusco's work (1995) on Pentecostal women in Colombia, simply do not address the dimension of belief, choosing instead to focus primarily on the strategic nature of women's accommodation to religious patriarchy. In contrast to these analyses, the Korean case illuminates the important salience of belief, as well as of ideological consent, that can frequently be involved in women's engagement with religious patriarchy, and in the process, conversion. Although most Korean women do approach submission strategically at one level and even possess a keen awareness of the injustices of the churches' views on gender, many of them experience conversion as a process of developing a sincere ideological commitment to the churches' views.

The following narratives are examples of the kinds of ideological commitment expressed by many of the female converts within Korean churches. In response to the question about her current feelings toward submission, Sung-ja, the woman who earlier described her agonized struggles with the ideology of submission, declared:

Obedience is the most fundamental basis of God's message. A man is the head, and the head rules everything. You can only issue orders from the head and only when your body and limbs follow can the body function. When the body or limbs go the wrong way, nothing can function; so for me, not obeying is out of the question. It can't happen. . . . Within Jesus Christ, obedience has to be one hundred percent, no exceptions.

Sung-ja believes that submission is something that one carries out not only because it is ordained by God or because it is useful, but also because it has inherent validity as the proper and effective principle for guiding gender relations in the world. According to her view, women must uphold submission and other forms of proper feminine conduct to the best of their ability because these principles are foundational to the proper functioning of the social order. Another member of the South River Church expresses a similar view:

You know Korean culture, it's so Confucian, with women at the bottom. . . . So especially among younger women, there is this thing where they want to get back at men a little for all those years of oppression Korean women suffered. But everyone has these thoughts before they gain faith. That's just natural. But I believe that you must obey the Bible absolutely, and believe that men are the head and that women must obey/submit to them no matter what.

A number of women seemed to hold a strong conviction about the fundamental correctness and validity of the principle of gender hierarchy and male superiority/female inferiority, especially as a rationale for feminine submission. One woman stated: "Of course I rebelled. Obedience? What kind of a word was that? I mean, a man and a woman are equal, so how does obedience make sense? But this was because I didn't know what God wanted. But now I understand. I see that a woman is the 'bottom' of man. Why? Because women's thoughts are not as deep as men's. I see that I am so narrow." Another woman remarked:

You see, my husband and I are only one year apart in age, so I had a tendency not to be all that respectful toward him.[15] So when he said something, I would think, yeah, right. Other people might call him doctor, but to me, he wasn't anything grand. But the seminar taught things like, treat your husband like God and Lord [*ju*]. I thought this was funny at first but then I came to realize, wow, I am really being wrong. So I came to feel very embarrassed about myself so I began to use honorifics to my husband like they told me to do at the seminar. Gradually, I realized that I really didn't know anything. My husband should be treated like God because the Bible says so.

Even within the context of the Christian conjugal "partnership" (*dongyeokja*), most women do not believe that such relationships should happen on equal terms, or that Christian partnership should and can be based simply on love. As one woman commented:

Husbands and wives should be partners. Once you become born again, you realize you want to be good to your husband because you love him and you share physical intimacy. But it goes beyond love. Your husband is a human being before God, and he must be obeyed because *he* is the one made in the image of God—women are not made in the image of God. I am merely a helpmate [*baepil*], and when I fulfill that role well, I believe that God will raise me, the helper, along with my husband.

Within the South Korean evangelical context, these narratives provide compelling testimony not only to the degree to which many women take seriously at the ideological level the traditionalist notions of gender and family advocated by the evangelical establishment, but also to the successful efforts by the churches in reforming women's gender consciousness and fundamentally redefining women's worldviews and self-conceptions. Not all women, of course, become fully persuaded of these views—indeed, a small number of converts in my sample were highly skeptical of these perspectives and a few even rejected them—while others seemed to approach submission primarily as a strategy, but we cannot ignore the extent to which the evangelical churches are able to serve as effective disciplinary agents that can reshape and reorient women's fundamental values and gender consciousness.

To effect changes in the worldview of their female members, the churches employ a well-defined set of rhetorical and disciplinary strategies that are designed to situate women's views within a new interpretative framework and help them develop a new religious and gender-specific habitus. The main part of the churches' strategy for fostering women's recommitment to the evangelical notions of gender, family, and femininity consists first of all in persuading women to recognize and accept their central role in and responsibility for the domestic conflicts they are experiencing and the need to rectify their wrongdoings. Indeed, one measure of the churches' success at reshaping female consciousness is how women come to accept sincerely the churches' redefinition of their problems and their various "sins" and begin to genuinely repent for them.

Cell meetings and family seminars are venues in which much more occurs than emotional release and collective sharing of personal problems; they are spaces in which members are taught to deal practically with domestic problems by identifying their true causes and attempting to find solutions for them. As such, these meetings are sites of realization in which women are expected to recognize their wrongdoings not just intellectually, but by way of sincere reflection and self-critique that lead to genuine repentance. Indeed, the level of self-criticism in which women engage is intense as they struggle collectively with their domestic dilemmas. Considerable time and energy, whether through discussion or through tearful prayers, are devoted to confessing and atoning for disobedience and various other types of domestic misconduct that the women come to believe are the causes of the greater part of their domestic discord.

This process of penitence begins with defining the varieties of major and minor female domestic misconduct as terrible "sins" to be eradicated. Aside from disobedience, most of the "sins" to which women are most frequently led to confess are those thought to directly undermine the fundamental principles of the ideal gender and family order—namely, male/female hierarchy and proper gender roles—including all the "sins" that the churches define as arising from "egoistic" and "arrogant" attitudes, such as selfishness, willfulness, and pride. Women become particularly remorseful about their sins of willfulness, assertiveness, and inability to endure and forgive, which they come to believe are primarily responsible for marital discord and the misconduct and alienation of husbands.

Another "sin" that is often a special cause of contrition for women is their perceived inability to endure difficulties. Agreeing with the church's diagnosis, women frequently express the belief that suffering in marriage may be inevitable but that it is their inability to endure these trials that leads to many domestic problems. The inability to forgive, in particular, is seen as a central source of conflicts. Women are also led to reflect harshly upon emotions of anger, resentment, and bitterness that arise from feelings of pent-up hatred and frustrated desires, feelings that are destructive to other family members, but most of all, to themselves.

As a remedy, women, in one gathering after another, are reminded continually that proper obedience and submission, principles that are the bedrock of social order, must then be pursued because they are the means through which gender and family harmony can be restored. While discussing the variety of means by which proper obedience can be better carried out and the role of the virtuous mother and wife fulfilled, the members are exhorted to devote a great part of their time to prayers in which they are to entreat God to help them obey, endure, and better forgive, regardless of others' behavior toward them, and to better carry out their family responsibilities.

An interesting aspect of the churches' discourse regarding these matters is the oft-repeated declaration about the difficulty of achieving *genuine* internal transformation. That is to say, according to this discourse, to recognize and to repent for one's sins is one thing, but to truly reform one's behavior and thinking and live out the proper Christian life is quite another. Many of the committed women often stated in their interviews that proper obedience is not something that can be achieved without a sincere and deeply felt faith in God. As one woman explained: "I don't think you can obey completely unless your heart is open with the Holy Spirit. The women who say they can't do this—well, I think it's because they haven't really been 'awakened' properly yet. It's hard to go home and try to serve and wait on your husband totally. You must have faith to do this. But with faith, one can succeed in complete submission and obedience."

To help female members achieve proper internal transformation, the churches carry out programs of behavioral, psychic, and emotional discipline that are often remarkable for their depth and intensity. For instance, one cell meeting at the South River Church took as its mission the task of transforming the self to approximate the virtuous feminine ideal, not only by attempting to change the members' beliefs regarding gender relations, but also by disciplining the internal subjectivities of women by directing them to repress—and eradicate, if possible—all of the underlying "negative" desires and emotions deemed responsible for defiant or unruly female behavior.

In one approach to this effort of disciplining and normalizing women's subjectivities, the group consistently employed language related to the concept of "dying of self." To "die" in sin is a classic metaphor in evangelical conversion that is considered a prelude to rebirth (Gordon 1984). In the context of Korean evangelical women, the idea of "dying of self," while referring to the conversion process, also clearly carries another meaning: the process of eradicating the "sins" associated with gender violations, such as arrogance, egoism, or impatience. In the Korean evangelical context, it is furthermore seen as an act of even more fundamental self-repression in which the "death" of a person's "self" or "ego" (*ja-ah*) indicates the suppression of all deep-down desires, emotions, and impulses considered responsible for generating the "sins" in the first place.[16]

Reflecting the influence of this discourse on church members, a number of women in both churches frequently used the related language of "killing of self" to refer to the repression of feminine desires and impulses—in particular, the desire to have things one's way, the impulse to assert these desires, and the desire to change other people. One cell leader, who displayed in her living room a large plaque with the phrase "I die everyday," repeatedly advised her members: "One of the things we have to do is to 'kill' [*jugida*] ourselves everyday. We keep coming back alive but that's no good. Everyday, we must die with Christ."[17]

One church member talked about how she learned to handle her domestic situation: "The most important thing I had to do in my marriage was to learn to 'die.' I had to 'kill' myself. Before, I used to talk back to my husband, get mad or upset, but now, I don't do that any more. I always try to be happy even though I have difficult problems to contend with." The degree of self-repression and sacrifice often demanded by this process of feminine self-transformation is revealed vividly in the following narrative related by a former cell leader at the North River Church:

I'd say that I dealt with my marital difficulties by "dying." I am a learned woman. I have the ability to teach and lead others. And I have a passionate [*yeoljeong han*] personality. When I was a cell leader, so many people would come to my meetings and listen to me. I became someone to whom people with difficulty would come for help. I have so much love, so much ability. But my husband disregarded me and this caused a lot of conflict. I like to study, I don't like to just gad about. And I think he didn't like that. And I also try to do everything best; I tend to be a perfectionist. And I think he couldn't stand this, so at a certain point, he put a stop to me. He blocked my way, kept me from developing, rising beyond. Like, at one point, I wanted to learn flower arrangement, for God's sake, and he didn't even like me to do this. When I'd be practicing at home, he would grab the flowers from me and fling them away.

You know, whenever I tried to do something that would give me a sense of achievement or fulfillment, he tried his best to put a stop to it. Another example is that I wanted to take cooking classes once, so I asked him to give me money for the classes. But he said to me what did I need to do that for, all I needed to know was how to make hot pepper paste [*kkochujang*]. See, whenever I tried to go beyond myself to be a little more professional in anything, he put a stop to it. So now, I just obey before God, and He helps me overcome, no matter how difficult things get. For me, "dying" means "killing" myself. Before, I used to talk back to my husband, but now, even when I'm upset, I pray and I get instantly turned around. Now, I am very happy even though I have difficult situations to contend with. And my husband has changed a lot in the last few years. He sees that I've changed and this has softened him up considerably. I realize now that in the past, a big part of it was that he was very jealous that I was doing all this for God, that I was neglecting him.

For many followers, killing the ego in such a manner is the only way to be able to obey "properly," and therefore to accomplish the task of transforming others. Another member attested: "I realized that only by totally 'getting rid' of myself and 'dying,' could I change the other person. If you try to do things by asserting your own temper and personality, it doesn't work. And that's how I deal with my husband, too."

"Dying" or "killing" of self, however, is not easy. There is often much struggle and anger from the sense of injustice at having to submit to such a degree of self-denial and repression. As another cell member admitted: "Despite all my training in the church, the most difficult thing about the life of faith is not being able to apply everything I've learned properly in life, and especially, still having a strong ego/self [*ja-a*]." When their situations become very difficult, women turn to prayer, of course, to aid them in this inner struggle. A cell member explained; "When I lowered myself before my husband, he softened. But still, you know, there are many times when anger just rises up within me. But I know I have to press down my self/ego. When this starts to happen, I just pray a lot."

Prayer is the primary vehicle—that is, a key disciplinary instrument—through which women are expected to acquire the strength and inspiration needed to submit properly, and through which women can truly realize and experience repentance for their sins. According to one leader: "Praying always helps you to realize that things are your own fault. And when you approach your husband and kids with such a humble attitude, admitting your fault, they will be moved to admit their fault and this will encourage love among you." But more importantly, just as prayer gives women the strength to transcend sufferings, it bestows the power to better endure, obey, and fulfill duties. Commanding women to pray ceaselessly, one leader observed:

Putting into practice God's wishes is so difficult because our faith is weak and our prayers are inadequate. Total obedience, for example, is so hard with only one's own strength. We just have to entrust everything to God and find out all the ways to make Him happy through prayer. . . . The answer to everything is prayer and the Word. When you pray hard enough, you will receive resolution. We are prayer warriors! We have to keep fighting!

By helping to reconstruct women's gender consciousness through a process that goes beyond mere ideological reindoctrination to the cultivation of intense internal self-discipline for "rebirth," the church is not only a place where women acquire consolation, peace, and empowerment in their efforts to cope with domestic stress, but also where they are ideologically and psychically redomesticated for the patriarchal system. To be sure, the degree of success achieved by the churches in this regard is by no means uniform; at the very least, it is a process that requires a great deal of collective effort and ideological reinforcement. Nevertheless, many of the female converts in my study display sincere belief in the legitimacy of the traditionalist notions of family and gender, suggesting the extent of their ideological transformations.

Indeed, despite their initial struggles, many evangelical women discover through their conversions not only the realization of the inherent "correctness" of obedience and women's gender roles, but also the meaning, value, and virtues of "true" womanly submission and endurance, as well as the proper ways to carry these out in life. As one woman summed up this view:

I think obedience is the fundamental basis. But if it's not obedience that comes from meeting God, it won't work, since it is something that just ends up making you surge with hatred and resentment later on. You can endure from moment to moment, but if you do it without prayer to God, it just becomes a barrier in the end. It's got to be obedience that comes from inside, from God. So at first I resisted, but God soon showed me how beautiful true obedience can be, and how valuable a thing it really was, that it was like a gem, and all my years of trying to live with obedience weren't a waste. Before, I used to reproach myself all the time, like, why am I so stupid that I can't express my thoughts and desires properly? But now I'm so thankful that I endured the way I did.

Conclusion

The practice of submission in the Korean evangelical context is a highly charged and contested process that signals on the part of many women genuine ideological acquiescence as well as resistance. At an important level, submission is viewed by women as a strategy to cope with their domestic problems and improve domestic situations; for many, however, it is also a practice that signifies sincere commitment to the religiously defined views of gender and family—that is, something that is valid and worth pursuing for its own sake—which, in the end, bespeaks the considerable success of the church in reconstituting women's gender identity.

Indeed, given the popular perception of how challenging "proper" submission is for most people, it is difficult not to imagine that women accommodate to religious patriarchy without some degree of genuine ideological conviction. Furthermore, since the project of reforming men—an uncertain and sometimes unsuccessful undertaking in itself—is often a long-term process, it is more than likely that women cannot affirm the principle of absolute submission without having or developing the strong belief that it is something to be pursued for its own sake. After all, women might hope that their acts of obedience might turn others around, but they must embrace the momentous lesson that it is they who must ultimately change themselves in order to bring about and ensure family peace and harmony.

What, then, are the implications of such religious engagement on the lives of evangelical women and on the role of their faiths? The next chapter explores this question and addresses an issue vital to understanding the religious engagement of Korean evangelical women: their "consent" to religious patriarchy.

SIX

Women's Redomestication
and the Question of Consent

In the lives of Korean evangelical women explored in this study, the intensely contradictory nature and role of evangelical faith have made the church not only a primary site of gender emancipation and women's struggles, but also an effective catalyst in women's "redomestication." As such, evangelical faith possesses both an emancipative and subjugative potential that engenders ambiguous consequences in their lives.

Beginning with an exploration of the effects of women's acquiescence, or their subjective redomestication, on their religiosity and domestic struggles, this chapter examines the ways in which evangelical beliefs, despite their emancipatory significance, serve as a powerful vehicle for preserving the status quo by countervailing the empowering possibilities of women's faiths, effectively securing women's "consent" to the current gender regime. Approaching the issue from the perspective of women's interests and subjectivity, we can investigate the motivational dynamics behind female "consent" to religious patriarchy.

The Two Sides of Religious Power

Various observations can be made about the ways in which existing gender/family arrangements are maintained through women's acquiescence to religious patriarchy, but one useful approach is to observe how this occurs through the ways in which women's recommitment to the ideology and practices of the traditionalist gender/family structure—that is, their subjective redomestication—ultimately offsets, circumscribes, and limits the emancipatory potential inherent in the women's faiths. As I alluded to in previous chapters, the mechanisms of submission through which women struggle for gender negotiation and resistance can, no matter how strategically they are deployed, lead to the reinforcement of their subordination. Women's attempts to reform male behavior through submission, for instance, implicate them in a process of their own behavioral transformation, intensifying their role adherence and thereby helping to maintain existing power structures.

An especially ironic dimension, however, is the ways in which women's efforts to *resist* through submission can result in an even greater intensification of their redomestication. For example, women's attempts to pursue domestic negotiation and power through strict adherence to the demands of the virtuous female can, despite their potential for long-term returns, result in binding women even more securely to their traditional roles. Although the experience of moral superiority that arises from acts of extreme self-sacrifice and submission can act as a source of women's internal resistance, it can also serve as a kind of compensatory mechanism that intensifies women's attachment to the domestic sphere. Furthermore, establishing God as the main authority in life may offer women a measure of psychic autonomy from men, but this decision also enables them, in the long run, to submit better to their husbands because to obey God properly is to learn to acquiesce to other forms of male authority.

However, insofar as the accommodation of women to religious patriarchy signifies a level of ideological acceptance, women's recommitment to these principles is not secured simply through a kind of mechanistic process of "unintended consequences" but through an effective transformation of gender consciousness. Given this, a key approach to viewing how evangelical faith influences the lives of women is by examining how this reconfigured gender identity—more specifically, a deeply family-centered, traditionalist feminine subjectivity—undercuts the liberationist possibilities and powers implied in the women's religiously empowered selves as Christians. The kinds of feminine self-conceptions that women develop through "rebirth," especially as the obedient, forbearing, self-sacrificing, and other-directed self, ultimately seem to countervail the full development and exercise of women's religious powers derived from their individual relationships with God, as well as the women's potential to contest the status quo.

To begin with, women's recommitment to and belief in the principles of obedience and submission imply the creation of a gendered self that is fundamentally oriented toward submission to and acceptance of authority, particularly male authority, which tends to deflect the potential for challenge inherent in women's evangelical faith. Although the spiritual experiences of evangelical women, as described in Chapter 3 can serve as powerful vehicles for individual empowerment, female spirituality and spiritual empowerment in the Korean evangelical context rarely enable challenges against male status and authority, covert or overt, that might help alter the social status of women and provide the impetus for the transformation of the basis of existing social arrangements. Women may acquire through their spiritual experiences and individual relationship with God a new sense of dignity, self-respect, self-esteem—not to mention personal consolation—but these experiences appear to stop short of developing into impulses for public challenge or critique of men as has been described in other cultural contexts; instead, they remain at the level of internal empowerment and resistance.[1]

By the same token, such submissive orientations toward authority can also explain why the sense of newfound power, ability, and knowledge women gain through church participation and activities rarely seem to translate into a sense of individual authority or independence that can lead to the forging of new social power and boundaries by women. Instead, we find among many women not only a continued belief in their own fundamental inferiority, but also a belief that their powers, seen as "borrowed" from God, are not their own, and that these powers cannot be used to assert themselves or their abilities, nor to challenge male authority. Reflecting their firm belief in the necessity of submission and subordination to men, women disown these felt powers, exercising them only to serve others or God and to enable themselves to better obey, endure, and forgive.

Furthermore, any felt powers or extraordinary abilities a woman may claim or experience are often rationalized as an act of or reward for obedience to God or to churchly authority, effectively undercutting possibilities for contestation, even though empowerment may be experienced subversively. As one woman commented:

I am still inadequate, but this is my belief now: that through obedience I can do anything. I always keep that close to my heart as I go through my life of faith. So when someone asks me to do something, I try not to say I can't, but reassure myself that God may be calling me to do this, so I try to obey. So at church, I do if told to do, go if told to go, and come if told to come. I don't know what other people think of me, but maybe because of that [my obedience], God makes things happen for me and when things get difficult, he gives me ability [*neungryeok*].

It is no wonder, then, that many evangelical women feel a deeply conflicting sense of personal power and identity, a sense of an essentially powerless self existing alongside an image of an empowered self, mirroring their domestic self-conceptions as both weak and strong.

The churches' call for the fulfillment of other virtuous feminine qualities, such as self-sacrifice and endurance, also serves greatly to limit the impetus toward the pursuit of new social power and change on the part of women. First, the ideals of self-sacrifice and endurance, in general and for the family, clearly foster an attitude of forbearance toward difficult circumstances, discouraging active efforts to change the status quo. Also, the ideal of self-sacrifice effectively delegitimizes any goals or actions on the part of women that are interpreted as being oriented toward personal or individual gain and fulfillment, including those related to personal freedom and equality.

As the above narrative hints, the submissive/obedient attitudes in women are also fostered through the nurturing of another aspect of feminine Christian identity implied in the Korean evangelical process of conversion, that of a highly dependent self that must rely on the will of God, and others in authority positions, to realize things in life. Chapter 3 showed how the process of totalistic surrender to God's control, a central dimension of Korean evangelical beliefs and conversion, can paradoxically serve as a source of liberation from pain and personal strength for many female believers. It is possible that women can indeed experience obedience and complete dependence as empowering in many senses, but such an emphasis nevertheless suggests the development of a distinctive conception of selfhood that can have particular implications for women.

The encouragement toward a total dependence upon and surrender to the divine will often facilitate the development of a self and self-conception in the believers that is empowering but also devoid of a conscious sense of agency. Put another way, the idea of oneself as an essentially helpless and dependent being utterly reliant upon God for all things—an attitude observed in many evangelical women in this study—implies, no matter how empowered in practice, a fundamentally submissive and dependent personality orientation that can have disempowering consequences (see also S. Park 1993).

The fostering of obedient and dependent orientations in women, moreover, is not hurt by the churches' attitude of anti-intellectualism that emphasizes unquestioning obedience over thinking and appears to discourage questioning.[2] Women, for instance, are urged to completely surrender their will to God and to live solely by faith, expressed through simple and unquestioning obedience to God. The churches often interpret conflicts in women's lives as a battle between the spirit and the intellect, with the intellect seen as the source of all problems. As one cell leader remarked: "Everyday, we are dragged around by the power of sin. All sin comes from the intellect. The spirit inside you has to counteract." Getting rid of the intellect is also presented as a precondition for God's grace and blessings. As a pastor from the South River Church explained: "If we want beautiful miracles in our lives, we have to become stupid [*babo*]. If we are too clever, no miracles will happen. When you make yourself stupid, and try your best to do so, God makes miracles." Resolution of personal conflicts and empowerment can only come by submitting to one's faith in the power of the Holy Spirit, who can help one to submit and obey properly.

In examining the contradictory role and impact of Korean women's evangelical faiths, we have observed the conflicting nature and operation of religious power as it plays out in these women's lives and identified the dual possibilities inherent in religious beliefs and power: to uplift, heal, empower, and liberate, but also to control and oppress the subordinated in ways that secure their participation in perpetuating the conditions of their subordination (Appleby 2000; Beckford 1983; McGuire 1983).

In the case of Korean evangelicalism, the conflicting operation of religious powers through the beliefs and practices of women is closely tied to a particular development of conflicting religious identities nurtured through evangelical conversion and faith experience: the individually empowered self that has been generated through a personal, individualized relationship with God, and the obedient, dependent self-conceptions whereby such individual felt powers are either disowned or domesticated. As I explore further, the domestication of women's powers is reinforced by the encouragement toward the development of a role-defined, relational self-identity that ultimately defines a person in relation to the welfare and goals of the family. As women appropriate their religious faiths to seek healing, transcendence, self-dignity, and personal power, women's domestically oriented self-conceptions and subjectivities also ensure that their powers are quite effectively suppressed for the purposes of individual liberatory stuggles, preventing substantial changes in the existing gender power structure.

Explaining Consent

Although this study has examined the process by which the churches undertake female redomestication and how this system affects women's lives and religiosity, it has yet to resolve one of the most difficult issues in Korean evangelical women's engagement with religious patriarchy: the willingness of women themselves to submit to the ideological demands of religious patriarchy—that is, the question of women's ideological "consent" to oppression. Insofar as we accord women a degree of agency and view female acquiescence not simply as a result of religious indoctrination but as an act that involves an element of choice on the part of women within a given set of ideological and structural constraints, we must address this issue accordingly.[3]

Influenced by the recent theoretical developments in the field of feminist theory and social sciences, many recent studies of women and religious traditionalisms have displayed an emphasis on women's agency and "resistance," an approach that has enabled us not only to reevaluate "oppressed" females as self-aware actors with choices and interests but to view conservative religions as contested terrains characterized by dissent. This has been a useful corrective to the totalizing formulations about power and domination, but one result of this has been an increasing tendency both to sentimentalize resistance (Abu-Lughod 1990; Dirks, Eley, and Ortner 1994; Rubin 1996) and to neglect the crucial question of consent to oppression on the part of women and other subordinate groups.[4]

The emphasis on women's agency we find in these recent analyses has led to a closer attention on women's interests and perspectives in explaining their choice to convert and has improved our understanding of these women's "puzzling" decision to embrace what seem ostensibly to be the instruments of their continued subordination. However, in their efforts to avoid presenting women simply as fools or victims of oppression, many of these works have also revealed too great a tendency to analyze the phenomenon of women's accommodation to religious patriarchy in terms of their efforts to challenge, resist, or subvert existing power relations while overlooking the important issue of women's compliance to domination. I have no problems with such an approach per se, but I believe that in neglecting the problem of consent, such interpretations can ironically undermine our efforts to analyze the dynamics and conditions of gender transformations.

To avoid this pitfall, we should address head on this thorny question of female consent as it concerns Korean evangelical women. Having seen that Korean women's engagement with religious patriarchy is a process involving simultaneous and contradictory acts of accommodation and resistance, we will next explore some of the deeper motivations and reasons for women's consent, especially *ideological* consent, that takes us beyond the views of submission primarily as a "rational" and/or conscious strategy for addressing domestic problems and negotiating the relations of gender, or as "resistance" to oppression. Instead, we will turn our attention to the following key issue: the desires on the part of women for *maintaining* and *preserving* the system as shaped by the opportunities provided by the Korean gender/family system, and the deeper levels of culturally constituted gender subjectivity, identity, and consciousness, all of which are embedded in and shaped by the structural, ideological, and power configurations of the Korean family and gender system.

Often overlooked in current research or discussions on gender domination/resistance is the reality of women's interests in or desires for maintaining existing gender arrangements. This oversight has partly to do with the recent poststructuralist turn in the social sciences and feminist studies—influenced significantly by the work of such scholars

as Michel Foucault (1979, 1980, 1990)—that has encouraged the uncovering of acts and spirits of resistance everywhere, especially in small
or everyday actions. This move, however, has been somewhat problematic in that it has tended to deflect our attention from the very real
problems of power and domination, as well as the desires or interests
people have in maintaining the status quo, not just resisting it.[5] Despite
his concern with illuminating the de-centered nature of power and its
mechanisms, Foucault's intellectual projects, after all, centered also on
the identification and delineation of the productive operations of disciplinary power, especially through the ways human subjectivities were
constituted "really and materially" through a "multiplicity of organisms,
forces, energies, materials, desires, thoughts, etc." (1980: 97). Through
such processes of subjectivization, women as well as other subordinate
groups often end up cooperating in the perpetuation of their own
subordination, even all the while resisting it, and their acquiescence in
many cases stems from an impulse to preserve the existing structures
of power (see Genovese 1972; Willis 1977).

In their attempts to resist male domination and the abuses of the
current gender/family system, many women in my study display a simultaneous but undeniable desire to preserve that very system, and
their places within it. This is curious since many of them, though not
all, appear to possess clear knowledge of, and resentment toward, the
injustices of the system. Hence, the key to comprehending the ideological consent of evangelical women—their willingness to embrace
and even defend the legitimacy of the current family/gender system—
lies in trying to understand some of the reasons behind this powerful
conservative impulse, as it arises both out of women's interests and the
deeper levels of their gender subjectivities as these are shaped within
the current patriarchal regime.

In any society, women have specific interests in challenging or defending the social order, depending upon the particular set of opportunities and constraints offered by the social system in which they live.
In the case of South Korea, as in other locales, societal constraints define and limit the options and choices available to women in the most
basic sense. Most Korean women are, first of all, economically disadvantaged relative to men and are not provided with many life options
that are viable alternatives to marriage or identities beyond that of wife

or mother.[6] Unlike many American evangelical women for whom the adoption of religious patriarchy can be seen as a result of their rejection of alternative forms of lifestyles that are available to them, the vast majority of contemporary Korean women, across generations and classes, confront an existence in which they are far more societally constrained and limited in their range of choices. Lacking viable options and fearing change, many of these women are probably driven by strong incentives to remain married and to survive within the existing family system to the best of their abilities.

We should not, however, view the interest or impulse of South Korean women to maintain or restore the traditional family order in purely negative terms—that is, as driven simply by societal constraints or lack of choices. Women, unlike other subordinate groups such as slaves, do not lack the ability to change or to leave their situations, nor are they uniformly oppressed by the system. To understand more fully the willingness of Korean evangelical women to defend and support the existing social arrangements, we must look beyond the issue of constraints to the "opportunities" provided by the system as well.

The most significant of these opportunities lies in the feature of the traditional and contemporary patriarchal family system that places tremendous value on women's domestic roles, especially motherhood, which provides a compelling structure of rewards and power for women (H. Cho 1988, 1986, 1996). As described at some length in the second chapter, one of the distinguishing characteristics of the traditional patrilineal/patrilocal Confucian family system, despite its belief in women's inferiority, is the high degree of worth it bestows on the sphere of women's activities, a phenomenon related to the intensely rigid domestic/public division of gender roles and the focus on women's reproductive and nurturing capacities. By bearing and raising boys, mothers in particular enjoy a great deal of power and status within the family, especially as young brides themselves become mothers-in-law in their old age.

The conservative impulses that I have observed among many Korean evangelical women have their source in this opportunity structure; given the high value accorded to women's roles and the significance of these roles as the sole origin of female status and power, women are powerfully motivated to embrace these positions, especially as mothers.

As mentioned in Chapter 2, Haejoang Cho (1986) has even claimed that legitimating "mother power" in such a way might be an effective way of accommodating women under the male-dominated social system, making women active agents in the continuation of their subordination. In such a system, furthermore, incentives for women to preserve their places within it and to actively collude in its maintenance are provided also by the cyclical nature of women's power positions, that is, the reward of domestic power that accrues to women in old age as they become mothers-in-law. Deniz Kandiyoti (1988), in speaking of women in what she calls areas of "classic patriarchy" puts it this way:

Thus, unlike women in sub-Saharan Africa who attempt to resist unfavorable labor relations in the household, women in areas of classic patriarchy often adhere as far and as long as they possibly can to rules that result in the unfailing devaluations of their labor. The cyclical fluctuations of their power position, combined with status considerations, result in their active collusion in the reproduction of their own subordination. (281)

Although the extent of and possibilities for such female domestic power—especially the power that accrues to women in old age—have become somewhat attenuated in the modern age in South Korea, the roles as mothers and wives still serve for contemporary Korean women as extremely important loci of power, status, and social identity that hold considerable appeal for women as positions to uphold and maintain.

To understand more fully the impulse of Korean women toward "consent," we must move beyond the explanatory level of "interests" to explore the realm of women's gender identity, subjectivity, and consciousness. As various authors (Baron 1991; Gerson and Peiss 1985) have pointed out, an examination of the specificity of women's gender identity and consciousness, especially in its varied, culturally specific forms, is necessary to understanding the dynamics of women's resistance or accommodation to male domination across different social settings. As Kandiyoti (1987) has stressed in particular, the impulse of women to accommodate to the conditions of subordination does not derive from some universal cause—biological, cultural, or material—but is mediated by the particular modes of gender identity and consciousness as they are shaped by the specific experiences of gender within each society, experiences that are shaped, in turn, by each society's particular configurations of gender/family ideologies and practices. Discussing the control of female sexuality in the Middle East and Turkey, Kandiyoti writes: "Different cultural modes of control of female sexuality create different subjective experiences of femininity. Insofar as subjective experiences of femininity and/or oppression have a direct bearing on the shaping of what we might imprecisely label a 'feminist consciousness,' they have to be taken seriously and analyzed in far greater detail than they have been" (324).

Chandra Mohanty (1991) makes a similar case for attending carefully to the cultural constitution of gender identities and subjectivities, especially in how women are constructed differently as mothers, wives, or sisters in and through a particular social system. Decrying the totalizing and monolithic character of Western feminist representations of the Third world "woman" and of "patriarchy" and kinship systems, she states:

Rather, it is *in* the family, as an effect of kinship structures, that women as women are *constructed*, defined within and by the group. . . . Not only is it problematical to speak of a vision of women shared by Arab and Muslim societies (i.e., over twenty different countries) without addressing the particular historical, material, and ideological power structures that construct such images, but to speak of the patriarchal family or the tribal kinship structure as the origin of the socio-economic status of women is to again assume that women are sexual-political subjects prior to the family. So while on the one hand women attain value or status within the family, the assumption of a singular patriarchal kinship system (common to all Arab and Muslim societies) is what apparently structures women as an oppressed group in these societies! . . . Not only are *all* Arab women seen to constitute a homogeneous oppressed group, but there is no discussion of the specific *practices* within the family which constitute women as mothers, wives, sisters, etc. (61)

In studying the actions of Korean evangelical women as well, we need to consider carefully the nature of their gender identity, subjectivity, and experience as they are constituted within the Korean family/gender system. To understand more comprehensively women's reasons for accommodating to or resisting domination within a specific cultural context, we must attend not only to their "interests" but to the dimension of the deeper levels of women's self-definition as gendered subjects as these are constituted by the discursive and social practices embedded in power relations that shape women's gender consciousness and choices.[7]

In the Korean context, the first step in comprehending the specific mode of women's gender subjectivity is to consider the ways in which the distinctive ideological and social configurations of the current patriarchal family regime—namely, the unique centrality given to motherhood and women's domestic responsibilities—give rise to a form of feminine subjectivity and experience that is characterized by a particularly strong identification with and attachment to mothering and domestic roles. The high valuation still placed on domesticity and motherhood in contemporary South Korea, along with the rewards of power, status, and identity that accompany this, may result in women's experience of their familial roles as much less depriving or confining as compared to the experience of their Western counterparts, rendering these roles worthier in the eyes of women. Although many well-educated women are beginning to feel an increasing sense of restriction with these roles, for many middle-class women it appears that motherhood and domesticity are still viewed and experienced as fulfilling and desirable.[8]

The second issue to consider in evaluating female subjectivity in the Korean context relates to another important dimension of the family/social system: the intensely relational—as opposed to individualistic—and family-centered vision of Confucian human and social relations that privileges obligations to others, especially to family members, over individual fulfillment.[9] Unlike in the West, where the ideology of individualism has supported the development of the conception of an individualistic self-identity that powerfully competes with, if not dominates, familial identities, the gender identities of Korean women in particular tend to be inseparably tied to their family-oriented self-conceptions as mothers, wives, and daughters-in-law, and all of the expectations and responsibilities that are bound up with these roles. And within such a social/family regime, Korean women have been accorded a distinctive task that has had the effect of further intensifying this other-directed and family-centered orientation.

Korean society has invested tremendous energy in maintaining family cohesion, a task for which women were traditionally given primary responsibility. In this family-centered social system, women were viewed as the "guardians" of the household, responsible not only for meeting the physical and emotional needs of the household, but for its ultimate integrity and survival.[10] As a consequence, Korean women have come to evolve not only intensely domestic identities, but an extraordinarily strong sense of moral responsibility and commitment to ensuring their family's welfare, and more significantly, to preserving the family structure, which works in significant ways to countervail emancipatory impulses.

Researchers in the West have also pointed to the salience of other-directed female moral responsibility as an important dimension of female consciousness (see Gilligan 1982). In Korean women, however, the sense of moral responsibility toward the family—a sensibility that moves beyond mere "other-directedness"—appears to occupy a central place in women's gender consciousness; the force of this internalized moral sense is such that, next to frustration, the most common emotion expressed by the women is guilt, over what they perceive as their "neglect" or "failure" to fulfill proper domestic and mothering duties because of marital conflicts or their feelings of unhappiness within the marriage. One member of the South River Church, reflecting upon her failed attempts to continue her studies after marriage, described her situation:

You know, all that studying was in a way worthless—I caused too much pain to my family. God helped me realize this. It's not something somebody like me could or should do. And it made me also realize that a mother needs to be with her kids through schooling. I realized that it's so important for a mother to be a model for her kids. I am so afraid that one day, my kids will turn to me and accuse me of not doing things that a mother should do. I don't want that to happen. I also realize that for all my troubles with my husband, it's better for my kids to be raised with their father. I also realize that for me, it's better to be with someone than not. If I didn't get married, I don't know what kind of a person I would be now—very twisted and unhappy probably. I would probably be a really terrible person.

To be sure, the above narrative does hint at the woman's efforts to rationalize her failed academic attempts. Nevertheless, the powerful sense of guilt and internal conflict the woman feels at not having been the ideal mother, as well as her deep conviction in the necessity and "rightness" of marriage, is unmistakable. Given narratives like these and the level of guilt apparent among many other women, it would not be an overstatement to suggest that a large part of Korean women's traditionalist longings are driven, even at the expense of their own personal happiness, by the need to alleviate the enormous burden of guilt at not having lived up to the demands of being "proper" mothers and wives.

In explaining Korean women's conservative desires regarding the family, we must look to one final and distinctive feature of the Korean family system: what we might call familism. In the Korean social context, familism can be defined as the overriding centrality of the family to the organization and ethos of society, and by extension, to the welfare, status, and identity of its members. To this we can add Dongno Kim's (1990) recent definition of "modern familism" in contemporary South Korea: "the priority of family interests, the dominance of economic interests in kinship ties, and exclusiveness of the kinship network" (415). Such a system, as mentioned earlier, facilitates the development of intensely role- and family-centered identities in its members, in which a woman's familial roles take precedence over her identity as an individual.[11] At the level of subjectivity, another significance of such a system for women is that the belief in the centrality of the family, and in the ties of the family's fortunes and well-being to their own welfare and status within society, is productive of a desire not only to defend the family and its collective welfare but to *advance* it as a unit.[12] And given that Korean women have traditionally been, and still are, vitally responsible for the task of enhancing the family's well-being and status, women not only serve as active participants in maintaining the integrity of the family, but also as its staunchest promoters.

In light of these understandings regarding the subjectivities and desires of contemporary Korean middle-class women, we can then view religious submission in a more complex light. For many Korean women, embracing the evangelical perspective on gender is clearly significant as more than just a rational strategy for improving their domestic situations and resolving conflicts, or even for furthering their positions within the family—although these motivations are certainly relevant—but as a response to some of the women's most powerful conservative desires and yearnings regarding the family, particularly, the deeply held goal of ensuring and promoting family well-being and integrity, and fulfilling their feminine obligations within the family.

Finally, there are a few other general factors related to women's location in the matrices of gender power relations that contribute to the development of a particularly complex feminine subjectivity and consciousness, factors that have to do in particular with women's unique status as a subordinate group. Aside from their various material or psychological interests in maintaining the system, women are implicated, unlike other subordinate groups such as workers or slaves, in particularly complex power relations with men. One major consequence is that many women find it difficult to clearly define men as *the* enemy. Given the complex emotional ties within the context of a family in which women also exercise a measure of power, women do not necessarily develop straightforward ideas of men as enemies or "oppressors," nor do they have uniform experiences of domination.

In fact, more often than not, women identify with men and their aims and aspirations particularly as these relate to the interests of the family unit. Furthermore, unlike peasants or workers who might want to eliminate and take the place of landlords or capitalists, women do not always wish to be rid of their husbands or men in general but are in fact seeking the creation of a more equal and harmonious cooperative situation with them, all of which suggests a lack of impetus toward the development of a clear-cut oppositional consciousness (MacLeod 1992).

Ambivalent Subjectivities and Consciousness

Taking seriously the motivations and reasons women have for embracing the legitimacy of the traditionalist views of gender and not for just challenging it, we should be alert to the necessity of moving away from any simplistic assumptions about women's emancipatory impulses and toward thinking about the complexities of female motivations and desires that often underlie contradictory female behavior. The contradictory impulses and behaviors of women—namely, their simultaneous efforts to resist and liberate themselves from oppression while acquiescing to the validity of hegemonic gender ideologies—stem ultimately from the kinds of complex power relations that enmesh them within society and the family, bonds that constrain women in certain ways and produce particular types of gender self-conceptions and subjectivities. The exact configurations of these power relations, and the nature of gender subjectivities to which they give rise, are culturally shaped and delineate the direction, potentialities, and limits for gender struggle.

The story of Korean evangelical women presents us with an important lesson regarding the nature of female subjectivity: its fundamental contradictoriness and ambiguity. To varying degrees and across different social contexts, such fragmentary subjectivities of women, and the conflicting desires that they often imply, can hinder the formation of a straightforward, oppositional consciousness against situations of oppression, the kind that is often assumed for women in "modern" societies and has also been imputed to other types of subordinate groups.

One instance of the latter, for example, appears in the work of James Scott (1986) on "everyday forms" of peasant resistance. In interpreting the acts of daily accommodation to class domination among Malaysian peasants primarily in terms of pragmatic tactics for dealing with their difficult everyday situations—acts that mask the actuality of underlying struggles involving little ideological consent—Scott not only gives short shrift to the possibilities of peasant consent to existing class relations, but ascribes a kind of uniform, clearly formed oppositional subjectivity in peasants that does not take into account the possibilities of contradictory consciousness. Dorinne Kondo (1990) sums up this problem:

Scott's individual who hides the transcript still retains the character of the whole, consciously intentional subject who holds well-formulated, uncontradictory opinions apart from the imposed values of the dominant ideology. . . . That people inevitably participate in their own oppressions, buying into hegemonic ideologies even as they struggle against those oppressions and those ideologies—a familiar fact of life to women, people of color, colonized and formerly colonized people—is a poignant and paradoxical facet of human life given short shrift in Scott's drama. (221)

In the Korean case, we can say that women's contradictory subjectivities are constituted primarily by two opposing underlying impulses: the desire to be free from patriarchal relations and the urge to preserve the family system. This complex nature of female subjectivity stems from the increasing ideological heterogeneity of South Korean society; although it is not yet as competitively pluralistic as many developed Western societies, South Korea unquestionably *is* a field of competing cultural discourses and schemas that is evermore becoming a breeding ground for extensive value confusion and conflicts. Very few of my informants assented to the demands and legitimacy of religious patriarchy without ambivalence or because these worldviews simply rang true for them. To the contrary, many of the middle-class evangelical women made choices and took action that can definitely be understood as efforts to resolve and negotiate a highly conflicting and contradictory set of messages about gender, family, and morality that dominate the cacophonous discursive field of modern day Korean society.

Taking a larger view, we can then perhaps understand women's church involvement as a response to the two distinct and conflicting feminine desires cited above: to resist the injuries of the patriarchal family while at the same maintaining its cohesion and the women's own sense of integrity as moral persons. In response to these contradictory yearnings, the evangelical church serves a double role: providing women the socially legitimate means with which to cope with the problems and sufferings of patriarchal oppression, and enabling women to fulfill their obligations via the family by revalidating their conservative longings and helping to combat their internal ambivalence. This double role of Korean evangelicalism, as a vehicle for helping women negotiate their domestic frustrations *and* for redomesticating them within the family, has made it, thus far, an effective instrument for maintaining the cohesion of the current family and gender order.

The effort to identify and bring to light the various forms of resistance and liberationist struggles occurring frequently in hidden places and in hidden ways is an important project. In pursuing such a project, we must be mindful, however, not only to refrain from making lofty assertions about small acts, but to avoid focusing on "resistance" at the expense of alternative analyses of human behavior, in particular, at the expense of ignoring the real complexities and contradictions of human subjectivities, consciousness, desires—as well as the structures of power that limit and constrain human struggles for liberation—all of which are crucial in helping us identify and explain the dynamics of and conditions for the stasis and transformations of social structures.

CONCLUSION

This book has investigated the intriguing "paradox" of middle-class women's enthusiastic involvement in and conversion to Protestant evangelical religion in contemporary South Korea. By means of an in-depth, on-the-ground ethnographic study of two evangelical congregations, we have delved into and explored the complex nature and meaning of women's religiosity and congregational participation within these settings, both with a view toward better understanding the dimension of gender in the development and functioning of Korean evangelicalism and the larger issue of the growing female involvement in patriarchally oriented religious groups around the world.

An important premise of this study has been that although we must situate our understanding of the actions and choices of these women within the context of the larger global, social, and cultural forces impinging on their lives, we can arrive at an adequate understanding of the significance and appeal of evangelicalism for women in South Korea only through a carefully contextualized analysis of how these individuals are affected by these forces and the ways they respond to them. Toward this end, I have undertaken an analysis that is as culturally informed and sensitive as possible, both with regard to the ways in which a particular generation of South Korean women has experienced the dramatic economic and socio-cultural transformations generated by the forces of modernity and modernization over the past several decades, and the specific ways in which many middle-class women have responded to these changes through their participation in evangelical religion. Although focused on concrete experiences of women in two churches, the assumption of this study, as of ethnographic research in general, has been that specific insights produced by well-done case studies can help discern larger social patterns and provide important understanding about the broader picture.

Women and Evangelicalism in South Korea: Blessing or Burden?

An important insight generated and detailed by this study is the intensely ambiguous and contradictory nature of evangelical women's religious beliefs and practices. As a response to the acute cultural tensions generated by recent social and economic changes as these are felt and experienced at the level of family and gender relations, evangelical involvement for many middle-class Korean women plays, on the one hand, a clearly liberating and empowering role as a resource for helping women cope with an array of domestic conflicts and problems arising from the contradictions of contemporary family and gender relations.

Evangelical faith, first of all, serves as a critical spiritual resource for women, particularly in its capacity to foster psychic/emotional healing from the injuries inflicted by the patriarchal family system, as well as to promote a sense of empowerment that enhances the ability of women to deal better with their situations. Institutional involvement in the form of church work reinforces such empowering and self-transformative processes by providing women with the opportunity to expand themselves beyond the domestic arena and gain a measure of self-fulfillment. As an important and unique community institution, the evangelical church is particularly important in a society lacking in a wide array of other institutional mechanisms for assisting women deal with domestic challenges. Despite its role as an instrument in women's efforts to cope with and struggle against patriarchy, evangelicalism in the South Korean context, however, can serve simultaneously as an important vehicle for maintaining the conditions of gender inequality. In particular, despite women's appropriation of evangelical faith to liberate themselves from patriarchal injuries and constraints, their efforts to utilize evangelical teachings as solutions to their domestic dilemmas often result in the women's effective redomestication to the family system.

As noted throughout this book, the emphasis on the "subversive" or emancipatory aspects of religious membership by female participants in recent studies of conservative religions has played a large role in opening our eyes to some of the unexpected dimensions of conservative religions, as well as to the more complex and multifaceted dynamics of women's engagement with these religions that go beyond the discourse of victimization. Although such insights and approaches very much inform this study, I have endeavored to show the extent to which neglecting the more disempowering dimensions of religious involvement for women obscures our ability to clearly understand the situation of women within contemporary religious traditions around the world and the conditions for the transformation and maintenance of existing gender arrangements. Although the specific impact of religious membership for women varies according to social context, the less libratory aspects of women's involvement in contemporary religions therefore warrant sustained examination.

The South Korean case has provided a valuable opportunity to explore this dimension regarding the relationship of contemporary women to religious traditionalism because the situation of middle-class women within Korean evangelicalism compels us to take seriously the role of religion in perpetuating the conditions and structures of women's existing position in society and the family. As we have seen, the Korean evangelical church, despite its role in women's gender struggles, has, for the most part, managed to serve as a highly effective vehicle and mechanism for maintaining the existing system of patriarchy, particularly through the reinforcement of the ideological basis and structure of the modern patriarchal family system. Indeed, not only does women's acceptance of evangelical patriarchy, even if inscribed with acts of resistance, result in a process that furthers women's subjection, the churches themselves are highly successful institutions in the project of redisciplining female desires and subjectivity, for securing women's recommitment and allegiance to the existing gender and family regime. Conversion to evangelicalism does not simply serve for women as a means for renegotiating gender and family relations or as a kind of "feminist" tool for pursuing gender interests, but also as a double-edged process that appears at the same time to involve a profound transformation and reformation of women's beliefs and consciousness.

Throughout this book, I have contrasted my findings from the South Korean case with the interpretative perspectives arising from recent studies of evangelical women in the United States and Latin America. Analyses emerging from Latin American cases have particularly emphasized the ways in which women are able to foster successful reformations or transformations of their patriarchal family contexts through their "subversive" appropriations of the evangelical ideology of gender and family relations. We can find another particularly interesting comparison in an example from the United States: black women in the Sanctified Church, an independent African-American Protestant denomination studied by Cheryl Gilkes. According to Gilkes (1985), despite the real structural inequalities between the sexes in these African-American congregations, women not only enjoy a high degree of de facto power, influence, and authority within the church, but various factors related to the situation of blacks in the American context mitigate against the development and exercise of extreme forms of patriarchy in terms of both ideology and practice, in these churches. Gilkes uncovers that black women within these congregations, despite the problems of access to the highest positions of authority, actually experience less structural marginality within their churches than their white female counterparts, and over time, "black women in the Sanctified Church have drawn on the strength of their skills and historical experiences to create structural conditions tending toward equality." (697).[1]

In contrast to these examples, the cases featured in this study represent instances in which women, despite their active and important roles, for the most part have not been able to overcome their structural inequality within the churches in any significant sense, which would lead to "conditions tending toward equality." To the contrary, the paradoxical and dual role of evangelicalism—as both a coping mechanism for women's suffering from patriarchal oppression *and* as an ideological mechanism for strengthening the integrity and legitimacy of that very system of oppression—appears to have rendered Korean evangelicalism as a uniquely effective instrument for preserving the cohesion of the current family/gender system.

That said, it is, at the same time, important not to ignore or overlook the fundamental worth of evangelical beliefs and practices from the women's point of view, their role as a critical instrument for helping women deal with the patriarchal system and their ongoing struggle for survival and happiness in the face of sometimes insurmountable domestic and personal difficulties. Even if they do not challenge the overall structure of gender arrangements, the religious commitments of these women provide a means of coping with emotional injuries and imply certain possibilities for improving their situations within the family by way of newfound powers to affect changes in themselves and others. The situation of Korean women indeed underscores the unavoidable and ironic tension between the empowering and disempowering natures of religion, as well as the reality of women within these churches as both powerful and powerless.

Furthermore, we must be careful not to homogenize the experiences of the Korean middle-class women within this study, or in general. Although the women in this study share a remarkable range of similarities in terms of gender- and class-related life experiences and values, the subjective experiences of their religious engagements, as well as their responses to their situations, are by no means uniform. In other words, although we can discern a number of observable, identifiable patterns in women's religiosity in collective terms, the quality of individual religious engagements and their effects are varied as well as distinctly evolving. For example, some women may find the power of evangelical spirituality and the teachings of the churches valuable resources for negotiating their domestic problems, but they might remain somewhat distant from, or even resist, the patriarchal messages; for others, reembracing the traditionalist ways truly serves as a compelling set of guidelines for fashioning their domestic relations. Not only do women's diverse responses reflect the particularities of individual circumstances, class positions, needs, desires, and interests, but this diversity underscores the view that "hegemonies" are never complete but always contested—and therefore must be repeatedly reasserted—and that reproduction of "structures" and power relations are never automatic (see Sewell 1992).

Implications for the Study of Women and Religious Traditionalism

This study of South Korean evangelical women supports the view that religious traditionalism in various forms continues to possess strong appeal for a variety of women around the globe, especially in times and places undergoing disjunctive processes of socio-cultural transformation that leave certain groups within the society particularly vulnerable to the challenges and contradictions of such transformations. For many women around the world, traditionalist religions offer attractive and viable means for negotiating these difficult tensions and conflicts of modernity and social change.

A major aim of this study, however, has been to show the ways in which the impact and the specific causes of women's religious membership and conversion in these religious groups are culturally and situationally shaped and determined, and that these factors, hence, must be examined in their social specificity. We have seen that the particular contradictions of the rapidly modernizing society of post–World War II South Korea have given rise to a distinct set of problems for Korean middle-class women, and that the reasons motivating these women's church participation and conversion, as well as the type of remedy they seek through religion, display a number of unique characteristics.

Much more than other recent studies of women and traditionalist religious movements, the Korean case highlights the prominence of healing, particularly from the injuries of the patriarchal family, as a motivation for church participation, and the key role the church plays in alleviating this problem. Indeed, an important objective of this study has been to capture and highlight how this healing process comes about and is attained by the women within the context of their spiritual experiences, a dimension of analysis that is frequently neglected in sociological studies of religion. Also notable is the centrality of the church as an institutional outlet for women, a form of non-domestic social community that provides a venue for the expression of their talents and energies. Furthermore, although the insight that religion can be both oppressive and liberating may not be new, the arguments in this study have cast light upon the particular ways in which the impact of evangelical religious beliefs are shaped by the particular exigencies of the local cultural and social contexts, and are influenced by the conditions that affect both how evangelicalism is transformed within a particular context and the ways in which the believers appropriate the religious beliefs and practices for their own purposes.

We have considered, for example, how the ideological and structural conditions inherent to Korean family and gender regimes provide the context within which the women's motivations to resist or consent to patriarchy have been constituted. In discussing the particular impact of Korean evangelical beliefs and practices on its members, we should therefore remember that this book is in important ways a study of religious indigenization and adaptation, an investigation of the ways in which an imported religious tradition, a hegemonic one to be specific, interacts and syncretizes with local religious and cultural elements to produce a distinctive religious product, constituting a form of "re-invented tradition." By shaping the ways in which a religion's messages and doctrines are interpreted and transmitted through a particular cultural lens, and the ways in which these are received and understood by its members, the indigenizing process, then, generates a particular set of consequences for the ways in which religious beliefs and practices are appropriated by its members and the effects these have on them. While clearly offering avenues for experiences of individual liberation from suffering, Korean evangelicalism has forged a symbiotic relationship with Confucian ideological traditions in particular that has channeled evangelicalism, thus far, as a force for social stabilization.

The Politics of Resistance and Consent

Insofar as the conversion experience of many female believers involves an ideological acceptance of the legitimacy of the patriarchal system, even while they struggle against its injustices, the question of women's consent to male domination and patriarchy has remained central to our investigation. The question of why women might want to cooperate in their own oppression is a complex and difficult issue to tackle. While recognizing the ways in which female "submission" to religious patriarchy might reveal a range of unexpected or hidden efforts at resistance and challenge to male domination, we must pay equal attention to women's conservative impulses that might underlie such actions in any society, especially their desires and interests for maintaining, defending, and preserving the existing gender arrangements.

For the Korean evangelical women studied in this book, the "puzzling" impulses for preserving the status quo are rooted in the particular character of women's interests and subjectivities as these are shaped by the ideological and structural configurations of the Korean family and gender system. Within the framework of the general economic and social constraints that no doubt limit the options of women in South Korean society, the Korean family and gender system still offers women of this generation powerful incentives to preserve their positions within the family as wives and mothers, due largely to the high degree of power and status such positions, especially motherhood, accords women. In fact, I would contend that the question of compulsory motherhood, as well as of heterosexuality, is an issue that demands greater in-depth investigation in the South Korean context. At the level of subjectivity, the tenets of Confucian human and social relations and familism in Korean society are also significant factors behind the conservative impulses of women found in these pages. Aside from binding women's interests inextricably to those of the family, these factors have traditionally helped to engender in women a strong family-centered identity as well as powerful moral obligations for preserving and promoting the family that have served to militate against the development of an impulse for change.

There are several lessons to be learned from this. As stated earlier, there is the need for renewed attention to the question of "consent," or why women actively collude in perpetuating the conditions of their own subordination in the contemporary world, even while they actively resist. Of particular importance is the need to develop a more complex model of gender identity and subjectivity that can account for the complexities of women's intentions and behaviors across cultures, particularly the capacity of women to participate simultaneously in reproducing and resisting gender hierarchies. Women, across societies, are enmeshed in complex matrices of power relations and cultural/ideological fields that can give rise to ambivalent or contradictory gender consciousness, inhibiting the emergence of a clearly formed oppositional gender consciousness. Pursuing a more accurate understanding of the dynamics of gender relations, power, resistance, consent, and subjectivities requires, of course, a culturally nuanced analysis of the systems of patriarchy, family, and the operations of power within which the desires, goals, and identity of women are formed.

Focusing on the issue of consent also brings our attention to another general lesson: the need to problematize any simplistic notions regarding the emancipatory impulses of women and how the very meanings and goals of gender liberation might vary across social settings. The reality for many groups of women around the world, as well as for some subgroups of women within the United States, is perhaps far more complex and "messy" than it is for the white middle-class women in the West whose experiences have traditionally been taken as the standard. Understanding the situations and motives of many diverse groups of women requires careful and contextually sensitive analysis of their interests and subjectivities and close attention to the ways these are constituted within their cultural milieu and regimes of patriarchy.

In the case of the evangelical women in this study, I would stress the particular significance of the radically family-centered conceptions of the self, gender identity, and interests, in mitigating the development of the kind of gender or "feminist" consciousness that can orient women toward individual-centered gender struggles. To put it another way, despite their awareness of and ongoing struggles against gender injustices at various levels, the evangelical women of this generation do not seem to channel their aspirations in the direction of the kind of equality or "liberation" we would traditionally associate with the Anglo-American feminist visions of individualistic fulfillment, affirmation, or realization because their primary allegiance appears to lie first and foremost in defending and promoting the well-being and cohesion of the family unit, which they see as an important moral and cultural goal. The evangelical church reinforces these desires.

Of Women, Gender, Modernity, and the Future of Korean Evangelicalism

In many ways, this book has been about women; more specifically, it has documented the experiences of a particular generation of South Korean middle-class married women engaged in the challenging task of negotiating the quandaries of the tumultuous and dizzying socio-cultural changes that have characterized South Korea since the early 1960s. Coming into adulthood and married life during a period in which the cultural and social landscape of their society was being profoundly and dramatically altered by the complex processes of modernization, industrialization, urbanization, and political changes, the women in these pages relate stories of the difficult predicaments of a generation of women who have faced the immense tensions and contradictions spawned by the rapidly shifting terrain of modernization, modernity, and even "postmodernity." Observing South Korea in the mid-2000s, we can continue to note the rapidity and even urgency with which society continues to shift and evolve in all senses; the pace of this change has only intensified through the heightened speed and reach of globalization that continues to alter the cultural and economic landscape of South Korea, including cultural understandings of family, morality, gender, and sexuality.

Thus far, evangelicalism appears to have thrived on the circumstances and situations of social, cultural, and moral upheaval that have beset South Korean society and have left many people thirsting for a sense of community, a remedy for suffering, and a return to foundational values. For middle-class women in particular, evangelicalism has played a critical role in their efforts to deal with and negotiate a range of domestic dilemmas, especially those arising from the turmoil of the changing definitions and relations of gender and family. Aside from its role in helping women deal with the tensions of domestic and gender relations, the evangelical religion has also played a conservative role for many female members, helping to stabilize the existing system of family/gender and the role of women within it, especially by helping women deal with and resolve the conflicting desires between their family-centered and "modern" gendered self-conceptions.

What role, then, will the evangelical religion play for women, and society at large, in the future? The answer to this question depends a great deal on how the situation of women changes over the next several decades. As long as there are acute social contradictions in the South Korean society, evangelicalism will continue to have a great deal of appeal for many groups of women. On the other hand, as society undergoes further transformations through intensified engagement with Western modernity and forces of globalization, especially with regard to gender relations and the family, cracks and fissures will begin to appear in the current moral authority of the church as women, especially the younger generation, become increasingly frustrated with, and begin perhaps to challenge, the restrictions and the conservative ideals of the church.[2]

Indeed, according to my follow-up observations in the mid-2000s, there are indications among the younger generation of certain major changes, especially regarding gender relations, that may be driven by some of the structural transformations that have occurred in South Korean society through the 1990s and 2000s. The two most important trends have been an overall increase in the level of women's workforce participation throughout this period for married as well as for unmarried women and a dramatic further decline in fertility.[3] My own interviews, observations, and studies of prevailing discourses in the mid-

2000s have revealed that these structural changes have been accompanied by perceptible ideological and attitudinal transformations in the younger generation of women, particularly those born in 1970 and later, regarding gender relations, gender equality, and the role of women.[4]

It was not surprising to hear, for example, that many young women in their 20s and 30s desire egalitarian marriages and are much less willing to brook mistreatment from their husbands or in-laws. Younger women, according to my interviews, are nowadays much more "self-assertive," and are likely to perceive men as equals; by the same token, younger men have become better in their "manners" and more respectful toward women—at least, in comparison to their fathers. Furthermore, although divorce and remarriage are still difficult for women in South Korea, many more young women say that they now are willing to risk divorce because the difficulties of a bad marriage for them are less tolerable than the difficulties of being on their own; indeed, they say they can hold such a view because many of them can now imagine, though not easy to do in reality, being able to make a living on their own. Finally, there is no question that the institution of marriage has become far more "couple-centered" than for the older generation.[5]

There have been a number of recent discussions about the newly subjugated subjectivities of the younger generation of South Korean women (referring especially to the "daughters" of middle-class housewives from the 1960s and 1970s) who "define themselves within a consumer-oriented society that bombards them with commoditized visions of a new femininity, telling them to be attractive, sexy, and compliant" (Kendall 2002: 16). Although we can regard the constraining effects of this newly sexualized femininity and consumer-driven subjectivity on the younger generation of women as valid and well-evidenced in the current social context, we cannot ignore the real ideological/attitudinal shifts that are beginning to alter the fundamental dynamics of male/female relationships in heretofore unseen ways.

These are changes, then, with which the Korean evangelical establishment may seriously have to contend. Indeed, if such a trend continues, the evangelical establishment in South Korea will surely have to consider modifying, for the sake of its own survival, its rigorously conservative ideological stance, or it will face the possibility of increasing attrition among the next generation of female members. Indeed, as we have learned from numerous studies of conservative/fundamentalist religions in the United States, traditionalist religions must often compromise with modernity, that is, accommodate to the larger cultural environment and trends, to remain viable and relevant to its followers (Davidman 1991; Hunter 1983). Studies of women and evangelical/fundamentalist Protestantism and Orthodox Judaism in the United States have shown, for instance, that many of these patriarchally oriented religions have managed to be continuously viable to their female constituents by incorporating certain aspects of feminist ideology. If Korean evangelicalism seeks to maintain its popularity and growth, then it, too, may have to follow this path.

In discussing the current situation of Korean women, I would like to conclude with a note of caution about the current direction and character of these cultural changes; more specifically, it is important not to overstate the extent to which South Korean society may be moving toward a situation of full gender equality. There is no doubt that there have been important ideological and structural changes in contemporary South Korean society in recent years. At the very least, most younger South Koreans now appear to hold the ideal of women's equality as a positive ideal. Beneath the discourse and the hopes, however, the fundamental structural and ideological conditions for gender inequality still remain and most of the women to whom I have talked are clearly cognizant of this. Most significantly, despite the fact that many more younger women now work and are willing to work after marriage due to the need for two incomes, the situation of women in the labor market is far from equal. Indeed, the basic disadvantages women face in the workforce still buttressed by the conventional understandings of gender roles and femininity/masculinity are now accompanied by the problem of the double work-household burden for women and the secondary nature of women's incomes.[6] Furthermore, the norms of the patriarchal family might be changing, but they are by no means disappearing, and they still pose ongoing dilemmas for women.[7] In sum, as Susan Greenhalgh (1985) observes, during periods of rapid capitalist development, women may make great absolute strides, but lose relative to men (303).

The direction of change in South Korea is difficult to predict; for certain, though, is that we must be open to the possibility that South

Korea will chart its own unique course regarding gender and family relations, one that will represent the distinctive negotiation of "modern/
Western" and native values within the context of their own cultural
struggles—but where that path leads is uncertain. Although economic
necessity, in dialectical interaction with ideological shifts, seems to be
serving as an engine of change that is forcing certain wanted or un-
wanted modifications on gender/family relations across classes, will
this help give rise to fundamental ideological and structural changes in
gender and gender/family relations, as well as the workplace, in the
foreseeable future? Will Korean women attempt to forge a new feminine ideal and blaze a path that somehow reconciles motherhood and
paid work in a unique way, that is, toward "social and sexual destinies
different from Western (male-dominated or feminist) visions" (Ong
1988: 86), or will they head in the direction of greater individualism and
individual autonomy—accompanied by a lesser emphasis on family-
centeredness—particularly if and when they begin to acquire greater
economic parity with men? This remains to be seen, as is the viability,
relevance, and significance of the Korean evangelical establishment in
this newly emerging social milieu.

Reference Matter

Notes

Introduction

1. Although Korean Protestantism encompasses almost all known Protestant denominations, I would strongly argue that a majority of these denominations and their churches can be categorized as "evangelical" because their beliefs and practices display the distinctive and salient characteristics of what we typically understand as evangelical (see also T. Lee 2006). Although evangelicalism as a religious phenomenon is quite diverse and notoriously difficult to define, what we generally recognize as evangelical can be doctrinally identified, according to Hunter (1983), by the following three conservative tenets: first, the belief that the Bible is the inerrant Word of God; second, the belief in the divinity of Christ; and third, the belief in the efficacy of Christ's life, death, and physical resurrection for the salvation of the human soul (7). Behaviorally, Hunter adds that evangelicals are characterized typically by "an individual and experiential orientation toward spiritual salvation and religiosity in general and by the conviction of the necessity of actively attempting to proselytize all nonbelievers to the tenets of the Evangelical belief system" (Hunter 1983: 7). Other central features noted about evangelicalism (Read 1992) include the importance accorded to the belief in salvation by grace through faith, a stress on a more personal and emotional kind of belief rather than on the institution and its disciplines, and an emphasis on personal decision in the salvation process, especially through the development of a personal encounter and relationship with Jesus as a savior. Many scholars view such characteristics of Korean Protestantism as a legacy of the evangelical-revivalist tradition of the earliest American missionaries in Korea.

2. The total Christian population constitutes almost 30 percent of South Korea's religious population. Buddhists are the next largest group, with about 24 percent of the religious population. The rest are either non-affiliated or adhere to other marginal religious groups (Gallup Korea 1998: 9).

3. By 1984, Yeoido Full Gospel Church was estimated to have 350,000 members and had grown to over half a million members by the mid-1990s (Ro 1995: 32). Korea also has the world's first and second largest Presbyterian churches, Yeongnak and Choonghyeon Presbyterian churches, with about 60,000 and 19,730 members respectively. By 1993, Korea also had the world's first and second largest Methodist churches, Gwangnim Methodist church and Geumnan Methodist church, both with about 60,000 members, as well as the world's largest Baptist church, Seongnak Baptist Church (T. Lee 1996: 169).

4. One piece of evidence that points to this evangelistic and spiritual zeal is that South Korea has, in the 1970s and 80s, staged some of the largest revival rallies in world history, involving millions of participants and their "conversion."

5. See, for example, D. Clark 1986; G. Han 1994; B. Kim 1985; I. Kim 1985; J. Kim 1996; T. Lee 1996; W. G. Lee 1994; Martin 1990; Song 1985; Suh 1985; Yoo 1988.

6. Works on the development of Protestantism in Latin America include the following: Aguilar et al. 1993; Annis 1987; Bastian 1990; Ireland 1991; Lalive D'Epinay 1968; Martin 1990; Mariz 1994; Nida 1960; Reina and Schwartz 1974; Roberts 1968; Sexton 1978; Stoll 1990; Willems 1967.

7. Here, it is useful to distinguish between "modernity" and "modernization." Laurel Kendall's articulation of this distinction is helpful (2002). According to her, while modernization can mean "the measurable material process of industrialization, technological innovation, expanding capitalist markets, and rapid urbanization," modernities, on the other hand, are the "cultural articulations of modernizations as self-conscious experiences and discourses, judgments, and feelings about these experiences" (Kendall 2002: 2). To put it in another way, I take modernity as a cross-cultural concept that is not realized similarly in all societies, but is that which arises from a culturally grounded process resulting from local/global interaction and negotiation. See also Rofel 1999 for a good discussion on the cultural politics of modernity.

8. The literature on conservative-fundamentalist religious groups in the United States includes Ammerman 1987; Bartkowski 2001; Brasher 1998; Davidman 1991; Gallagher 2003; Griffith 1997; Kaufman 1989; Manning 1999; Rose 1987; Stacey 1990. There is an emerging body of literature regarding women within the Islamic tradition as well, especially focused on the issue of contemporary veiling. See, for example, Ahmed 1992; Bartkowski and Ghazal

Read 2003; Brink 1997; El Guindi 1999; Hoffman-Ladd 1986; Mahmood 2001, 2004; MacLeod 1992; Mernissi 1987; Rugh 1993; J. Williams 1980.

9. Examples of such studies include Brusco 1995; Burdick 1993; Gill 1990; Maldonado 1993; Mariz 1994; Smilde 1997.

10. See Bartkowski and Ghazal Read 2003; Brasher 1998; Griffith 1997; Rose 1987; Stacey 1990.

11. See Ammerman 1987; Gallagher 2003; Manning 1999.

12. According to Debra Kaufman (1989), Orthodox Jewish women gain a powerful sense of themselves and identity by idealizing feminine roles and virtues such as nurturance, mutuality, family, and motherhood, and linking the feminine and the female with the sacred and spiritual meaning of life within the Orthodox community.

13. See Brusco 1995; Burdick 1993; Gill 1990; Maldonado 1993.

14. In his study of Sicilian Pentecostals, Cucchiari (1990) has called Sicilian Pentecostalism a "haven for rebellious women" that offers women power and opportunities for a liberating struggle and helps to transform the ideology and practices of hegemonic patriarchy in a more egalitarian direction.

15. For critiques of "totalizing" or "essentializing" notions of male domination and power, see Baron 1991; Butler 1990; Connell 1995; Mohanty 1991; Nicholson 1995.

16. Some notable exceptions to this are works by Arlene MacLeod (1991) and Julie Ingersoll (2003).

17. See Abu-Lughod 1990 for her discussion on the recent preoccupation with and romanticization of resistance in the human sciences.

Chapter One

1. These missionaries were Horace N. Allen of the Northern Presbyterian Church in 1884, followed by Horace G. Underwood of the Northern Presbyterian Board of Missions and Henry Appenzeller of the Northern Methodist Mission in 1885. Horace N. Allen first came not as a missionary but as a physician to the U.S. legation in Seoul. It is, however, worthwhile to mention that before this group of missionaries arrived, there had already been a few attempts by Western missionaries, most of them working in China, to evangelize the Koreans; these earlier attempts, however, did not meet with great success (see Grayson 2006).

2. See I. Kim 1985: 229; K. Min 2005; Song 1985; Suh 1985; M. Yi 1991; Yoo 1988. These circumstances are in direct contrast to those of the Roman Catholic mission, which launched its efforts in 1784. Unlike Protestantism, Catholicism had little success in Korea in its beginning phases because of its continuous persecution by the Yi government. One reason for the rejection of Catholicism

was its clash with traditional Confucian practices, especially ancestor worship, which the Catholics considered idolatry. Several major persecutions against Catholics occurred in 1801, 1815, 1827, 1839, and 1866–1871, resulting in the executions of numerous French priests and Korean Catholics. Implicit sanctions were given to the Catholic church by the Korean government only after the Friendship Treaty with the United States was signed in 1882 (Grayson 2006).

3. David Martin (1990: 138) observes parallels between the Korean situation at this time and the situation in the late nineteenth century Latin America.

4. There were some differences in the methods and practices of Presbyterians and Methodists. Presbyterians tended to emphasize direct evangelistic efforts and church planting, while Methodists laid stronger stress on education and medical work as evangelistic instruments (A. Clark 1971: 122).

5. In 1886, Henry Appenzeller, the first Methodist missionary, opened the first school providing modern education for boys (known as Baejae Hakdang, "Hall for Rearing Useful Men"). Mary F. Scranton, also a Methodist, founded the first school for girls in 1887 (known as Ewha Hakdang, "Hall for Pear Blossoms"), which grew into Ewha Womans University in Seoul, the largest Christian women's university in the world today (A. Clark 1971: 93–94). In the first two decades of the twentieth century, the missionaries established a Western system of public education from primary school to college.

6. The queen's nephew was Min Yong-ik, a leading figure in the conservative faction within the Yi government. Min's injury was incurred during the attempted coup d'etat of December 4, 1884, by the progressive faction within the government against the conservative faction. The progressives, largely educated in Japan and interested in pursuing modern reforms, were supported by the Japanese government and keen to extend their influence in Korea.

7. Portions of the New Testament had already been translated and in circulation by 1882. The Bible was translated in Manchuria through the efforts of an early missionary to China, John Ross, with the help of a group of Korean merchants.

8. To avoid duplicating their efforts, the major missions divided up the country. For example, the "Comity Agreement" of 1893 was a territorial agreement among the American Northern and Southern Presbyterians, American Northern and Southern Methodists, the Presbyterian Church of Victoria, Australia, and the Canadian Presbyterian Church (A. Clark 1971: 105; D. Clark 1986: 6; J. Kim 1996: 103–4). While big cities were subject to open competition, different provinces of the Korean peninsula were distributed to these six groups, a policy which lasted 30 years. The most successful work in terms of numbers and church growth was accomplished in northwest Korea around Pyongyang, in the territory of the American Northern Presbyterian Mission. Pyongyang, now

the capital of communist North Korea, thrived for many years as a center of Christian activity.

9. In 1886, the total figure for the number of adherents was 4,356; in the following year, the figure increased by over 50 percent to 6,614. By 1890, the number reached 20,918, nearly a five-fold increase; by 1907, the year of the first Great Revival, the figure had increased to 106,287, a growth of more than 24 times in an 11-year period (T. Lee 1996: 35).

10. The Nevius plan was devised by John Nevius, a missionary in Shantung, China.

11. With heavy emphasis on witnessing and personal testimony as the marks of true faith, the Gospel messages were spread around the country in large part by itinerant volunteers who pledged or "tithed" certain days and months to personal evangelicalism and tract distribution around the country (Yoo 1988: 58–60; A. Clark 1971: 171). Scholar Illsoo Kim (1985: 230) speculates that one of the reasons for the success of this method may also lie in its tapping into the unofficial self-governing organizational patterns of Korean villages and their penchant for forming personalistic communities, but there is no doubt that, among other things, the strategy was successful among ordinary Koreans because of the opportunities it provided for learning and leadership long denied to them.

12. Reports of missionaries contain astounding accounts of religious experiences and responses arising from women converts in particular. According to one report: "Though inferior in intellectual capability to males, the simplicity of faith, agility in mental adaptability, and the depth of religious experiences of women converts were far more excellent than that of men" (Korean Repository, vol. 4, no. 5, May 1897, 192; quoted in H. Yi 1985a: 94). Women, once converted, were catalysts in the early revival movements and came to play a prominent role in evangelization, working alongside Western female missionaries, even in the face of much family opposition. See also Yang 1991; D. Clark 2006.

13. According to the Presbyterian rules and bylaws of 1896, the Bible woman is described as "a Christian Woman employed in the distribution of Christian literature, and in Biblical instruction" (J. Kim 1996: 168).

14. H. Yi (1985a) describes an example: "One woman evangelist called on 1,481 houses, sold 239 copies of Christian booklets, and obtained the conversion of 31 persons a year. In the 1900s they also propagated books of information on daily life such as childcare, schooling, home sanitation, and social etiquette in church attendance. In tandem with the growing number of churches and revival meetings, the role of women evangelists for the church also greatly increased. Particularly in opening up a pioneer church or in taking care of a small church, they were the only available church officers. In the formation of

the Korean church, women evangelists acted as assistants to women missionaries and as church officers as well, greatly influencing the pattern of faith
prevalent among women believers in the understanding of the Bible" (96).

15. The missionaries actually had explicit non-involvement and pro-Japanese
policies (See Song 1985: 23–24). Although some missionaries did write letters
of protest about Japanese atrocities out of humanitarian concern, they generally
eschewed direct involvement in politics. This gave rise to some anti-American
sentiment and contributed to the gradual undermining of missionary influence
in Korea (T. Lee 1996: 40–41; Suh 1985: 16; Yoo 1988: 104).

16. For example, Christians played a key role in the famous March 1 Independence Movement of 1919, the first peaceful nationwide demonstration by
Koreans against the Japanese. The brutal suppression of this march by the Japanese brought worldwide attention to Korea. Of the 33 leaders who signed
the Declaration of Independence on that day, 16 were Protestant Christians.
Furthermore, Christians made up 2,113 of the 9,456 people imprisoned as of
June 1919 (G. Han 1994: 63).

17. Church growth alternated between expansion and recession, but on the
whole, Protestantism still grew ten times as fast as the population between
1905 and 1960. In periods of decline, missionaries launched several revival
movements, most notably in 1919 and in 1929 (Moffett 1962: 50–51). Many his-
torians point to an interesting development when the church was forced to
cope with repression: it turned increasingly inward, mystical, and other-worldly,
and a wave of mysticism swept Christianity in the 1920s and 30s (Song 1985).
Tim Lee (1996) observes that these mystical and introversive tendencies are
exemplified by the orientations of the three great Korean revivalists, Kil Son-Ju,
Lee Yong-Do, and Kim Ik-Du, all of whom had enormous influence on Korean
Christianity during that period and the times to follow. They constructed the
world as an iniquitous place to be endured rather than transformed. Indeed,
if Korean Protestantism before 1920 can best be characterized by its activist
spirit—with which to reform individuals, remake society, and regain the nation's
political independence—then the church in the two decades after the 1920s
can be characterized by an introversive mood, as people turned inward, passive,
and pietistic (T. Lee 1996: 135–40; see also Song 1985). Grayson (2000) points
out that after the 1919 March First Movement, two strands of Protestant Christianity emerged: one theologically liberal and the other socially conservative and
concerned purely with church affairs. Through the 1920s, the conservative
group began to dominate.

18. See W. Han 1980: 495–96. This forced "cultural assimilation" policy, an
attempt by Japan to "Japanize" its colonial subjects, was initiated in 1936. Aside
from the dictate that Koreans must worship at Shinto shrines, this policy also

decreed the exclusive use of the Japanese language in all schools, the closure of Korean-language newspapers and publications, and the requirement of convening all meetings and ceremonies with an oath of allegiance to the Japanese Emperor. This policy culminated with the directive that all Koreans were to adopt Japanese names.

19. Despite the initial resistance, most of the denominations eventually complied, going along with the claim by the Japanese that the Shinto ceremony was a patriotic act, not a religious one. The policy was met with the most vigorous resistance by the Presbyterians, who, after the liberation, also became most deeply divided over this issue. But the Presbyterians, too, were forced as a denomination to capitulate at gunpoint during their twenty-seventh general assembly in 1938. Nevertheless, between 1938 and 1948, around 2,000 Protestants were arrested for non-compliance to this policy; as many as 50 Protestants died at the hands of the Japanese (Grayson 2006; T. Lee 1996).

20. The Presbyterian church first split in 1951, when a very conservative faction (now called Koryo Presbyterian Church) composed of those who had opposed Shinto during the occupation left the denomination, charging the parent body of complicity with the Japanese as well as of "liberalism" (Moffett 1962: 114). The main body split yet again in 1954, but this time, the liberal wing of Presbyterians (now called the Presbyterian Church in the Republic of Korea, known informally as Gijang) split from the parent body, charging that it was too conservative (A. Clark 1971: 306–7). The most virulent schism occurred in 1959 when the remaining Original Assembly—the Presbyterian Church of Korea—again split into two fighting factions; the ultra-conservative group (aligned with the National Association of Evangelicals in the United States and also called the Presbyterian Church of Korea) left the main body. As a result of these splits, there are now four major Presbyterian denominations in Korea: the Presbyterian Church of Korea (ecumenical), unofficially called Donghap; the Presbyterian Church of Korea (non-ecumenical), called Hapdong; the Presbyterian Church in the Republic of Korea, called Gijang; and the Koryo Presbyterian Church. It is important to remember, however, that these splits were not simply over theological issues; much of the conflict was driven by personal, political, or regional rivalries. In fact, one scholar has observed that "One can find churches . . . accusing each other of being liberal or conservative or modernistic or fundamentalistic, but none of them seemed to know clearly what these terms really mean" (Yoo 1988: 148).

21. The numbers of adherents tripled between 1940 and 1961 (Martin 1990: 143). In 1955 alone, two years after the Korean War, the Presbyterians reported 1,200 new churches built, the Methodists, 500, and the Holiness Church, 250.

New denominations entering the country in the postwar period built hundreds more. In all, a total of over 2,000 new church buildings were constructed by 1955 (J. Kim 1996: 118).

22. According to Illsoo Kim (1985), this is because the splintered churches are constantly vying to increase membership. Indeed, according to statistics, schisms in Korea have often been followed by membership increases in both the "parent" church and the churches formed after the split. Kim also offers the following piece of evidence: the Methodist church, which has not experienced as many church schisms as the Presbyterian church, shows correspondingly lower rates of growth (230).

23. See T. Lee 1996: 169–79 and Vaughan 1984. At least ten local churches in Seoul are gigantic in size with a membership over 30,000 each, plus hundreds of other churches with membership between 500 and 1,000. On the other hand, there are many small-sized churches, especially in rural areas and small towns (Ro 1995: 27). Jae Bum Lee (1986) notes that the mission theology of the Korean church in the 1970s may have been partly influenced by the Church Growth Movement, especially by its leading spokesmen Donald A. McGavran and C. Peter Wagner (221).

24. The number of missionary organizations increased from 21 in 1970 to 89 in 1986. In these 89 mission societies, there were 511 missionaries (including wives) working in 47 different countries (J. Kim 1996; J. Lee 1986). The two Presbyterian Churches of Korea, Hapdong and Donghap, are the largest sending groups. The Full Gospel World Mission Association is the third largest sending organization (J. Lee 1986: 237).

25. The two most notable crusades, the five-day Explo '74 and the four-day '80 crusade called "Here's Life, Korea," both held at Yeoido Plaza, totaled 6.55 and 17.25 million in attendance, respectively (T. Lee 1996: 195, 221). These crusades also hosted American Protestant luminaries of all shades, including televangelist Robert Schuller, campus crusader Bill Bright, church growth theorist Donald McGavran, and Billy Graham (T. Lee 1996: 171).

26. See C. Park 2003. In the Rhee regime, for instance, there was a disproportionate number of Christians in positions of leadership. For example, 25 percent of the National Assembly was Christian, in a country of less than 7 percent Christians (Moffett 1962: 80). On the other hand, although the image of the Korean church as "pro-Rhee" or "pro-American" was helpful for increasing church membership, many people, especially university students and intellectuals, were acutely critical of the church's collusion with the dictatorial regime and the American influence on Korean affairs (B. Kim 1985: 64).

27. See Chung-Shin Park (2003) for a comprehensive study of the history of Korean Christianity and politics. Park further notes that many of the Gijang

pastors did not participate in anti-government activities or critiques; the major reason was the constraints placed on their actions by their conservative congregants, many of whom were established members of the community. He also points out that the government often used these conservative lay leaders—in effect exploiting the tension commonly present between clergymen and lay leaders within many churches—to persuade or pressure the pastors not to become involved in national politics. Nevertheless, the Gijang denomination served as one of the organizational bases/political centers for anti-government activists of all stripes, including students, politicians, and secular intellectuals (192).

28. Another factor considered by some scholars to explain Christianity's growth in Korea was the oversupply of clergy that fueled intense competition for positions and for congregants (G. Han 1994: 89). The number of theological training centers went from two in 1884 to over 80 by 1983—many of which were illegal and unregistered with the Ministry of Education. Although there was a review of theological training centers in 1980, leading to the closings of many substandard and illegal operations, enrollments still increased by about 600 percent in 1991 (G. Han 1994: 89). According to one estimate, as of the mid-1990s there were 270 theological colleges and seminaries, of which 6 had more than 1,500 students (Ro 1995: 32). The theological schools are more crowded in Korea than anywhere else in Asia, Africa, or Latin America. This oversupply of clergy generates intense competition among theological graduates to find ministerial positions. One way of solving this problem has been to get the seminary graduates to "pioneer" a new congregation and try to build it up to a size at which it can fully support the minister. There is no doubt that this process has contributed to the overall church growth process.

29. Gidokgyo Munsa 1993.

30. Although Korean churches are largely independent from foreign funding and control, they are not completely free from foreign influence: whereas the major denominations are now largely quite independent, the newer missionary organizations are still growing and channeling foreign funds into Korea (D. Clark 1986: 18).

31. See D. Clark 1986: 22; Hong, Won, and Kim 1966; Moffett 1962: 117; T. Lee 1996: 234; C. Lee 1966; Rhee 1966; Oh 1995. The exceptions are a branch of Christianity built around so-called *minjung* theology, and Gijang, one of the major "liberal" Presbyterian denominations mentioned earlier. *Minjung* (meaning "masses" or "ordinary people") theology is a radical form of Christian theology developed in the 1970s that has been focused on social gospel and political activism on behalf of the poor and the "oppressed." It shares many similarities to Latin American liberation theology.

32. Many missionaries were trained at the Princeton Theological Seminary, the seat of classical Calvinistic orthodoxy.

33. Because of their strong emphasis on biblical literalism and the centrality of the Bible, Korean churches are often characterized by high levels of doctrinal rigidity that derive both from the practices of the missionaries—who not only promoted "simplified" theology to the Koreans but also encouraged strict adherence to doctrine—and the tendencies in traditional Confucianism to stress orthodoxy, authority, and reverence for books and learning. Indeed, as Donald Clark (1986) observes, orthodoxy within the Korean church is reinforced by a strong emphasis on group Bible study in which "scriptural issues are discussed in fine detail, strengthening group beliefs" (22).

34. According to the survey by the Hanguk Gidokgyo Sahoe Munje Yeonguso (1982: 56), 97 percent of clergy and 85 percent of the laity, believe in the inerrancy of the Bible. See also surveys in the Hyeondae Sahoe Yeonguso (1982), by Gallup Korea (1998), and by Hanguk Gidokgyo Munje Yeonguso (1982). As one observer puts it: "The Bible is the one textbook emphasized and studied. . . . Presbyterians, with their historic Calvinistic background, accepting the Westminster standards and Presbyterian form of government have, as of old, unquestioningly accepted the Scriptures as the very Word of God. On this basis the gospel story centering in the cross of Christ, with its frank Pauline supernaturalistic interpretation, has been taught by the missionaries and accepted by the Korean church without reserve" (Oh 1995: 173).

35. See J. Lee 1986; Moffett 1962. See also surveys mentioned in note 34.

36. The reliance of early missionaries on the religious enthusiasm of Pentecostal-type revivals as a means of bringing about conversion cannot be ignored as a factor in the development of this Korean "Pentecostal ferment." However, according to Tim Lee (1996), during the Japanese occupation, the missionaries' reliance on these revivals may also have been motivated by political reasons; although sincerely desiring to save souls, these revivals were perhaps also an effort to sublimate nationalistic fervor and prevent political agitation. See Andrew Kim (2000) for a discussion on the relationship between Korean evangelicalism and shamanism.

37. See Riesebrodt 1993 and Riesebrodt and Chong 1999 for more details on the typological distinction between "rational" and "charismatic" fundamentalisms. Donald Clark (1986: 26) refers to the two main strains of Korean Protestant churches as "conservative and ultra-evangelical," with the latter exemplified by the Yeoido Full Gospel Church.

38. Throughout history, there have been ongoing attempts within the Protestant establishment to try to circumscribe Pentecostal practice and influence (J. Lee 1986: 6). More specifically, although the established churches did not

reject outright the role of the Holy Spirit, especially in relation to the conversion experience, the conservative/fundamentalist Protestants rejected certain signs of gifts as having validity in the modern world. Thus, some of the earlier mystical or Pentecostal-type revivalists have been outcast as heretical, and contemporary pastors such as Cho Yonggi of the Yeoido Full Gospel Church—the founder and leader of the fastest-growing Pentecostal/charismatic congregation in South Korea and perhaps the world—is considered something of an outlier. Jae Bum Lee (1986) explains that there are two main streams of conservative, anti-Pentecostal theological movements in Korea: what he calls Rational Orthodoxy, the seventeenth-century scholastic Calvinism represented by Orthodox Presbyterianism, and Dispensational Fundamentalism, which also rejects the validity of spiritual gifts and other Pentecostal experiences and practices, asserting that these experiences ceased with the Apostolic church and are not valid today (22, 34–35).

39. See J. Lee 1986; Ryu 1982; Suh 1982; Yoo 1988. Calling these elements of Pentecostalism "Pentecostal Distinctives," Jae Bum Lee (1986) describes these "distinctives" as including the baptism in the Holy Spirit, the use of "charismatic" gifts such as divine healing, miracles, speaking in tongues, prophecies, exorcism, and the structuring and regularizing of all-night prayer sessions (iii, 251).

40. The Baptism of the Spirit refers here to the idea of charismatic experience that may or may not include speaking in tongues. According to various major surveys on aspects of Protestant experience in South Korea, the majority of the laity and even a larger majority of the clergy regard the Holy Spirit experience as absolutely necessary to salvation (Hanguk Gidokgyo Sahoe Munje Yeonguso 1982; Hyeondae Sahoe Yeonguso 1982). And the importance given to prayer reflects the belief that the power and hand of God can be experienced primarily through the workings of the Holy Spirit, but especially through devoted and ardent prayer (C. Han 1995: 75).

41. This favoring of "experience" may seem as if the church is exposing itself to the danger of the challenges of lay charisma, but that which constitutes "appropriate" experience is also quite well defined and transmitted by the churches to the lay, with charisma carefully controlled and circumscribed within proper bounds. See Brasher (1998: 15) for a similar observation.

42. Jae Bum Lee (1986) observes the following: "The non-Pentecostal Korean churches traditionally (until the 1970s) understood the Baptism in the Holy Spirit to be conversion-initiation into the Body of Christ. But in the 1970s, the concept of the action of the Holy Spirit within the Korean church was changed through mass evangelistic revivals, a movement which was characterized by many of the beliefs and practices intrinsic to Pentecostalism. During

this time, various popular charismatic revivalists . . . began to understand the work of the Holy Spirit in the Pentecostal manner. In their revival meetings, they began to emphasize the two aspects of the Spirit's work: his work in bringing a person to repentance and faith, leading to water baptism, and the subsequent work of grace which they termed the baptism of the Holy Spirit. They urged believers to receive baptism, a vital charismatic experience with God, which may or may not include speaking in tongues" (214).

43. I am arguing here that this is a *general* character of Korean evangelicalism. There are, of course, exceptions to these generalizations, not only in the small percentage of liberal churches (such as Gijang) but also in what can be considered "high" churches (such as Episcopalian and Lutheran).

44. The dawn prayer meetings have their origins in the traditional Buddhist practice of early morning meditation (Ro and Nelson 1995: 98). The structure of an early morning prayer gathering is simple: there is a corporate worship service, which is commonly made up of hymns, scriptural readings, short sermons, more hymns, and unified vocal prayer, all lasting about 20 to 30 minutes. Afterward, the participants can stay to pray individually for as long as they desire. For many Koreans, participation in these dawn prayers is a daily ritual and seen as a mark of religious zeal. As I was told in the churches I investigated, participation in these prayer meetings is almost mandatory for those holding positions, such as elders or deacons. All-night prayer gatherings, also traced to the 1907 revival, are a regular feature of Korean churches. Usually held on Friday evenings, all-night services are designed to last through the night and even until early Saturday morning. Friday night prayer meetings are usually more elaborate in structure than the daybreak meetings, with an extended session of hymns, followed by a longer corporate worship, testimonies, and extended time for prayers, both individual and unified.

45. Even in the more fundamentalist churches, revival meetings provide opportunities, if somewhat circumscribed, for charismatic experiences and expressions that would normally not be encouraged, including loud prayer and other physical expressions of spiritual fervor. Many people report charismatic experiences or conversions for the first time in revival meetings. According to an opinion poll of Presbyterian pastors (from the Donghap church) about the value of revival meetings, 81.5 percent of them responded that revival meetings are necessary to the growth and function of their churches (J. Lee 1986: 251).

46. Healing prayers may consist either of the "laying of hands" by the minister as he walks through the congregation or asking the members to lay their own hands on the part of the body that ails them and having them join him in a fervent unified vocal prayer.

47. According to Tim Lee (1996), nondescript prayer houses may have existed in Korea during the years of the Japanese occupation, but the first noteworthy prayer house was built in October 1945 in Cheolwon, a town to the north of the 38th parallel. Immediately after the Korean War, many more were constructed throughout South Korea. A study found that by 1981, there were about 210 prayer houses in operation. Currently, there are about 521 prayer houses throughout South Korea. The variety of prayer houses runs the gamut: small prayer houses, where one cannot engage in much more than prayer or small group worship; larger prayer houses, where one can also partake in healing services sponsored by the institution; and huge prayer complexes run by mega-churches that operate many different kinds of activities and programs. One example of the latter is the mammoth prayer center of the Yeoido Full Gospel Church called Osanli Prayer Mountain. This is the largest prayer house in Korea, built on 81 acres of hilly land, able to accommodate up to 20,000 people at one time (T. Lee 1996: 273). Such prayer houses are equipped with several worship halls, office space for administration and the ministry, food and lodging facilities for members, as well as individual prayer rooms. In many ways, these retreats resemble traditional Buddhist monasteries that are also located deep in mountain locations and where Koreans have for centuries gone to meditate.

48. The following excerpt from John Nevius's book (1899: 16–35; quoted in J. Kim 1996: 143) on his missionizing method appears under the heading of "Instruction of inquirers and church members": "Basic instruction should be given by local lay-leaders. Emphasize teaching, more than preaching of the Gospel, since the oriental peoples are less accustomed to our western methods of long rhetorical addresses. Manuals of instruction should be provided. In all teaching, lay heavy stress upon the Scripture text itself. Bible classes should be established. The Bible is the basis of all work, and the aim is to fill the minds of the people with it so that it will control conduct. The Bible is the only authoritative guide to answer questions. Depend on all teaching upon the guidance of the Holy Spirit."

49. See surveys in the Hanguk Gidokgyo Sahoe Munje Yeonguso (1982) and Hyeondae Sahoe Yeonguso (1982). Since the first decades of Christianity in Korea, an extensive system of Bible study classes, and later Bible Institutes, was established around the country to encourage Bible study and to train local leaders. The first Bible study class was held in 1890, with seven male members. Bible classes or conferences, lasting from four to ten days, were held annually (or more often) in nearly every church and in central locations for both the lay and the leaders, and Bible Institutes were held practically in all mission stations for several months out of the year. It was in these classes that colporteurs,

evangelists, and helpers to the missionaries were also discovered and appointed to work. Many were enthusiastic to learn the Bible because Bible study
provided ordinary Koreans with the only opportunity to learn *hangeul,* the
Korean writing system. Indeed, by translating the Bible into *hangeul* and not the
Chinese writing system, the missionaries are often credited with helping to
rescue *hangeul* from disuse, which had been rejected by the elites as too simple
since its invention in the fifteenth century.

50. According to many observers, cell groups are a key to the successful
growth of Korean churches. Cho Yonggi, for example, credits the success of his
church to the cell system. As of the mid-1990s, the Full Gospel Church was
estimated to have 52,000 cell groups, according to one estimate (Ro 1995: 32).
Cell groups trace their origins back to John Wesley's class meetings in the eighteenth century and were first introduced to Korea by missionaries; since then,
they have become a regular feature of almost every Protestant church, irrespective of denominational affiliation. See also Hadaway, DuBose, and Wright 1987.

51. The Korean Methodist Church in South Korea, for example, has a similar structure of lay leadership centered around the administrative board largely
consisting of *jangno* (elders), *gwonsa* (exhorting deacons), and *jipsa* (deacons).
Although the Korean Methodist "elders" do not perform the same administrative functions as their Presbyterian counterparts, they are the most influential
lay leaders in church government. See I. Kim 1985: 234.

52. Critical analyses of the conservative and anti-feminist orientation of contemporary Korean Protestantism abound, both from Christian feminists and
academics. See, for example, Ewha Institute for Women's Theological Studies
1996, 1998; Gidokgyo Yeoseong Pyeongwha Yeonguwon 1992; Kang 1995,
1996; Ai Ra Kim 1996; W. G. Lee 1994; W. J. Lee 1985; K. Min 2005; Hanguk
Gidokgyo 100-Junyeon Gineom Sa-eop Heop-uihoe Yeoseong Bungwa Wiwonhoe 1985; Hanguk Yeosinhakja Hyupuihoe 1994; Hanguk Yeoseong Sinhakhoe 1994; H. Yi, 1985a, 1985b.

53. The South River Church belongs to the Hapdong (Presbyterian Church
of Korea) Presbyterian denomination.

54. The Korean Methodist Church is a member of the Korean National
Council of Churches (KNCC), an affiliate of the World Council of Churches
(WCC).

55. It should be noted, however, that there is a considerable debate among
sociologists working on Korea about the applicability of the traditional objective indicators of class to determine class position for Koreans. The complexities of determining class locations, both subjective and objective, challenge the
traditional Western criteria for determining class. For instance, regardless of
the objective economic status, the majority of Koreans identify themselves as

"middle class." See Abelmann 1997 for a summary of this debate and a discussion of the complexity of determining class position in South Korea.

56. This age distribution is confirmed in the survey taken by Gallup Korea (1998: 158), which shows that women between ages 30 and 50 were most numerous. In Buddhism, on the other hand, older women tend to predominate.

57. Methodological empathy differs from sympathy in that "empathy" does not necessarily require agreement with a perspective in order to understand it. McGuire's (1982) distinction between "empathy" and "sympathy" is applicable here: "Empathy is the ability to feel with, to see things from the standpoint or perspective of the individual being studied rather than to identify with or act from this standpoint" (20).

58. The scholarly literature includes a number of instances in which ethnographic efforts within religious communities had to be aborted prematurely because of the researcher's failure to convert or resolve other conflicts. See Lofland 1966 and Robbins, Anthony, and Curtis 1973.

59. For discussions on the issue of identity or role-management in fieldwork, see Glesne and Peshkin 1992; Lofland and Lofland 1995; Shaffir 1991.

60. Lila Abu-Lughod (1986) describes this problem as the "sense of inauthenticity" that resulted from having felt compelled at times to lie to her Bedouin informants about her life so that they would not shun her as a modern American woman.

61. See Abu-Lughod 1990; Adams 1999; Hsiung 1996; Kondo 1986; De Andrade 2000.

62. See Ayella 1993; Klatch 1988; Blee 1998; Peshkin 1984; Richardson 1991; Shaffir 1991.

63. One of the more notable critiques of social scientific "objectivity" is Donna Haraway's (1990) article, "Situated Knowledges: The Science of Question in Feminism and the Privilege of Partial Perspective." For succinct critiques of classic objectivism and realist narratives, see Clough 1992; Van Maanen 1988; Rosaldo 1993.

Chapter Two

1. See Snow and Machalek 1984 and Bruce and Wallis 1983 for examples of two opposing perspectives regarding this debate.

2. The first five-year plan focused on export of agricultural products and raw materials (such as pork, laver, and rice) and some minerals (iron, graphite, and tungsten), but not industrial products. The plan also emphasized the development of infrastructure and energy production, as well as of import-substitute industries, including chemical fertilizers, cement, and synthetic fibers (Lie 1998: 56). Despite a huge amount of economic aid from the United States,

the South Korean economy did not perform well during the first few years of Park's industrialization efforts. Park's domestic-oriented growth strategy was generating large international trade deficits, and the U.S. government feared that curtailing aid would result in a major foreign debt crisis and the collapse of the South Korean economy.

3. The immediate result of the highly controversial 1965 Korea-Japan Normalization Treaty was a large influx of cash in the form of direct grants ($300 million in 1965 dollars), public loans ($200 million), and private investment ($300 million). It also resulted in the transfer of Japanese technology and business expertise to South Korean enterprises. But this new economic relationship between Japan and South Korea also tied South Korean businesses to the Japanese production cycle; that is, South Korea took over the low-technology, labor-intensive, pollution-producing, low value-added industries that Japanese companies were abandoning. Japan also became a major export market for South Korea. Externally, South Korea's entry to export-based industrialization also received a push from Korea's support of the United States in the Vietnam War, both in the form of war-generated demand for Korean exports and American aid in exchange for contributing troops to the war effort. By the end of the war, about 300,000 Korean soldiers had served in Vietnam (Cumings 1997: 321).

4. Unlike many developing economies, South Korea was quite successful at protecting its domestic economy from foreign capital throughout the 1960s and 1970s by controlling the autonomy and influence of multinational corporations. Preferring direct foreign loans that could be channeled to targeted export industries, the government strictly limited and controlled direct foreign investment in South Korean companies. For detailed studies of the South Korean interventionist state, see Amsden 1989; Haggard et al. 1994; Hart-Landsberg 1993; E. M. Kim 1987; Woo-Cumings 1991.

5. As late as 1986, South Korean employees in manufacturing worked the longest hours in the world and their wages were lower than those of workers in Brazil, Mexico, Hong Kong, and Singapore. South Korea also had one of the highest rates of industrial accidents in the world.

6. For instance, protectionist policies kept domestic prices high and blocked access to affordable bank loans for individual consumers.

7. This crisis prompted President Kim Dae Jung to push forward a number of liberalizing economic reforms that moved the South Korean economy in a more market-oriented direction.

8. For studies of South Korea's economic development, see Amsden 1989; Clifford 1998; Deyo 1987; Haggard 1990; Hart-Landsberg 1993; Janelli and Yim 1993; Lie 1998; S. Moon 2005; Woo-Cumings 1991. Only recently have scholars in the Western academy begun to pay direct and in-depth attention to issues of

wider socio-cultural change related to economic development. Some recent examples include Abelmann 2003; Kendall 1996, 2002; Lett 1998; Nelson 2000. Indeed, Laurel Kendall (2002) states: "The social consequences of South Korea's rapid transformation from an agricultural to an urban and highly industrialized society have only just begun to be digested" (115).

9. For Kyung-sup Chang (1999), the contemporary "authoritarian political aristocracy" of South Korean politics is a legacy of post–Korean War political culture in which the native efforts at the construction of a genuine democratic process and culture failed partly because political democracy had been externally imposed. Despite what he terms a "democracy alliance between professional politicians and civil intellectual leaders" that has existed since the Park era, the culture and procedures of authoritarian aristocracy were never fundamentally altered in South Korean politics, which are still characterized by, among other things, "patriarchal despotic control, rigid hierarchy, and uniform political opinion." For Chang, this includes the governments of oppositional parties led by Presidents Kim Young Sam and Kim Dae Jung, whom he sees as "aristocratic civilian politicians" ultimately interested in capturing, not democratizing, state power.

10. The underdevelopment of the public welfare system in South Korea has been in no small part due to the reliance of government and the corporate sectors on the "traditional" family—and by extension, on women—to provide financial and caregiving support to members of society. See the insightful discussion on this topic in K. Chang (1999).

11. This is expressed not only in corporate appropriation of Confucian patriarchal and familial ideology in the workplace—embodied foremost in the idea of the company as a Confucian-style family—but also in the corporations' attempt to cultivate management-labor harmony. It is important, also, to note that the South Korean corporate culture has been shaped as much by the application of modern military management principles, a legacy both of the character of Japanese colonial institutions and American military management practices. See Janelli and Yim 1993; Lie 1998: 100–104; Pye 1985.

12. The central figure in the articulation of Neo-Confucianism was Chu Hsi (1130–1200 C.E.), whose writings became highly influential in Korea (Deuchler 1992).

13. Indeed, although Confucian patriarchy was also the organizing and cultural principle in neighboring countries such as China and Japan, many scholars agree that the system of Neo-Confucian patriarchy developed and instituted in Korea during the Yi dynasty was probably the most rigid and "ideal" form of Confucian patriarchy ever achieved. Popular aphorisms suggest that Koreans "out-Chinese the Chinese" and "if Confucius were to come back to

earth at any time, he probably would have been most pleased with the society of the later Yi dynasty" (P. Chang 1996: 19, 24–25).

14. More specifically, the five major principles, or moral imperatives (*illyun*) of human relationships were: between sovereign and subject guided by righteousness (*ui*); the relationship between father and son guided by parental authority (*chin*); the relationship between husband and wife guided by the separation of their function (*byeol*); the relationship between the elder and younger brothers guided by the sequence of birth (*seo*); and the relationship between senior and junior guided by faithfulness (*sin*) (Deuchler 1977: 2).

15. Men, as family heads, had three major rights and obligations: representing their families to the public, supervising family members, and controlling family property. Another vital responsibility was performing ancestor worship (D. Lee 1986: 65).

16. Once married, a woman was considered a *chulga oein*, "she who left the family and has become a stranger."

17. In works such as *Naehun* (Instructions for Women), one of the most influential books for women compiled in 1475 by the mother of King Seongjong, girls were indoctrinated into the four basics of womanly behavior: moral conduct (women need not have great talents but must be quiet and serene, chaste, and disciplined), proper speech (women need not have rhetorical talents but must avoid bad and offensive language and speak with restraint), proper appearance (women need not be beautiful but must be clean in dress and appearance), and womanly tasks (women need not be clever but must pay attention to such duties as weaving and entertaining guests) (Deuchler 1977: 6). These practices became cardinal rules of conduct for upper-class women by the latter period of the Yi dynasty. Although lower-class women, especially entertainers, shamans, and slaves could not, by necessity, fully adopt these practices, these were, nevertheless, the models and standards of behavior to which all women were held and to which all women strove .

18. Pilwha Chang (1996) comments that the few notable women who appear in the historical record fall into the following basic categories: mothers whose sons passed the civil service examinations, women who sacrificed themselves in various ways for their husbands and family and to preserve their chastity, and those who enabled their husband's household to prosper through hard labor and wisdom (28).

19. Inability to produce an heir was the most common cause for a woman's dismissal. There were, however, certain legal measures to protect women from the most extreme forms of abuse. For example, even if a wife was found to be guilty of one of the "seven sins," she could not be dismissed if she served three years of mourning for her husband's parents, if the husband had gone

from poverty to wealth since marrying, or if the wife had no family to which to return when divorced (Y. C. Kim 1996: 6).

20. Compare Margery Wolf's (1972) concept of the Chinese "uterine" family.

21. In 1916, for example, there were 447 primary schools, 74 vocational schools, 3 high schools, and 4 colleges in Korea, but only a handful of girls' schools (W. Han 1980: 470). In 1940, primary school attendance was 47 percent for Korean boys, but only 18 percent for girls, and secondary school attendance was only 4 percent for Korean boys but less than 1 percent for girls. In 1944, one year before the end of colonial rule, 7,272 Korean men had completed four-year college, while only 102 women had done so (Yu 1987: 22). Furthermore, it is important to remember that education for Korean youths, as part of the Japanese cultural assimilation policy, was highly discriminatory and was aimed primarily at indoctrinating Koreans to become the loyal subjects and workers for the Japanese empire, and ultimately at extinguishing Korean national identity. In addition to mandating the sole use of the Japanese language in schools, the Japanese completely prohibited the teaching of Korean history and language by 1938 (Y. C. Kim 1996: 13). As Denise Lett (1998) states: "The purpose of the education provided by the Japanese was to benefit the Japanese politically, by converting Korean youth into loyal subjects, and economically, by training them for subordinate roles in both agriculture and industry. Koreans, however, took advantage of whatever educational opportunities were available" (36).

22. The highest rate of increase in labor force participation for women, and men, has been in the manufacturing sector. The rate of increase for women's labor force participation in the secondary (manufacturing) sector between 1960 and 1990 was from 9.3 percent to 42.2 percent, an increase of 12.7 times (from 0.16 million to 2 million) in the last three decades (Economic Planning Board 1990). And although South Korea does not seem to have experienced the feminization of tertiarization that other developing countries have experienced, both the number and proportion of female workers in clerical occupations, especially in business firms related to light manufacturing, have also rapidly increased (M. Kim 1992: 160). According to government statistics, the proportion of women in clerical occupations increased from 5.7 percent in 1960 to 39.7 in 1990 (Economic Planning Board 1960, 1990).

23. The revised Family Law of 1989 grants women the right to head a family. Although the law still disadvantages women in regard to property division in divorce, it does include some important changes: for example, husbands no longer gain automatic custody of children, and children of both genders and any birth order are now entitled to receive equal shares of property (Palley 1990: 1148; Korea Institute for Social Information and Research 1995: 18).

24. There is a large body of literature in both English and Korean about contemporary Korean patriarchy. See, for example, K. Chang 1997; H. Cho 1986, 1988, 1995, 1996; Kendall 1996, 2002; D. Lee 1986; S. Lee 1995; Research Center for Women's Concerns, Yonsei University 1995, 1996; Yeoseong Hanguk Sahoe Yeonguhoe 1994; H. Yi 1996.

25. Dongno Kim (1990) explains the persistence of familism in modern Korea: "The change in family structure, however, means neither that the network of interactions among individuals has become confined narrowly to the nuclear family members, nor that an individual is liberated from the constraints of the traditional extended family" (414).

26. Also see S. Lee 1995; H. Yi 1996.

27. According to Heidi Hartmann (1981), although women made large economic contributions to the domestic economy in the preindustrial family, they were still subject to the patriarchal system and subordinate to the male household heads during this era. However, despite its equalizing potential, capitalism as it developed during the industrial development of Europe deepened the unequal position of women by building onto that hierarchical authority structure an economic one—a compromise, she suggests, between men and capitalists in their struggle over women's labor power. When labor was organized capitalistically in factories away from the home, women were either excluded from labor by men who were better organized, or given undesirable jobs and lower wages. See also Zaretski 1973. For a discussion of Korean/Asian capitalist patriarchy and neo-conservatism, see H. Cho 1995, 1996 and H. Yi 1996.

28. According to UNDP 1995, South Korea ranked 54th out of 55 countries with respect to the ratio of men's to women's wages, at 53.5 percent of male wages. See also U. Cho 1996. The wage disparity is particularly great for older workers, with female earners over the age of 40 being paid only about one-third of their male counterparts (Yu 1987: 23).

29. As of 1987, there were, for example, fewer than fifteen active female lawyers in South Korea (H. Cho 1986: 48), although the situation has been improving in recent years (see Korea Institute for Social Information and Research 1995). The medical profession has been somewhat better, with women comprising about 18.7 percent of medical doctors in 1992 (Korea Institute for Social Information and Research 1995). In general, the system of occupational sex segregation is also reflected in sectoral gender segregation as well; that is, the more prestigious the sector, such as public enterprises and larger firms, the smaller the proportion women employed in them. At present, over 70 percent of female workers are employed in firms with fewer than ten employees, and the older the woman is, the more likely she works in a smaller firm (U. Cho 1996: 61).

30. Another clear illustration of Hartmann's perspective appears in Makoto Kumazawa's (1996) study of women's place in the postwar structure of the Japanese labor market. Kumazawa illustrates how the entrenched system of gendered division of labor in the Japanese workplace indeed results in a kind of "partnership" between capitalism and patriarchy, a consequence of conscious corporate labor policy built upon the system of domestic division of labor. In the years immediately after the Second World War, Japanese women were shepherded into simple unskilled or semi-skilled jobs at low wages in both the manufacturing and service sectors, and expected to quit after marriage. After 1965, however, when it no longer became feasible to effectively maintain wage discrimination simply based on gender, Japanese corporations launched a systematic restructuring of discrimination—a process that Kumazawa describes as a "modern" form of gender discrimination—by establishing a grade system based on qualification and ability, and restricting women to low-level job assignments with low wages. Thus, these policies resulted in the persistent use of women in the ever-expanding domain of menial work. By taking away any incentive to remain in the workplace, the consequences of such industrial discrimination in Japan, according to Kumazawa, was to turn women toward marriage, strengthening the domestic division of labor and women's roles and identities at home. Caught in the most boring and routine jobs at low wages, many women, especially college-educated women, actually saw marriage as a welcome escape from the drudgery of the work world. As Kumazawa documents, many young women during the affluent recent decades engaged in passive forms of resistance by turning their backs on labor, rejecting the "desirable image of the office lady" who had dedicated herself to the managerial principle of efficiency, and engaging instead in a "determined pursuit of leisure" that embraced an irresponsible attitude toward work (176).

31. It is helpful to point out, however, that this pattern has been gradually shifting, especially since the 1990s. Because of the rise in marriage age for women (and men), the rate of labor force participation does not display a significant drop in the 25–29 age range, but at the 30–34 age range. And even in the 30–34 age range, the drop in workforce participation from the pre-marital years is not as dramatic as it had been in the 1970s and 1980s. These figures suggest that more married women with infants and young children continue to work (See Economic Planning Board 1991, 1995, 2000, 2005).

32. According to UNDP's Human Development Report (1995), South Korea ranked 79th out of 153 nations in terms of women's labor force participation rate. See also U. Cho (1996: 59) for a fuller comparison with other nations. According to a more recent study by Young Lan Kim and Kyung Ock Chun (1996), South Korea has seen some increase in the overall rate of women's

labor participation, but again, most of these working women are ghettoized in traditional female occupations (134).

33. As of 1990, only 8.3 percent of the female workforce in South Korea held college or university degrees (Lett 1998: 162). Interestingly, according to the study of Korean women's political and social consciousness by Kim and Chun (1996: 136), as many as 87.8 percent of all unemployed women in the survey expressed a desire to be employed. Those who did not want jobs at all represented only 8 percent of the women surveyed.

34. At present, it is in fact easier for South Korean women with high school educations to find jobs than those with college degrees. Given this, it actually makes more sense for highly educated women to translate their educational capital into marriage and find a husband with high earning power than to seek a career. Furthermore, for upper-class women, there is a stigma attached to working as a sign that their husbands are not providing adequately for them.

35. By pointing out that economic development does not automatically guarantee the enhancement in the status of women because of government policies, interests of men, and various traditional forces, Esther Boserup gives a more comprehensive explanation combining structural and cultural factors, including "traditional ideologies and customary behavior" that serve to keep women in their traditional positions. She states, "Traditional attitudes affect women's positions in the family, in the labor market, and in public life, and the effects of the changes caused by economic development in all three spheres interact and produce a complicated pattern. . . . Governments promote industrialization and other technological modernization, but do what they can to prevent economic development from changing the traditional position of women" (1995: 52, 58).

36. Moon (2005) notes how the economic marginalization of women became more conspicuous as industrial development shifted from light consumer goods manufacturing to heavy and chemical industrialization in the 1970s. She cites as evidence the relative exclusion of women from both public and private vocational training programs, especially from more technologically skilled areas that paid more, contributing to the masculinization of skilled labor in South Korea. During the latter heavy industrialization phase (1975–85), women's exclusion from these programs intensified.

37. Elaborating on Hartmann's thesis, Susan Greenhalgh (1985) finds that the Taiwanese patriarchal family, on whose sexual hierarchies the capitalist economic system was built, drives the perpetuation and even intensification of the Taiwanese system of gender stratification and the subordination of women throughout the industrialization process. Going beyond Hartmann's macro-

level analysis, Greenhalgh analyzes the specific agents and mechanisms by which the Taiwanese patrilineal family system perpetuates gender inequality. She reports that Taiwanese parents respond to the disadvantaged position of women in the labor force and the status of women as "temporary" and "marrying-out" household members by discriminating against their daughters in such things as education and employment options and expecting "quick returns" from them in the form of economic repayment. Studies by Kung (1994) and Salaff (1981) on young working women in Taiwan and Hong Kong, respectively, also support Greenhalgh's thesis that the root cause of women's continued unequal status lies in the form of the traditional family, which prevents women from improving their status though their earning power by exerting control over their lives and finances —a model that Salaff calls the "centripetal family" (8). Such behavior by the families, of course, is intimately tied to the ideology and the reality of women's subordinate position in the family economy (Salaff 1981: 12).

38. Compare with R. W. Connell's (1995: 81–86, 200–203) conceptualization and discussion of the "crisis tendencies" of the modern gender order.

39. In South Korea, housewives are often caricatured as a "non-working leisured group," but as many as one-third of middle-class women, and 44 percent of working-class women, are engaged in some form of informal earning activities that are often hidden from conventional labor statistics (O. Moon 1990: 31; Cho and Koo 1983).

40. Common tutoring activities by middle-class women include teaching English or giving music lessons. For poor or working class women who are forced to work out of necessity, informal incomes may be generated through participation in informal labor markets, typically by means of manual work such as petty trading, domestic service, and home-based craft production (M. Kim 1992).

41. One structural basis for this discrepancy, which also provides evidence of the cultural contradictions in contemporary Korean society, is that despite the modernized expectations of a companionate marriage, the majority of matrimonial unions in Korea are still arranged or semi-arranged. Denise Lett (1988: 197) estimates that at least half of all marriages in Korea are arranged or semi-arranged, with the proportion becoming higher as class level rises. (From my own sample, however, I estimate an even higher proportion.)

42. Not only do many women say that they are subject to unbending traditional role expectations from husbands who disregard their wives' basic needs and humanity while expecting obedience, but many women, having married men they do not know very well, also point to the disappointments, conflicts, and loneliness stemming from the lack of close emotional bonds, communica-

tion, and companionship for which they had hoped. This is, of course, also an inevitable part of the situation of strictly gendered division of spheres that inevitably leads to emotional and physical distance between husbands and wives. See also Lebra 1986.

43. Although many couples now live apart from their parents, their sense of obligation still remains strong; though the nuclear family form as a residential unit has become the statistical norm in South Korea (Tsuya and Kim 1991: 22), the middle-class family system, due to the continuing economic interdependence between children and parents, exists as what one scholar calls a "modified stem family," keeping alive the traditional mutual obligations of parents of children throughout life (See K. Lee 1986: 13).

44. Indeed, as late-industrialization has been premised upon learning the production processes and management characteristics of more advanced economies, South Korea's economic expansion has been dependent upon a highly educated labor force (Amsden 1989). Especially for men, credentials from prestigious colleges have led to a fast track for good and secure employment and leadership positions in the national economy (M. Kim 1992).

45. This intensification of attention on children tends to intensify the powerful traditional bond between the mother and her children, aided by contemporary women's isolation with their children in the nuclear family setting. While the lives of men are focused on work, a young mother's identity and aspirations become intensely entwined with those of her children. There has been much concern and fuss in South Korea over these child-centered mothers, whose obsessions with their children are presumed to have adverse affects on the emotional lives of their offspring.

46. This situation has been described in the following way: "Before a woman is married, she is treated like a queen. After she marries, she is treated like a slave" (quoted in Lett 1998: 143).

Chapter Three

1. Unified vocal prayer in Korea is believed largely to be a product of the great revival of 1907 in Wonsan, which has since become a regular feature of worship in a significant number of Korean churches, irrespective of their denominational affiliation. The following is an excerpt from a report on one of the meetings during the 1907 Great Revival by a Presbyterian missionary which may very well describe the origin of unified vocal prayer in Korea: "After a short sermon, Rev. Graham Lee took charge of the meeting and called for prayers. So many began praying that Dr. Lee said, 'If you wish to pray like that, all pray,' and the whole audience began to pray out loud, all together.

The effect was indescribable. Not a confusion, but a vast harmony of sound and spirit, a mingling together of souls moved by an irresistible impulse to prayer. It sounded to me like the falling of many waters, an ocean of prayer beating against God's throne. It was not many, but one, born of one Spirit, lifted to one Father above. . ." (Blair 1946, quoted in A. Clark 1971: 161–62).

2. A notable exception here is the work of R. Marie Griffith (1997).

3. Judging from the frequency with which people mentioned the active efforts of acquaintances and neighbors in getting them to go to church, the role of proselytization seems to be particularly central in attracting people to Protestantism. Almost all childhood and adult converts report that the evangelizing efforts of other Christians were important in getting them into church. In fact, I would guess that almost every Korean has been subjected to intense proselytization efforts by churchgoers at some point in their lives. As one woman convert recalls of her earlier experiences: "As it happens, wherever I lived, there were always some crazy Christians near me. For instance, in our first apartment, there was this crazy Christian woman upstairs from me who kept pestering me. I was really not very happy about this. And for some reason, there was always a church near me, too. Anyway, because of this woman's pestering, I was dragged to the church all the time. My husband went too, but we weren't into it at all at first. When the end of the service was near, my husband would pinch our child so he would start crying and we could leave."

4. Here I assume an "activist" view of conversion, a view that focuses on the activities of a person as an active, reality constructing, strategizing "seeker" of conversion and problem resolution, rather than simply a passive "convert" to whom conversion just "happens." Unlike some scholars however, I do not believe that seekers are necessarily fully conscious of their "quest." See Lofland and Stark 1965; Richardson 1985; Straus 1979.

5. See Rambo 1992: 165; Bainbridge 1992; Lofland and Stark 1965; Scroggs and Douglas 1967; Simmonds 1977; Stark and Bainbridge 1980; Ullman 1982. This perspective is generally referred to as the "crisis" or "strain" theory of religious conversion.

6. For an interesting discussion on this issue, see also David Smilde's recent article (2005) on Venezuelan evangelicalism.

7. Whether conversion is a dramatic, sudden, single-event change or a gradual process is one of the central issues in the literature on conversion (see Scroggs and Douglas 1967). The former model can be seen as similar to the traditional prototype of conversion based on the "Pauline experience" on the road to Damascus: one that is considered sudden, dramatic, emotional, and implying a radical transformation of the self and break with the past (Richard-

son 1985: 153–65). My view, based on my observations of the conversion experiences of Korean evangelical women, suggests that though we do not have to reject the view of conversion as sudden or dramatic, we should remember that conversion may not occur as a single event, and that even after "conversion," there may not necessarily be a total resolution of one's conflicts nor a drastic or life-long self-transformation (Simmonds 1977). "Conversion" may also require repeated experiences and reinforcements throughout one's lifetime.

8. In their article about conversion to the Unification Church, Lofland and Stark (1965) also describe the same kind of "experimenting" activity by the "seeker" converts prior to joining the Unification Church. For the authors, the process of seeking has as its main purpose the resolution of personal problems and tensions, a conclusion that my research also supports.

9. Indeed, the importance of healing, particularly for lower-class women, as well as the centrality of healing ministries in many Korean churches, have also been amply described and documented in various studies of Korean Christianity, and are credited as major factors in the vigorous expansion of Korean Protestantism. In particular, there are various studies by Korean scholars regarding the members of charismatically or Pentecostally oriented churches, which demonstrate that church participation of many poorer women is motivated by a desire to find a supernatural cure for severe physical illness or disease, after other medical or religious attempts at a cure, such as shamanistic rituals, have failed. This seems similar to what Burdick (1993: 75, 101) calls the "cult of affliction" among Brazilian Pentecostal women; and indeed, in response to these needs, a number of the Pentecostally oriented churches in South Korea operate healing ministries—though many have yielded ambiguous results. Many observers have criticized these ministries, their healing practices, and doctrines not only as a sham, but as an attempt to "take advantage" of the shamanistic, supernatural orientations of poor, under-educated women. See J. Lee 1986; Yoo 1988; S. Park 1993.

10. One example of such a church is the Yeoido Full Gospel Church, where I also conducted a set of interviews. Although this mammoth church (with membership estimated to be around half a million) is certainly a "multi-class" congregation, it contains, on the whole, a much higher proportion of lower-middle-class, working-class, and poorer individuals than the South or North River Churches.

11. The literal meaning of the term *sijipsari* is "life at the husband's household"; figuratively, however, it is used by women to denote the difficult and arduous life a daughter-in-law has to endure in the husband's household, and has the connotation of life imprisonment.

12. "Mouth-turning" (*Ib-i dolda*) is a common colloquial expression to denote loss of muscle control on the face, usually as a result of stroke or some kind of neurological or nervous disorder, such as Bell's palsy.

13. The cases described here are by no means particular to religious Korean women. There are various clinical-psychological studies done on Korean married women that document similar kinds of psychosomatic-type illnesses. In an English-language study, Bou-yong Rhi (1986) interprets the various case studies of mental and physiological disorders of women he has treated in the context of conflicts caused by the patriarchal Confucian family structure and values.

14. In fact, Seong-gil Min (1989) goes as far as to say that based on his study, a large number of women became Christians after having experienced *hwatbyeong*, seeking the religion primarily as a strategy for obtaining healing for their illnesses or suffering often in concert with other religious strategies such as pursuing the services of shamans. According to Min, this has contributed to the growth of Christianity in Korea.

15. In their seminal article on conversion, Lofland and Stark (1965) astutely point out the importance of examining the failure of other types of "problem-solving perspectives" in explaining why certain persons turn to religion and others do not. Indeed, in the case of middle-class Korean evangelical women, the failures of other types of solutions, particularly medical and psychiatric, seem to be instrumental in their decisions to seek out religion. Among less-educated women, shamanism may be the most typical type of alternative solution.

16. See Bainbridge (1992) for a good summary of these perspectives. As opposed to the "strain" or "crisis" theory of religious conversion, the perspectives that focus on social processes in conversion can be categorized under what Bainbridge (1992) calls "social influence theory." Within this category, according to Bainbridge, we can distinguish between those views that focus on the strength of social ties/bonds in facilitating conversion, termed the "control theory," and those that emphasize the importance of repeated social interaction in promoting faith, called the "subculture" theory. In the Korean case, my data suggests that although social factors, in addition to crisis motives, can be crucial in bringing about conversion, "control theory" best explains the process of church attendance, while "subculture theory" is better applied to explaining the process of actual religious conversion. It is important to remember that social influence theories, however, can rarely explain conversion by themselves, but must be combined with crisis perspectives.

17. In Korea, then, conversion can be seen in many ways as both a personal and a collective accomplishment. See also Straus 1979.

18. In many cases, members might, at the behest of a neighbor or a friend, begin attending the cell groups even before attending the church. And even if members are not fully committed to the church, they nevertheless go regularly to the cell meetings, which become crucial sites both for gospel transmission and social integration into the church body.

19. Based on my "activist" view of conversion, I regard prayer and other ritualistic practices of evangelicalism as a learned process, an active achievement by the seeker who "accomplishes" conversion within a particular religious group context by mastering certain practices. These might include the relevant "technology," such as prayers, as well as language and interpretive schemes appropriate to the group (see Straus 1979). Indeed, one cell leader from the South River Church tells her cell members that praying is a "difficult thing to do," and especially difficult without "proper training." See also Sarbin and Adler (1970).

20. This emphasis on absolute or unconditional obedience to God within Korean evangelical churches has been amply documented in a number of studies (see, for example, articles in Hong, Won, and Kim 1966; H. Yi 1985a), even studies on Korean immigrant churches such as A. R. Kim 1996.

21. Interestingly enough, entrusting and surrendering is encouraged not just to God-Father, but to a strong man-figure equated with Jesus. As one South River Church member said to a potential recruit: "We all want a strong man who can "lead" us. Just as we want to entrust ourselves to such a man, we must entrust ourselves to Jesus, and let him lead us, like a man."

22. I should stress that these acts of surrender are not necessarily final once-and-for-all experiences that generate permanent release or healing. To the contrary, I have found that although these therapeutic effects are real in each act of surrender and encounter with God, such effects may not necessarily last, and must be renewed on a continual basis. This is one reason why prayer is seen as so central by the churches and by the members in their evangelical lives. Prayers foster repeated encounters with God, ever renewing experiences of surrender, conversion, and faith.

Chapter Four

1. See Kang 1996; A. R. Kim 1996; Lett 1998; Yu 1987. The first "modern" (non-Christian) school in Korea, where modern subjects were taught with traditional ones, was Wonson Haksa in Wonson, established in 1883 (Lett 1998: 35).

2. Interestingly, the Korean Methodist Church began ordaining women in 1931, many years before the Methodist Church in the United States. In fact, a group of American female missionaries traveled to Korea in the 1930s to become ordained (Yang 1992: 64).

3. See Yoon 1992 and P. Min 2008.

4. In the Korean evangelical establishment, most denominations have instituted an eldership system after the Presbyterian model. This seems to have been an innovation designed to create positions with which to reward status to highly contributing male members of the church.

5. Beyond these official guidelines, the exact pace at which a member becomes appointed to these different positions depends, as one elder said, on the believer's "enthusiasm" for the church.

6. When a person is recognized as worthy of such an appointment, she or he is either nominated by a high-ranking member of the church or simply appointed by the pastor. The nominee is usually expected to accept.

7. See also Yang 1992: 69. Three notable biblical passages justify these views: "Wives, be subject to your husbands as you are to the lord. For the husband is the head of the wife just as Christ is the head of the Church, the body of which he is the savior. Just as the church is subject to Christ, so also wives ought to be, in everything, to their husbands." (Ephesians 5:22–24); "Let a woman learn in silence with full submission. I permit no woman to teach or to have authority over a man; she is to keep silent. For Adam was formed first, then Eve; and Adam was not deceived, but the woman was deceived and became a transgressor. Yet she will be saved through childbearing, provided they continue in faith and love and holiness, with modesty." (1 Timothy 2:11–15); "A wife must put her husband first. This is her duty as a follower of the Lord. A husband must love his wife and not abuse her." (Colossians 3:18–19).

8. As the center of evangelistic efforts in Korean churches, cell groups are also encouraged to seek receptive individuals or groups and are the primary means by which new members are "brought in," connected, and overseen (J. Lee 1986: 255; J. Kim 1996: 178). Since a majority of the church members live in middle-class apartment complexes, most residents are likely to find at least one cell group in operation in their apartment buildings.

9. Monetary contributions, in the form of tithes, are considered an important part of church "service" and a mark of one's devotion and dedication. Reading off the names of tithers at the end of the Sunday service was until recently a common practice in most Korean Protestant congregations; however, this practice has fallen into disfavor in many quarters, with many churches ceasing to read off names. However, in the North River Church, tithing is still made public knowledge by listing people's names on the bulletin board.

10. Although considered to be in the minority, "Jesus-crazy" women are objects of incessant rumors as examples of perpetuators of "unhealthy" Christian practices. As such, an important task of a pastor is helping his members achieve a delicate balance between commitment to the church and to the home.

Chapter Five

1. It is worth noting that there is very little direct and public criticism of men in the all-women meetings. In the all-male group meetings that I observed, on the other hand, the participants spend far less time than women in agonized self-critique and self-reflection regarding family matters.

2. In this context, another possible translation for the term *jallancheok hada* is "to act self-important."

3. Ms. Cho is not simply making a straightforward critique of women for their gender "violations"; rather, she points subtly to some of the larger structural/cultural problems of the Korean family and social system, revealing her awareness of the structural causes of family problems. For instance, her remarks that Korean women these days "just meet someone, get married, and just live," and "don't really know how to maintain a family life" attempt to call attention to one of the great contradictions of the modern Korean institution of marriage and courtship—a system that despite the acceptance of the modern ideology of romance and conjugal love is still designed to encourage arranged or semi-arranged marriages in the majority of people and thus set people up for failure. Hence, it is no accident that "lack of marriage preparedness," along with "communication problems" and "personality incompatibility," are very often identified by church leaders, including Ms. Cho, as some of the most pressing problems facing contemporary Korean couples. According to this view, couples too often hurry into marriages without getting to know each other sufficiently, and often lack the relationship experience to work out successful marriages. In such situations, issues of communication—stemming from basic incompatibility, lack of relationship experience, and often a simple lack of goodwill—can become serious problems for couples.

4. The Korean expression "climbing on the head of a man" refers to this attitude.

5. Such remarks as the following by a seminar leader constantly serve to remind and reinforce women of their guilt: "Because women are too strong [*gang hada*], there are many homes in which men are turned into idiots [*byeongshin*]. But do you think this 'idiocy' stays in one place? No. So where does it go? To drinking and gambling. If you don't attend to your husband properly and obey him, and instead always point out his shortcomings, where do his feelings of inadequacy go? They go outside of the home. So whom does this make unfortunate? The wife."

6. In my observations of the South River Church, the female obligation to obey was not qualified even in the case of domestic abuse. In all my conversations with various leaders, only one admitted that he would condone divorce in extremely abusive situations, and only when I pushed him; most were very

vague about such limits and usually preached continuous obedience as the only solution. In my fieldwork, I did not hear anyone advocate mutual *obedience* between the husband and wife, only mutual love and caring.

7. In a lecture directed at both husbands and wives, the leader told the husbands to "live with your wives at the center" as well. This however, does not signify mutual submission, but is an encouragement for the husbands to "love" their wives.

8. Some of these notions on proper Christian marital relations take as their sources the American conservative/fundamentalist literature on gender and family relations that were adapted to the Korean situation. In his conversation with me, this particular seminar leader referred specifically to Phyllis Schlafly's (1977) book *The Power of the Positive Woman*. Thus, the views of these leaders often represent an interesting hodge-podge of American conservative-Christian and Confucian perspectives on marital/gender relations; this instance shows the incorporation of the Western/American vision of ideal contemporary womanhood: the double view of married women as both sexual/physically alluring and domestic/maternal rather than simply the latter (as is usual in the Korean context).

9. Kandiyoti (1988) uses the description "classic" to denote instances of patriarchy found in a geographical area that includes North Africa, the Muslim Middle East (including Turkey, Pakistan, and Iran), and South and East Asia.

10. It is clear here that despite the general stereotype of Korean men as "closed mouthed" and "silent," their silence and withdrawal are often expressions of anger and resentment toward their wives.

11. Gyeongsangdo is a state in the Southeastern part of South Korea known widely for its deep cultural conservatism, and particularly for its traditional and conservative men with silent and stubborn characters.

12. This passage is transcribed from an audio tape of a lecture given by a family seminar leader of one of the churches I investigated. To keep anonymous the identity of the seminar leader and the name of the church, the source of the recording will not be listed in the reference matter.

13. It is a common perception that quitting smoking and drinking is very difficult for men in South Korea because it is an important part of general male social etiquette, particularly in the workplace. To be social, men are generally expected to drink and smoke together, especially after work, and men not engaging in this behavior can be excluded from the group. Many believe that abstinence on the part of deeply Christian men often puts them at a professional and financial disadvantage because they cannot "socialize" properly with their clients and co-workers.

14. The word *jong* can be translated as both "slave" and "servant" in Korean.

15. Predictably enough, numerous women point to the fact of age-parity with their husbands as a major source of their own arrogant attitudes, revealing their belief in the necessity of maintaining gender hierarchy through marital age difference.

16. This theme of "dying" in conversion has been observed in studies of American evangelical conversion. For example, Gordon (1984), in his discussion of Jesus People groups, talks about "dying to self" in the process of surrender that ultimately leads to rebirth and reconstitution of a more empowered self; "dying of self" is a form of surrender through which one becomes more empowered to accomplish one's goals by "letting go" of oneself and one's sins and allowing God to direct one's life. Although the overall process appears similar in the case of Korean women, "dying of self" in the process of Korean women's reconstitution of domestic and gender identity seems to signify creation of a new self that, albeit spiritually and internally empowered, is a self reformed to better fulfill its traditional gender role through the negation or the submerging of the self's desires and ego.

17. My findings regarding the rhetoric of "killing" of self in evangelical women's discourse is corroborated clearly by Ai Ra Kim's (1996) study of first-generation Korean evangelical immigrant women in America, which suggests that this rhetoric is a central part of Korean female evangelical discourse. In Kim's findings as well, the concept of the killing of self is understood by the women as a kind of extreme self-denial and self-repression (96, 121–23), an enactment of Jesus's sacrificial example and Christian virtue.

Chapter Six

1. The role of the churches as public, discursive spaces for enabling female critique of male behavior and transgressions has been documented with particular clarity in studies of Latin American evangelicals. See Brusco 1995; Burdick 1993.

2. The anti-intellectual tendencies of the Korean evangelical establishment are documented in numerous studies. See, for example, articles in Hong, Won, and Kim 1966.

3. See Sewell (1992) for an excellent discussion and re-theorization of the notion of "agency." See also Risman 1998.

4. Among the notable exceptions are Arlene MacLeod's studies (1991, 1992) on working women and veiling on Cairo. Although she shies away from exploring the possibilities of deeper ideological/normative consent among the women of Cairo, she does attempt to pursue an analysis of the various cultural and subjective sources for their accommodation to veiling.

5. Jeffrey W. Rubin puts it this way: "Many of these works on resistance are attempts to combine broadly Marxist frameworks of political economy with poststructuralist notions of power as de-centered and of culture as a site of the inscription of power and of resistance to power. Within this body of work . . . the relative weights of political economy and culture, as well as of broad structures of power and local manifestations of power, are matters of considerable debate, including questions about the validity of these distinctions themselves" (Rubin 1996: 238). Some representative works in this vein include Comaroff 1985; Ong 1987; Scott 1985, 1986. In the last few years, several studies have critiqued such approaches, especially for their tendency to "romanticize" resistance and to ignore the conservative potential inscribed in the actions of the oppressed. Some scholars have even begun to question the utility of "resistance" as an analytical category, stating that such wide uses of the term tends to dilute the meaning of the term or that they reify the resistance/domination dichotomy (Dirks, Eley, and Ortner 1994; Isaacman 1990; Kondo 1990; Rubin 1996). Within the field of gender/feminist studies, such criticisms have been articulated by writers such as Lila Abu-Lughod (1990), who advocates our renewed attention to the study of power and power relations.

6. Even while glorifying their traditional female roles, many women will, in the same breath, express a sense of resignation at their situations and at their lack of choices, including their inability to return to work because of their loss of skills during child-rearing periods and at everything else they have had to give up through marriage.

7. For a critique of the neglect of the issue of female gender consciousness in the recent focus on female "resistance," see Rubin 1996. In their article on reconceptualizing gender relations, Judith Gerson and Cathy Peiss (1985) argue for attention to "consciousness," along with "boundaries" and "negotiation," as specific categories and conceptual tools for analyzing gender relations.

8. See Seung Kyung Kim's (1997) analysis of this issue within the context of working-class South Korean factory women.

9. See P. Chang 1996; A. R. Kim 1996; D. Kim 1990; S. Lee 1995. For theorizations of relational subjectivity/identity in the Middle East, see also Joseph 1993 and Gallagher 2007.

10. See H. Yi 1985a.

11. See D. Kim 1990 for an enlightening discussion on Korean familism and its evolution into what he calls "modern familism." See also K. Chang 1997.

12. Affirming the interpretation that the family continues be a "sacred unit" in South Korea, Haejoang Cho (1996) points out the ways in which many women, especially from the 1970s onward, had as their main preoccupation the socio-economic advancements of their families, "the task of heightening social

status of the family as a unit in the name of the 'family' and the 'nation.'" According to Cho, this was driven by the women's powerful, primary subjectivities as mothers within the family; moreover, working for the advancement of their families also further assured women's powerful positions as mothers. Cho also observes that the younger generation of married women, referred to commonly as "missy" housewives, are caught up in an even more vexing contradiction of "rejecting" the self-denying ethic and lifestyles of their mothers while adopting an equally anti-feminist but far more sexualized, individualistic, and consumerist feminine subjectivity. She calls this situation a "modern/postmodern patriarchy" and the "colonial-postmodern." See also H. Cho 1995.

Conclusion

1. See also Cott 1975, 1977 about the experiences of white evangelical women in the late eighteenth and nineteenth centuries.

2. Among some of the younger female members of the churches, there is already a growing sense of frustration and discontent with the ideological and structural rigidity of the evangelical establishment. In the course of my investigation, a number of these women expressed to me some dissatisfaction with the traditions and current situations of gender inequality and sexism within the churches, as well as the general authoritarian character of the leadership. However, they seemed to be "going along" with the situation for the time being.

3. See KWDI 2007. As of 2005, the total average fertility rate for women in South Korea was a mere 1.08 children per woman.

4. Various observers (Kendall 2002; H. Cho 2002) have commented that the compressed pace of social change in contemporary South Korean society has generated dramatically shifting notions of female gendered self-conceptions and desires not only between mothers and daughters, but even among siblings separated by a few years.

5. One interesting indicator of this new attitude is the report by some of my interviewees that many younger couples now desire delaying childbearing for several years after marriage because they want to live alone as a couple.

6. One of the major perceived causes of financial stresses on most families is the cost of education. This expense is often given as the primary reason many families feel that they need a second income earned by the wives. Indeed, given the current economic and ideological environment, women who view paid work as a full-fledged career pursuit still appear to be in the small minority.

7. It is a common impression that mothers-in-law can no longer mete out abuse with the kind of impunity entitled to those of the previous generation. Many individuals mentioned that mothers-in-law nowadays try to treat their daughters-in-law with greater reasonableness, mostly out of necessity. On the

other hand, many parents-in-law no longer wish to live with their children for the entire duration of their retirement because they, too, want to have their own freedom, although the belief persists that the children will have the responsibility to take care of them when the parents become infirm. Ironically, this poses a new set of dilemmas for young women because many mothers-in-law no longer wish to serve as full-time babysitters for their grandchildren.

Bibliography

Abelmann, Nancy. 1997. "Women's Class Mobility and Identities in South Korea: A Gendered, Transnational, Narrative Approach." *Journal of Asian Studies* 56, no. 2: 398–421.

———. 2003. *The Melodrama of Modernity: Women, Talk, and Class in Contemporary South Korea.* Honolulu, HI: University of Hawai'i Press.

Abu-Lughod, Lila. 1986. *Veiled Sentiments: Honor and Poetry in a Bedouin Society.* Berkeley, CA: University of California Press.

———. 1990. "The Romance of Resistance: Tracing Transformations of Power through Bedouin Women." *American Ethnologist* 17, no. 1: 41–55.

Adams, Laura L. 1999. "The Mascot Researcher: Identity, Power, and Knowledge in Fieldwork." *Journal of Contemporary Ethnography* 29, no. 4: 331–63.

Aguilar, Edwin Eloy, José Miguel Sandoval, Timothy J. Steigenga, and Kenneth M. Coleman. 1993. "Protestantism in El Salvador: Conventional Wisdom versus Survey Evidence." *Latin American Research Review* 28, no. 2: 119–40.

Ahmed, Leila. 1992. *Women and Gender in Islam.* New Haven, CT: Yale University Press.

Ahn, Byung-Mu. 1985. "A History of the Christian Movement in Korea." *International Review of Mission* 74 (January): 82–92.

Ammerman, Nancy. 1987. *Bible Believers: Fundamentalists in the Modern World.* New Brunswick, NJ: Rutgers University Press.

Amsden, Alice H. 1989. *Asia's Next Giant: South Korea and Late Industrialization.* New York: Oxford University Press.

Annis, Sheldon. 1987. *God and Production in a Guatemalan Town.* Austin, TX: University of Texas Press.

Anyon, Jean. 1983. "Intersection of Gender and Class: Accommodation and Resistance by Working Class and Affluent Females to Contradictory Sex-Role Ideologies." Pp. 19–37 in *Gender, Class and Education*, edited by Stephen Walter and Len Barton. Lewes, UK: Falmer Press.

Appleby, R. Scott. 2000. *The Ambivalence of the Sacred: Religion, Violence, and Reconciliation*. New York: Rowman & Littlefield.

Ayella, Marybeth. 1993. "They Must Be Crazy: Some of the Difficulties of Researching 'Cults.'" Pp. 108–24 in *Researching Sensitive Topics*, edited by Claire M. Renzetti and Raymond M. Lee. Newbury Park, CA: Sage Publications.

Bainbridge, William Sims. 1992. "The Sociology of Conversion." Pp. 178–91 in *Handbook of Religious Conversion*, edited by H. Newton Malony and Samuel Southard. Birmingham, AL: Religious Education Press.

Baron, Ava, ed. 1991. *Work Engendered: Toward a New History of American Labor*. Ithaca, NY: Cornell University Press.

Barrett, Michele. 1997. "Capitalism and Women's Liberation." Pp. 123–30 in *The Second Wave: A Reader in Feminist Theory*, edited by Linda Nicholson. New York: Routledge.

Bartkowski, John P. 2001. *Remaking the Godly Marriage: Gender Negotiation in Evangelical Churches*. New Brunswick, NJ: Rutgers University Press.

Bartkowski, John P., and J. Ghazal Read. 2003. "Veiled Submission: Gender Negotiation among Evangelical and U.S. Muslim Women." *Qualitative Sociology* 26: 71–92.

Bastian, Jean-Pierre. 1990. *Historia del Protestantismo en America Latina*. Mexico City: Casa Unida de Publicaciones.

Becker, Gary S. 1985. "Human Capital, Effort, and the Sexual Division of Labor." *Journal of Labor Economics* 3, no. 1, part 2 (January 1985): S33–S58.

Beckford, James A. 1978. "Accounting for Conversion." *British Journal of Sociology* 29, no. 2: 249–62.

———. 1983. "The Restoration of 'Power' to the Sociology of Religion." *Sociological Analysis*. 44, no. 1: 11–32.

Blee, Kathleen M. 1998. "White-Knuckle Research: Emotional Dynamics in Fieldwork with Racist Activists." *Qualitative Sociology* 21, no. 4: 381–99.

Boserup, Ester. 1995. "Obstacles to Advancement of Women during Development." Pp. 51–60 in *Investment in Women's Human Capital*, edited by T. Paul Shultz. Chicago, IL: University of Chicago Press.

Brasher, Brenda E. 1998. *Godly Women: Fundamentalism and Female Power*. New Brunswick, NJ: Rutgers University Press.

Brink, Judy, and Joan Mencher, eds. 1997. *Mixed Blessings: Gender and Religious Fundamentalism Cross Culturally*. New York: Routledge.

Brinton, Mary C., Yean-Ju Lee, and William L. Parish. 1995. "Married Women's Employment in Rapidly Industrializing Societies: Examples from East Asia." *American Journal of Sociology* 100, no. 5: 1099–1130.

Bruce, Steve, and Roy Wallis. 1983. "Rescuing Motives." *British Journal of Sociology* 32, no. 1: 61–71.

Brusco, Elizabeth E. 1995. *The Reformation of Machismo: Evangelical Gender and Conversion in Colombia.* Austin, TX: University of Texas Press.

Burdick, John. 1993. *Looking for God in Brazil: The Progressive Catholic Church in Urban Brazil's Religious Arena.* Berkeley, CA: University of California Press.

Bureau of East Asian and Pacific Affairs. 2007. "Background Note: South Korea." U. S. Department of State. http://www.state.gov/r/pa/ei/bgn/2800.htm. Accessed October 13, 2006.

Butler, Judith. 1990. *Gender Trouble: Feminism and the Subversion of Identity.* New York: Routledge.

Chang, Kyung-sup. 1997. "The Neo-Confucian Right and Family Politics in South Korea: The Nuclear Family as an Ideological Construct." *Economy and Society* 26, no. 1: 22–42.

———. 1999. "Compressed Modernity and Its Discontents: South Korean Society in Transition." *Economy and Society* 28, no. 1: 30–55.

Chang, Pilwha. 1996. "Korean Mothers, Daughters, and Wives." Pp. 18–33 in *Women of Korea: A History from Ancient Times to 1945.* Seoul: Asian Center for Women's Studies, Ewha Womans University.

Cho, Haejoang. 1986. "Male Dominance and Mother Power: The Two Sides of Confucian Patriarchy in Korea." Pp. 277–98 in *The Psycho-Cultural Dynamics of the Confucian Family: Past and Present,* edited by Walter H. Slote. Seoul: International Cultural Society of Korea.

———. 1987. "Korean Women in the Professions." Pp. 47–70 in *Korean Women in Transition: At Home and Abroad,* edited by Eui-Young Yu and Earl H. Phillips. Los Angeles, CA: Center for Korean and Korean-American Studies, California State University, Los Angeles.

———. 1988. *Hanguk-ui Yeoseong-gwa Namseong.* (Korean Women and Men). Seoul: Munhak-gwa Jiseong Sa.

———. 1995. "Women's Work and 'Development' in South Korea." *Yonsei Journal of Women's Studies* 1: 44–46.

———. 1996. "Feminist Intervention in the Rise of 'Asian' Discourse." Pp. 144–70 in *The Rise of Feminist Consciousness against the Asian Patriarchy.* Seoul: Asian Center for Women's Studies, Ewha Womans University.

———. 2002. "Living with Conflicting Subjectivities: Mother, Motherly Wife, and Sexy Woman in the Transition of Colonial-Modern to Postmodern Korea." Pp. 165–95 in *Under Construction: The Gendering of Modernity, Class, and*

Consumption in the Republic of Korea, edited by Laurel Kendall. Honolulu, HI: University of Hawai'i Press.

Cho, Uhn. 1996. "Female Labor in Korea: Economically Active but Not Empowered." Pp. 55–76 in *Asian Women.* Vol. 2. Seoul: Research Center for Asian Women, Sookmyung Women's University.

Cho, Uhn, and Hagen Koo. 1983. "Economic Development and Women's Work in a Newly Industrializing Country: The Case of Korea." *Development and Change* 14: 515–31.

Choi, Elizabeth. 1994. "Status of the Family and Motherhood for Korean Women." Pp. 189–205 in *Women of Japan and Korea: Continuity and Change,* edited by Joyce Gelb and Marian Lief Palley. Philadelphia, PA: Temple University Press.

Clark, Allen D. 1971. *A History of the Church in Korea.* Seoul: The Christian Literature Society.

Clark, Donald N. 1986. *Christianity in Modern Korea.* Lanham, MD: University Press of America.

———. 2006. "Mothers, Daughters, Biblewomen, and Sisters: An Account of 'Women's Work' in the Korean Mission Field." Pp. 167–92 in *Christianity in Korea,* edited by Robert E. Buswell, Jr. and Timothy S. Lee. Honolulu, HI: University of Hawai'i Press.

Clifford, Mark L. 1998 (revised edition). *Troubled Tiger: Business, Bureaucrats, and Generals in South Korea.* Armonk, NY: M.E. Sharpe.

Clough, Patricia Ticineto. 1992. *The Ends of Ethnography: From Realism to Social Criticism.* Newbury Park, CA: Sage Publications, Inc.

Comaroff, Jean. 1985. *Body of Power, Spirit of Resistance: The Culture and History of a South African People.* Chicago, IL: University of Chicago Press.

Connell, Robert W. 1995. *Masculinities.* Berkeley, CA: University of California Press.

Cott, Nancy F. 1975. "Young Women in the Second Great Awakening in New England." *Feminist Studies* 3: 15–29.

———. 1977. *The Bonds of Womanhood: "Women's Sphere" in New England, 1780–1835.* New Haven, CT: Yale University Press.

Cucchiari, Salvatore. 1990. "Between Shame and Sanctification: Patriarchy and Its Transformation in Sicilian Pentecostalism." *American Ethnologist* 17, no. 4: 687–707.

Cumings, Bruce. 1997. *Korea's Place in the Sun: A Modern History.* New York: W.W. Norton & Company.

Davidman, Lynn. 1991. *Tradition in a Rootless World: Women Turn to Orthodox Judaism.* Berkeley, CA: University of California.

De Andrade, Lelia Lomba. 2000. "Negotiating from the Inside: Constructing Racial and Ethnic Identity in Qualitative Research." *Journal of Contemporary Ethnography* 29, no. 3: 268–90.

Deuchler, Martina. 1977. "The Tradition: Women during the Yi Dynasty." Pp. 1–48 in *Virtues in Conflict: Tradition and the Korean Woman Today*, edited by Sandra Mattielli. Seoul: Royal Asiatic Society, Korea Branch.

———. 1992. *The Confucian Transformation of Korea: A Study of Society and Ideology.* Cambridge, MA: Council on East Asian Studies, Harvard University.

Deyo, Frederic, ed. 1987. *The Political Economy of New Asian Industrialism.* Ithaca, NY: Cornell University Press.

Dirks, Nicholas B., Geoff Eley, and Sherry B. Ortner. 1994. "Introduction." Pp. 3–45 in *Culture/Power/History: A Reader in Contemporary Social Theory*, edited by Nicholas B. Dirks, Geoff Eley, and Sherry B. Ortner. Princeton, NJ: Princeton University Press.

Economic Planning Board. 1960. *Ingu-wa Jutaeck Senseos Bogoso* (The Population and Housing Census Report). Seoul: Economic Planning Board.

———. 1990, 1991, 1995, 2000, 2005. *Hanguk Tongge Weolbo* (*Monthly Statistics of Korea*). Seoul: National Statistical Office, Republic of Korea, Economic Planning Board.

———. 1996. *Economic and Social Changes since the 1960s.* (In Korean.) Seoul: National Statistical Office, Republic of Korea, Economic Planning Board.

El Guindi, Fadwa. 1999. *Veil: Modesty, Privacy, and Resistance.* Oxford, UK: Berg.

Ewha Institute for Women's Theological Studies. 1996. *Gyohoe Yeoseong-gwa Chiyu* (Women of the Church and Healing). Seoul: Ewha Institute for Women's Theological Studies.

———. 1998. *Feminist Theology Review* 2 (August). Seoul: Ewha Institute for Women's Theological Studies.

Foucault, Michel. 1979. *Discipline and Punish: The Birth of the Prison.* New York: Vintage Books.

———. 1980 [1972]. *Power/Knowledge.* New York: Pantheon Books.

———. 1990 [1978]. *The History of Sexuality.* Vol. 1. New York: Vintage Books.

Galanter, Marc. 1978. "The 'Relief Effect': A Sociobiological Model for Neurotic Distress and Large-Group Therapy." *American Journal of Psychiatry* 135: 588–91.

Gallagher, Sally K. 2003. *Evangelical Identity and Gendered Family Life.* New Brunswick, NJ: Rutgers University Press.

———. 2007. "Agency, Resources, and Identity: Lower-Income Women's Experiences in Damascus." *Gender and Society* 21, no. 2: 227–49.

Gallagher, Sally K., and Christian Smith. 1999. "Symbolic Traditionalism and Pragmatic Egalitarianism: Contemporary Evangelicals, Families, and Gender." *Gender & Society* 13, no. 2: 211–33.

Gallup Korea. 1998. *Hanguk Gaesin Gyoin-ui Gyohoe Hwaldong mit Sinang-uisik Josa Bogoso* (Investigation and Report on the Church Activities and Religiosity of Korean Protestants). Volume: Analysis. Seoul: Gallup Korea.

Genovese, Eugene. 1972. *Roll, Jordan, Roll: The World the Slaves Made.* New York: Vintage.

Gerson, Judith M., and Cathy Peiss. 1985. "Boundaries, Negotiation, Consciousness: Reconceptualizing Gender Relations." *Social Problems* 32, no. 4: 317–31.

Gidokgyo Munsa (Christian Publishers). 1993. *Gidokgyo Daeyeongam* (The Christian Yearbook of Korea). Seoul: Gidokgyo Munsa.

Gidokgyo Yeoseong Pyeonghwa Yeonguwon (Christian Research Institute for Women's Peace). 1992. *Pyeonghwa-reul Mandeuneun Yeoseong* (Women Who Create Peace). Vols. 10 and 11. Seoul: Gidokgyo Yeoseong Pyeonghwa Yeonguwon.

Gilkes, Cheryl Townsend. 1985. "'Together and in Harness': Women's Traditions in the Sanctified Church." *Signs* 10, no. 41: 678–99.

Gill, Lesley. 1990. "'Like a veil to cover them': Women and the Pentecostal Movement in La Paz." *American Ethnologist* 17, no. 4: 708–21.

Gilligan, Carol. 1982. *In a Different Voice: Psychological Theory and Women's Development.* Cambridge, MA: Harvard University Press.

Glaser, Barney G., and Anselm L. Strauss. 1967. *The Discovery of Grounded Theory: Strategies for Qualitative Research.* Chicago, IL: Aldine Publishing

Glesne, Corrine, and Alan Peshkin, eds. 1992. *Becoming Qualitative Researchers.* New York: Longman.

Gordon, David F. 1984. "Dying to Self: Self-Control through Self-Abandonment." *Sociological Analysis* 4, no. 1: 41–56.

Gramsci, Antonio. 1992. *Prison Notebooks.* Vol. 1. Edited by Joseph Buttigieg. New York: Columbia University Press.

Grayson, James Huntley. 2006. "A Quarter-Millennium of Christianity in Korea." Pp. 7–28 in *Christianity in Korea*, edited by Robert E. Buswell and Timothy S. Lee. Honolulu, HI: University of Hawai'i Press.

Greenhalgh, Susan. 1985. "Sexual Stratification: The Other Side of 'Growth with Equity' in East Asia." *Population and Development Review* 11: 265–314.

Griffith, R. Marie. 1997. *God's Daughters: Evangelical Women and the Power of Submission.* Berkeley, CA: University of California Press.

Hadaway, Kirk C., Francis M. DuBose, and Stuart A. Wright. 1987. *Home Cell Groups and House Churches.* Nashville, TN: Broadman Press.

Haggard, Stephan. 1990. *Pathways from the Periphery: The Politics of Growth in the Newly Industrializing Countries.* Ithaca, NY: Cornell University Press.

Haggard, Stephan, Richard N. Cooper, Susan Collins, Kim Chungsoo, and Ro Sung-tae. 1994. *Macroeconomic Policy and Adjustment in Korea, 1970–1990.* Cambridge, MA: Harvard University Press.

Han, Chul-Ha. 1995. "Involvement of the Korean Church in the Evangelization of Asia." Pp. 74–95 in *Korean Church Growth Explosion,* edited by Bong Rin Ro and Marlin L. Nelson. Seoul: World of Life Press.

Han, Gil Soo. 1994. *Social Sources of Church Growth: Korean Churches in the Homeland and Overseas.* Lanham, MD: University Press of America.

Han, Woo-keun. 1980 [1970]. *The History of Korea.* Translated by Kyung-shik Lee and edited by Grafton K. Mintz. Honolulu, HI: University of Hawai'i Press.

Hanguk Gidokgyo 100-Junyeon Ginyeom Sa-eop Heopuihoe Yeoseong Bungwa Wiwonhoe (Women's Committee of the Task Force for the Centennial Celebration of Korean Christianity). 1985. *Yeoseong! Kkaeljieoda, Ireonalgieoda, Noraehaljieoda: Hanguk Gidokgyo Yeoseong 100-Nyeonsa* (Women! Awaken, Arise, Sing: One-Hundred-Year History of Korean Christian Women). Seoul: Daehan Gidokgyo Chulpansa.

Hanguk Gidokgyo Sahoe Munje Yeonguso (Christian Institute for the Study of Justice and Development). 1982. *Hanguk Gyohoe 100-Nyeon Jonghap Josa Yeongu* (The Centennial Comprehensive Study of the Korean [Protestant] Church). Seoul: Hanguk Gidokgyo Sahoe Munje Yeonguso.

Hanguk Yeoseong Sinhakhoe (Korean Association of Women's Theology). 1994. *Hanguk Yeoseong-ui Gyungheom* (The Experience of Korean Women). Seoul: Daehan Gidokgyo Seohoe.

Hanguk Yeosinhakja Hyupuihoe (Korean Association of Women Theologians). 1994. *Gyohoe-wa Yeoseong* (Church and Women). Seoul: Yeoseong Sinhaksa.

Haraway, Donna J. 1990. "A Manifesto for Cyborgs: Science, Technology, and Socialist Feminism in the 1980s." Pp. 190–233 in *Feminism/Postmodernism,* edited by Linda J. Nicholson. New York: Routledge.

Hardacre, Helen. 1993. "The Impact of Fundamentalisms on Women, the Family, and Interpersonal Relations." Pp. 129–50 in *Fundamentalisms and Society: Reclaiming the Sciences, the Family, and Education,* edited by Martin E. Marty and R. Scott Appleby. Chicago, IL: University of Chicago Press.

Harding, Susan F. 1987. "Convicted by the Holy Spirit: The Rhetoric of Fundamental Baptist Conversion." *American Ethnologist* 14, no. 1: 167–81.

Hart-Landsberg, Martin. 1993. *The Rush to Development: Economic Change and Political Struggle in South Korea.* New York: Monthly Review Press.

Hartmann, Heidi. 1976. "Capitalism, Patriarchy, and Job Segregation by Sex." *Signs* 1, no. 3: 137–69.

———. 1981. "The Unhappy Marriage of Marxism and Feminism." Pp. 2–31 in *Women and Revolution*, edited by Lydia Sargent. Boston, MA: South End Press.

Hochschild, Arlie. 1990. *The Second Shift.* New York: Avon Books.

Hoffman-Ladd, Valerie. 1986. "The Religious Life of Muslim Women in Contemporary Egypt." Ph.D. diss., University of Chicago.

Hong, Harold S., Ji Yong Won, and Chung Choon Kim, eds. 1966. *Korea Struggles for Christ: Memorial Symposium for the Eightieth Anniversary of Protestantism in Korea.* Seoul: Christian Literature Society of Korea.

Hsiung, Ping-Chun. 1996. "Between Bosses and Workers: The Dilemma of Keen Observer and a Vocal Feminist." Pp. 122–37 in *Feminist Dilemmas in Fieldwork*, edited by Diane L. Wolf. Boulder, CO: Westview Press.

Hunt, Everett N. 1980. *Protestant Pioneers in Korea.* Maryknoll, NY: Orbis.

Hunter, James D. 1983. *American Evangelicalism: Conservative Religion and the Quandary of Modernity.* New Brunswick, NJ: Rutgers University Press.

Hyeondae Sahoe Yeonguso (Institute for the Study of Modern Society). 1982. *Hanguk Gyohoe Seongjang-gwa Sinang Yangtae-e Gwanhan Josa Yeongu* (Investigation into the Growth and Religiosity of the Korean [Protestant] Church). Seoul: Hyeondae Sahoe Yeonguso.

Ingersoll, Julie. 2003. *Evangelical Christian Women: War Stories in the Gender Battles.* New York: New York University Press.

Ireland, Rowan. 1991. *Kingdoms Come: Religion and Politics in Brazil.* Pittsburgh, PA: University of Pittsburgh Press.

Isaacman, Allen. 1990. "Peasants and Rural Social Protest in Africa." *African Studies Review* 33, no. 2: 1–120.

Janelli, Roger L., and Dawnhee Yim. 1993. *Making Capitalism: The Social and Cultural Construction of a South Korean Conglomerate.* Stanford, CA: Stanford University Press.

Joseph, Suad. 1993. "Gender and Relationality among Arab Families in Lebanon." *Feminist Studies* 19, no. 3: 465–86.

Kandiyoti, Deniz. 1987. "Emancipated but Unliberated? Reflections on the Turkish Case." *Feminist Studies* 13, no. 2: 317–38.

———. 1988. "Bargaining with Patriarchy." *Gender & Society* 2, no. 3: 274–90.

Kang, Nam-soon. 1995. "Hanguk Gyohoe-neun Pyeongdeung Gongdongche inga?" (Is the Korean Church an Equal Community?). *Hanguk Yeoseong Sinhak* 24 (Winter): 62–73.

———. 1996. "Christianity in Korea and Women." Pp.50–59 in *Women of Korea: A History from Ancient Times to 1945.* Seoul: Asian Center for Women's Studies, Ewha Womans University.

Kaufman, Debra. 1989. "Patriarchal Women: A Case Study of Newly Orthodox Jewish Women." *Symbolic Interaction* 12, no. 2: 299–314.

Kendall, Laurel, ed. 2002. *Under Construction: The Gendering of Modernity, Class, and Consumption in the Republic of Korea.* Honolulu, HI: University of Hawai'i Press.

Kendall, Laurel, and Mark Peterson, eds. 1983. *Korean Women: View from the Inner Room.* Cushing, ME: East Rock Press.

Kim, Ai Ra. 1996. *Women Struggling for a New Life: On the Role of Religion in the Cultural Passage from Korea to America.* Albany, NY: State University of New York Press.

Kim, Andrew. 2000. "Korean Religious Culture and Its Affinity to Christianity: The Rise of Protestant Christianity in South Korea." *Sociology of Religion* 61, no. 2: 117–34.

Kim, Byong-Suh. 1985. "The Explosive Growth of the Korean Churches Today: A Sociological Analysis," *International Review of Mission* 74 (January): 61–74.

Kim, Dongno. 1990. "The Transformation of Familism in Modern Korean Society: From Cooperation to Competition." *International Sociology* 5, no. 4: 409–25.

Kim, Eun Mee. 1997. *Big Business, Strong State: Collusion and Conflict in South Korean Development, 1960–1990.* Albany, NY: State University of New York Press.

Kim, Illsoo. 1985. "Organizational Patterns of Korean-American Methodist Churches: Denominationalism and Personal Community." Pp. 228–36 in *Rethinking Methodist History*, edited by Russell Richey and Kenneth Rowe. Nashville, TN: Kingswood Books.

Kim, John T. 1996. *Protestant Church Growth in Korea.* Belleville, Ontario, Canada: Essence Publishing.

Kim, Myung-Hye. 1992. "Late Industrialization and Women's Work in Urban South Korea: An Ethnographic Study of Upper-Middle-Class Families." *City & Society* 6, no. 2: 156–73.

Kim, Seung Kyung. 1997. *Class Struggle or Family Struggle? Lives of Women Factory Workers in South Korea.* New York: Cambridge University Press.

Kim, Young Hee, and Jeong Shin Han. 1996. "Korean Women's Consciousness of Sex Roles, Marriage, and Child-Rearing." Pp. 149–72 in *Asian Women.* Vol. 2. Seoul: Research Center for Asian Women, Sookmyung Women's University.

Kim, Young Lan, and Kyung Ock Chun. 1996. "A Study of Political and Social Consciousness of Korean Women." Pp. 117–48 in *Asian Women.* Vol. 2. Seoul: Research Center for Asian Women, Sookmyung Women's University.

Kim, Yung-Chung. 1996. "Women of Korea: A Historical Overview." Pp. 1–17 in *Women of Korea: A History from Ancient Times to 1945*. Seoul: Asian Center for Women's Studies, Ewha Womans University.

Klatch, Rebecca. 1988. "The Methodological Problems of Studying a Politically Resistant Community." Pp. 73–88 in *Studies in Qualitative Methdology*, edited by Robert G. Burgess. Vol 1. London: JAI Press.

Kondo, Dorinne K. 1986. "Dissolution and Reconstitution of Self: Implications for Anthropological Epistemology." *Cultural Anthropology* 1, no. 1: 74–88.

———. 1990. *Crafting Selves: Power, Gender, and Discourses of Identity in a Japanese Workplace*. Chicago, IL: University of Chicago Press.

Koo, Hagen. 1991. "Middle Classes, Democratization, and Class Formation: The Case of South Korea." *Theory and Society* 20, no. 4: 485–509.

Korea Institute for Social Information and Research. 1995. *Women in Korea: A Statistical Profile*. Seoul: Korea Institute for Social Information and Research.

Korean Women's Development Institute (KWDI). 1997, 2007. *Statistical Handbook: Women in Korea*. Seoul: Korean Women's Development Institute.

Kumazawa, Makoto. 1996. *Portraits of the Japanese Workplace*. Boulder, CO; Westview Press.

Kung, Lydia. 1994. *Factory Women in Taiwan*. New York: Columbia University Press.

Lalive D'Epinay, Christian. 1968. *El Refugio de las Masas*. Santiago de Chile: Editorial del Pacifico. Published in English in London by Lutterworth in 1979.

Lebra, Takie S. 1986. "The Confucian Gender Role and Personal Fulfillment for Japanese Women." Pp. 221–42 in *The Psycho-Cultural Dynamics of the Confucian Family: Past and Present*, edited by Walter H. Slote. Seoul: International Cultural Society of Korea.

Lee, Chang Sik. 1966. "Rethinking Some Aspects of Devotional Life." Pp. 166–76 in *Korea Struggles for Christ: Memorial Symposium for the Eightieth Anniversary of Protestantism in Korea*, edited by Harold S. Hong, Ji Yong Won, and Chung Choon Kim. Seoul: Christian Literature Society of Korea.

Lee, Dong-won. 1986. "The Changes in the Korean Family and Women." Pp. 230–54 in *Challenges for Women: Women's Studies in Korea*, edited by Sei-wha Chung and translated by Shin Chang-hyun et al. Seoul: Ewha Womans University Press.

Lee, Hyo-Chae, and Kim Chu-Suk. 1977. "The Status of Korean Women Today." Pp. 147–56 in *Virtues in Conflict: Tradition and the Korean Woman Today*, edited by Sandra Mattielli. Seoul: Royal Asiatic Society, Korea Branch.

Lee, Jae Bum. 1986. "Pentecostal Distinctives and Korean Protestant Church Growth." Ph.D. diss., Fuller Theological Seminary.

Lee, Kwang-Kyu. 1986. "Confucian Tradition in the Contemporary Korean Family." Pp. 3–18 in *The Psycho-Cultural Dynamics of the Confucian Family: Past and Present*, edited by Walter H. Slote. Seoul: International Cultural Society of Korea.

Lee, Sook-in. 1995. "Yugyo Yulli-wa Hanguk Yeoseong" (Confucian Ethic in the Korean Woman's Life). *Feminist Theology Review* 1 (February): 93–118.

Lee, Timothy. 1996. "Born Again in Korea: The Rise and Character of Revivalism in (South) Korea, 1885–1988." Ph.D. diss., University of Chicago.

———. 2006. "Beleaguered Success: Korean Evangelicalism in the Last Decade of the 20th Century." Pp. 330–50 in *Christianity in Korea*, edited by Robert E. Buswell, Jr. and Timothy S. Lee. Honolulu, HI: University of Hawai'i Press.

Lee, Won Gue. 1994. *Hanguk Gyohoe-ui Hyungsil-gwa Jeonmang*. (The Reality and Prospects of the Korean Church). Seoul: Seongseo Yeongusa.

Lee, Woo-jeong. 1985. *Hanguk Gidokgyo Yeoseong Baeknyeon-ui Baljachwi*. (Korean Christian Women in the Last One Hundred Years). Seoul: Minjungsa.

Lett, Denise. 1998. *In Pursuit of Status: The Making of South Korea's "New" Urban Middle Class*. Cambridge, MA: Harvard University Asia Center.

Lie, John. 1998. *Han Unbound: The Political Economy of South Korea*. Stanford, CA: Stanford University Press.

Lofland, John A. 1966. *Doomsday Cult*. New York: Irvington.

Lofland, John A., and Lyn Lofland. 1995. *Analyzing Social Settings: A Guide to Qualitative Observation and Analysis*. Belmont, CA: Wadsworth.

Lofland, John, and Rodney Stark. 1965. "Becoming a World-Saver." *American Sociological Review* 30: 862–75.

MacLeod, Arlene Elowe. 1991. *Accommodating Protest: Working Women, the New Veiling, and Change in Cairo*. New York: Columbia University Press.

———. 1992. "Hegemonic Relations and Gender Resistance: The New Veiling as Accommodating Protest in Cairo." *Signs* 17, no. 3: 533–57.

Mahmood, Saba. 2001. "Feminist Theory, Embodiment, and the Docile Agent: Some Reflections on the Egyptian Islamic Revival." *Cultural Anthropology* 16, no. 2: 202–36.

———. 2004. *Politics of Piety: Islamic Revival and the Feminist Subject*. Princeton, NJ: Princeton University Press.

Maldonado, Jorge E. 1993. "Building 'Fundamentalism' from the Family in Latin America." Pp. 214–39 in *Fundamentalisms and Society: Reclaiming the Sciences, the Family, and Education*, edited by Martin E. Marty and R. Scott Appleby. Chicago, IL: University of Chicago Press.

Manning, Christel. 1999. *God Gave Us the Right: Conservative Catholic, Evangelical Protestant, and Orthodox Jewish Women Grapple with Feminism*. New Brunswick, NJ: Rutgers University Press.

Mariz, Cecilia Loreto. 1994. *Coping with Poverty: Pentecostals and Christian Base Communities in Brazil.* Philadelphia, PA: Temple University Press.

Martin, David. 1990. *Tongues of Fire: The Explosion of Protestantism in Latin America.* New Haven, CT: Yale University Press.

McGuire, Meredith B. 1982. *Pentecostal Catholics: Power, Charisma, and Order in a Religious Movement.* Philadelphia, PA: Temple University Press.

———. 1983. "Discovering Religious Power." *Sociological Analysis* 44, no. 1: 1–10.

Mernissi, Fatima. 1987 (revised edition). *Beyond the Veil: Male-Female Dynamics in Modern Muslim Society.* Bloomington, IN: Indiana University Press.

Min, Kyong-bae. 2005 [1972]. *A History of Christian Churches in Korea.* Seoul: Yonsei University Press.

Min, Pyong Gap. 2008. "Severe Underrepresentation of Women in Church Leadership in the Korean Immigrant Community in the United States." *Journal for the Scientific Study of Religion* 47, no. 2: 225–41.

Min, Seong-gil. 1989. "Hwatbyeong-ui Gaenyeom-e daehan Yeongu" (Research about the Concept of the Fire Disease). *Singyeong Jeongsin Uihak* 28, no. 4: 604–16.

Ministry of Labor, Republic of Korea. 1989. *Yeoseong-gwa Chieop* (Women and Employment). Seoul: Ministry of Labor.

Moffett, Samuel H. 1962. *The Christians of Korea.* New York: Friendship Press.

Mohanty, Chandra. 1991. "Under Western Eyes: Feminist Scholarship and Colonial Discourses." Pp. 51–80 in *Third World Women and the Politics of Feminism,* edited by Chandra Mohanty, Ann Russo, and Lourdes Torres. Bloomington, IN: Indiana University Press.

Mol, Hans. 1976. *Identity and the Sacred: A Sketch for a New Social-Scientific Theory of Religion.* New York: Free Press.

Moon, Okpyo. 1990. "Urban Middle Class Wives in Contemporary Korea: Their Roles, Responsibilities and Dilemma." *Korea Journal* 30, no. 11: 30–43.

Moon, Seungsook. 2002. "Carving out Space: Civil Society and the Women's Movement in South Korea." *Journal of Asian Studies* 61, no. 2: 473–500.

———. 2005. *Militarized Modernity and Gendered Citizenship in South Korea.* Durham, NC: Duke University Press.

Nelson, Laura C. 2000. *Measured Excess: Status, Gender, and Consumer Nationalism in South Korea.* New York: Columbia University Press.

Nicholson, Linda. 1995. "Interpreting Gender." Pp. 39–67 in *Social Postmodernism: Beyond Identity Politics,* edited by Linda Nicholson and Steven Seidman. Cambridge, UK: Cambridge University Press.

Nida, Eugene A. 1958. "The Relationship of Social Structure to the Problem of Evangelism in Latin America." *Practical Anthropology* 5, no. 3: 101–23.

Oh, Pyeng-Seh. 1995. "Keeping the Faith Pure." Pp. 170–93 in *Korean Church Growth Explosion*, edited by Bong Rin Ro and Marlin L. Nelson. Seoul: World of Life Press.

Ong, Aihwa. 1987. *Spirits of Resistance and Capitalist Discipline: Factory Women in Malaysia*. Albany, NY: State University of New York Press.

———. 1988. "Colonialism and Modernity: Feminist Re-Presentations of Women in Non-Western Societies." *Inscriptions* 3/4: 79–93.

Ortner, Sherry B. 1984. "Theory in Anthropology since the Sixties." *Comparative Studies in Society and History* 26, no. 1 (January): 126–66.

Palley, Marian Lief. 1990. "Women's Status in South Korea: Tradition and Change." *Asian Survey* 30 (December): 1136–53.

Papanek, Hanna. 1979. "Family Status Production: The 'Work' and 'Non-Work' of Women." *Signs* 4: 775–81.

Park, Chung-Shin. 2003. *Protestantism and Politics in Korea*. Seattle, WA: University of Washington Press.

Park, Hyung-Kyu. 1985. "The Search for Self-Identity and Liberation." *International Review of Mission* 74 (January): 51–60.

Park, Sung-Ja. 1993. "Hanguk Gyohoe Yeoseong-ui Singang Hyeongtae-e Daehan Yeoseong Shinhak-jeok Yeongu" ("A Feminist Theological Study of the Faith Patterns of Korea Church Women: Emphasis on the Religious Psychopathological Phenomenon"). Ph.D. diss., Ewha Womans University.

Patai, Daphne. 1991. "U.S. Academics and Third World Women: Is Ethical Research Possible?" Pp. 137–53 in *Women's Words: The Feminist Practice of Oral History*, edited by Sherna Berger Gluck and Daphne Patai. New York: Routledge.

Peshkin, Alan. 1984. "Odd Man Out: The Participant Observer in an Absolutist Setting." *Sociology of Education* 57, no. 4: 254–64.

Pye, Lucian W. 1985. *Asian Power and Politics: The Cultural Dimensions of Authority*. Cambridge, MA: Harvard University Press.

Rambo, Lewis R. 1992. "The Psychology of Conversion." Pp.159–77 in *Handbook of Religious Conversion*, edited by H. Newton Malony and Samuel Southard. Birmingham, AL: Religious Education Press.

Read, David H. C. 1992. "The Evangelical Protestant Understanding of Conversion." Pp. 137–46 in *Handbook of Religious Conversion*, edited by H. Newton Malony and Samuel Southard. Birmingham, AL: Religious Education Press.

Reina, Ruben E., and Norman B. Schwartz. 1974. "The Structural Context of Religious Conversion in Peten Guatemala: Status, Community, and Multicommunity." *American Ethnologist* 1, no. 1 (February): 157–91.

Research Center for Women's Concerns, Yonsei University. 1995. *Yonsei Journal of Women's Studies*. Vol 1. Seoul: Research Center for Women's Concerns, Yonsei University.

————. 1996. *Yeoseong, Namseong, Daejung Munhwa* (Women, Men, and Popular Culture). Seoul: Research Center for Women's Concerns, Yonsei University.

Rhee, Jong Sung. 1966. "Types of Church Leaders Today." Pp. 133–47 in *Korea Struggles for Christ: Memorial Symposium for the Eightieth Anniversary of Protestantism in Korea*, edited by Harold S. Hong, Ji Yong Won, and Chung Choon Kim. Seoul: Christian Literature Society of Korea.

Rhi, Bou-yong. 1986. "Confucianism and Mental Health in Korea." Pp. 249–76 in *The Psycho-Cultural Dynamics of the Confucian Family: Past and Present*, edited by Walter H. Slote. Seoul: International Cultural Society of Korea.

Richardson, James T. 1985. "The Active vs. Passive Convert: Paradigm Conflict in Conversion/Recruitment Research." *Journal for the Scientific Study of Religion* 24, no. 2: 119–236.

————. 1991. "Experiencing Research on New Religions and Cults: Practical and Ethical Considerations." Pp. 62–71 in *Experiencing Fieldwork: An Inside View of Qualitative Research*, edited by William B. Shaffir and Robert A. Stebbins. Newbury Park, CA: Sage Publications.

Riesebrodt, Martin. 1993. *Pious Passion: The Emergence of Modern Fundamentalism in the United States and Iran*. Berkeley, CA: University of California Press.

Riesebrodt, Martin, and Kelly H. Chong. 1999. "Fundamentalisms and Patriarchal Gender Politics." *Journal of Women's History* 10, no. 4: 55–77.

Risman, Barbara J. 1998. *Gender Vertigo: American Families in Transition*. New Haven, CT: Yale University Press.

Ro, Bong Rin. 1995. "The Korean Church: God's Chosen People for Evangelism." Pp. 11–44 in *Korean Church Growth Explosion*, edited by Bong Rin Ro and Marlin L. Nelson. Seoul: World of Life Press.

Ro, Bong Rin, and Marlin L. Nelson, eds. 1995. *Korean Church Growth Explosion*. Seoul: World of Life Press.

Robbins, Thomas, Dick Anthony, and Thomas E. Curtis. 1973. "The Limits of Symbolic Realism: Problems of Empathic Field Observation in a Sectarian Context." *Journal for the Scientific Study of Religion* 12, no. 3: 259–71.

Roberts, Bryan. 1968. "Protestant Groups and Coping with Urban Life in Guatemala City." *American Journal of Sociology* 73, no. 6: 753–67.

Rofel, Lisa. 1999. *Other Modernities: Gendered Yearnings in China after Socialism*. Berkeley, CA: Universisty of California Press.

Rosaldo, Renato. 1993 [1989]. *Culture and Truth: The Remaking of Social Analysis*. Boston, MA: Beacon Press.

Rose, Susan. 1987. "Women Warriors: The Negotiation of Gender in a Charismatic Community." *Sociological Analysis* 48, no. 3: 245–58.

Rubin, Jeffrey W. 1996. "Defining Resistance: Contested Interpretations of Everyday Acts." *Studies in Law, Politics and Society* 15: 237–60.

Rugh, Andrea B. 1993. "Reshaping Personal Relations in Egypt." Pp. 151–80 in *Fundamentalisms and Society: Reclaiming the Sciences, the Family, and Education*, edited by Martin Marty and R. Scott Appleby. Chicago, IL: University of Chicago Press.

Ryu, Dong-Shik. 1982. "Hanguk Gyohoe-wa Seongryeong Undong" ("The Korean Church and the Pentecostal Movement"). Pp. 9–21 in *Hanguk Gyohoe Seongryeong Undong-ui Hyeonsang-gwa Gujo* (A Study on the Pentecostal Movement in Korea). Seoul: Korea Christian Academy.

Salaff, Janet W. 1995. *Working Daughters of Hong Kong.* New York: Columbia University Press.

Sarbin, Theodore R., and Nathan Adler. 1970. "Self-Reconstitution Process: A Preliminary Report." *Psychoanalytic Review* 57, no. 4: 599–616.

Schlafly, Phyllis. 1977. *The Power of the Positive Woman.* New York: Jove Publications.

Scott, James C. 1985. *Weapons of the Weak.* New Haven, CT: Yale University Press.

———. 1986. "Everyday Forms of Resistance." *Journal of Peasant Studies* 13, no. 2: 5–35.

Scroggs, James R., and William G. Douglas. 1967. "Issues in the Psychology of Religious Conversion." *Journal of Religion and Health* 6: 204–16.

Sewell, William H., Jr. 1992. "A Theory of Structure: Duality, Agency, and Transformation." *American Journal of Sociology* 98, no. 1: 1–29.

Sexton, James, D. 1978. "Protestantism and Modernization in Two Guatemalan Towns." *American Ethnologist* 5, no. 5: 280–302.

Shaffir, William B. 1991. "Managing a Convincing Self-Presentation." Pp. 72–81 in *Experiencing Fieldwork: An Inside View of Qualitative Research*, edited by William B. Shaffir and Robert A. Stebbins. Newbury Park, CA: Sage Publications.

Simmonds, Robert B. 1977. "Conversion or Addiction: Consequence of Joining a Jesus Movement Group." *American Behavioral Scientist* 20, no. 6: 909–24.

Smilde, David. 1997. "The Fundamental Unity of the Conservative and Revolutionary Tendencies in Venezuelan Evangelicalism: The Case of Conjugal Relations." *Religion* 27, no. 4: 343–59.

———. 2005. "A Qualitative Comparative Analysis of Conversion to Venezuelan Evangelicalism: How Networks Matter." *American Journal of Sociology* 111, no. 3: 757–96.

Smith, Dorothy D. 1992. "Sociology from Women's Experience: A Reaffirmation." *Sociological Theory* 10, no. 1: 89–98.

Snow, David A., and Richard Machalek. 1984. "The Sociology of Conversion." *Annual Review of Sociology* 10: 167–90.

Song, Kon-Ho. 1985. "A History of the Christian Movement in Korea." *International Review of Mission* 74 (January): 20–37.

Stacey, Judith. 1990. *Brave New Families: Stories of Domestic Upheaval in Late 20th Century America.* New York: Basic Books.

Stark, Rodney, and William Sims Bainbridge. 1980. "Networks of Faith: Interpersonal Bonds and Recruitment to Cults and Sects." *American Journal of Sociology* 85, no. 6: 1376–95.

Stoll, David. 1990. *Is Latin America Turning Protestant?* Berkeley, CA: University of California Press.

Straus, Roger A. 1979. "Religious Conversion as a Personal and Collective Accomplishment." *Sociological Analysis* 40, no. 2: 158–65.

Suh, David Kwang-Sun. 1982. "Hanguk Gyohoe Seongryeong Undong-gwa Buheung Undong-ui Sinhak-jeok Ihae" ("The Understanding of the Pentecostal and Evangelical Movement of the Korean Church from a Theological Perspective"). Pp. 23–99 in *Hanguk Gyohoe Seongryeong Undong-ui Hyeonsang-gwa Gujo* (A Study on the Pentecostal Movement in Korea). Seoul: Korea Christian Academy.

———. 1985. "American Missionaries and a Hundred Years of Korean Protestantism." *International Review of Mission* 74 (January): 6–19.

Tsuya, Noriko O., and Choe Minja Kim. 1991. "Changes in Intrafamilial Relationships and the Role of Women in Japan and Korea." *NUPRI Research Paper Series*, no. 58.

Turner, Victor. 1974. *Dramas, Fields, and Metaphors.* Ithaca, NY: Cornell University Press.

Ullman, Chana. 1982. "Cognitive and Emotional Antecedents of Religious Conversion." *Journal of Personality and Social Psychology* 43, no. 1: 183–92.

United Nations Development Program (UNDP). 1995. *The Human Development Report.* New York: Oxford University Press.

Van Maanen, John. 1988. *Tales of the Field: On Writing Ethnography.* Chicago, IL: University of Chicago Press.

Vaughan, John N. 1984. *The World's Twenty Largest Churches.* Grand Rapids, MI: Jordan.

Wagner, C. Peter. "The Greatest Church Growth Is Beyond Our Shores." *Christianity Today* (18 May 1984): 25–31.

Wasserfall, Rahel. 1993. "Reflexivity, Feminism, and Difference." *Qualitative Sociology* 16, no. 1: 23–41.

Westley, Frances R. 1977. "Searching for Surrender: A Catholic Charismatic Renewal Group's Attempt to Become Glossolalic." *American Behavioral Scientist* 20, no. 6: 925–40.

Willems, Emilio. 1967. *Followers of the New Faith: Culture Change and the Rise of Protestantism in Brazil and Chile.* Nashville, TN: Vanderbilt University Press.

Williams, John Alden. 1980. "Veiling in Egypt as a Political and Social Phenomenon." Pp. 71–86 in *Islam and Development: Religion and Sociopolitical Change,* edited by John L. Esposito. Syracuse, NY: Syracuse University Press.

Williams, Raymond. 1973. "Base and Superstructure in Marxist Cultural Theory." *New Left Review* 82 (November/December): 3–16.

Willis, Paul. 1977. *Learning to Labor: How Working Class Kids Get Working Class Jobs.* New York: Columbia University Press.

Wolf, Margery. 1972. *Women and Family in Rural Taiwan.* Stanford, CA: Stanford University Press.

Woo-Cumings, Meredith. 1991. *Race to the Swift: State and Finance in Korean Industrialization.* New York: Columbia University Press.

World Bank. 1982. *World Development Report.* Washington, DC: World Bank.

Yang, Mi-Gang. 1991. "Chogi Jeondobuin-ui Sinang-gwa Yeokhwal-e Gwanhan Yeongu." (Research on the Beliefs and Role of Early Bible Women). *Pyeonghwa-reul Mandeuneun Yeoseong* 10 (December): 73–82.

———. 1992. "1930-Nyeondae-ui Gidokgyo Yeoseong Munje-ui Insikgwa Yeoseong Ansu Undong." (The Understanding of the Problems of the Female Christians of the 1930s and the Movement for Female Ordination). *Pyeonghwa-reul Mandeuneun Yeoseong* 13 (September): 60–71.

Yeoseong Hanguk Sahoe Yeonguhoe (Women's Association for Korean Society Research). 1994. *Yeoseong-gwa Hanguk Sahoe* (Women and Korean Society). Seoul: Sahoe Munhwa Yeonguso.

Yi, Eunhee. 1993. "From Gentry to the Middle Class: The Transformation of Family, Community, and Gender in Korea." Ph.D. diss., University of Chicago.

Yi, Hyo-Jae. 1985a. "Christian Mission and the Liberation of Korean Women." *International Review of Mission* 74 (January): 93–102.

———. 1985b. "Hanguk Gyohoe Yeoseong 100-Nyeonsa: Gaegwan-gwa Jeonmang." (100-Year History of the Women of the Korean Church: Outline and Prospects). Pp. 13–72 in *Yeoseong! Kkaeljieoda, Ireonalgieoda, Noraehaljieoda: Hanguk Gidokgyo Yeoseong 100-Nyeonsa* (Women! Awaken, Arise, Sing: 100-Year History of Korean Christian Women). Seoul: Daehan Gidokgyo Chulpansa.

———. 1996. "Hanguk Gabujangje-wa Yeoseong" (Korean Confucian System and Women). *Yeoseong-gwa Sahoe* 7: 160–76.

Yi, Man-Yŏl. 1991. *Hanguk Gidokyo-wa Minjok Uisik: Hanguk Guidokyosa Yeongu Nonmun* (Korean Christianity and National Consciousness: A Study of Korean Christian History). Seoul: Jisik Saneopsa.

Yoo, Boo-Woong. 1988. *Korean Pentecostalism: Its History and Theology.* Frankfurt am Main: Verlag Peter Lang.

Yoon, Moon-Ja. 1992. "Yeoseong Mokhoeja-ui Hyunjang iyagi" (Women Pastors' Stories from the Field). *Pyeonghwa-reul Mandeuneun Yeoseong* 11 (March): 31–35.

Yu, Eui-Young. 1987. "Women in Traditional and Modern Korea." Pp. 15–28 in *Korean Women in Transition: At Home and Abroad,* edited by Eui-Young Yu and Earl H. Phillips. Los Angeles, CA: Center for Korean-American and Korean Studies, California State University, Los Angeles.

Zaretski, Eli. 1973. *Capitalism, the Family, and Personal Life.* New York: Harper & Row.

Index

Abu-Lughod, Lila, 11
African Americans, 191
Agency, 10, 11, 175, 176–77
Aggressive women, 142–43, 144–45
Allen, Horace N., 17, 205*n1*
Amsden, Alice H., 54
Ancestor worship, 59, 78, 205–6*n2*, 220*n15*
Arrogance, 140, 144–45, 165, 167
Assemblies of God, 25, 31
Authoritarianism: in church culture, 29–30, 236*n2*; political, 54, 57, 219*n9*
Autonomy: of church women, 9, 107, 109, 133; of married women, 76, 77, 78, 172. *See also* Empowerment

Baptist churches: denominational schisms, 21; large, 2, 204*n3*; membership numbers, 25
Bible: interpretations supporting subordination of women, 113, 231*n7*; translations, 18, 206*n7*, 215–16*n49*
Bible study: groups, 29, 120–21, 132, 215–16*n49*; practice, 28, 29, 132

Bible women (*jeondo buin*), 19
Brazil, Pentecostal women in, 162
Brusco, Elizabeth E., 7, 162
Buddhism, 58, 59, 204*n2*, 214*n44*
Burdick, John, 162

Calvinism, 25
Capitalism, patriarchy and, 67–71, 222*n27*, 223*n30*. *See also* Economic development
Catholics: missionaries, 15, 205–6*n2*; persecution of, 205–6*n2*; in South Korea, 2
Cell groups: activities, 119–20; attendance by non-church members, 230*n18*, 231*n8*; conversion opportunities, 97; efforts to reform women, 136, 138–39, 165, 166–67; functions, 29; meetings, 29, 37, 43–44, 97–99; mutual assistance of members, 120; opportunities for emotional release, 97–99; origins, 216*n50*; prayers, 99; social interactions, 29, 118–19; at South River Church, 36, 98–99, 100, 118–20, 166–67; teachings on

gender and family relations, 137,
140–41; women's, 98–99
Cell leaders: educational levels, 126;
female, 31, 167–68; functions, 130;
responses to researcher, 43–44;
roles, 99; self-empowerment, 130;
training, 132; on women's obedience, 143–44
Chang, Kyung-sup, 67
Charismatic movements, 26–27,
213*nn*39–40, 213–14*n*42. *See also*
Pentecostals
Children: daughters, 80; education of,
78–79, 139, 236*n*6; fathers and, 103;
number in families, 63; obedience
by, 145–46; parental investment,
80; sons, 59, 60, 62, 80, 179. *See
also* Motherhood
Cho, Haejoang, 62, 180
Cho Yonggi, 212–13*n*38
Christians: class membership, 35–36;
liberal groups and denominations,
31, 32, 35, 211*n*31; number in South
Korea, 2; repression in North
Korea, 20, 24; resistance to Japanese colonial government, 19–20,
21, 208*n*16; in South Korean governments, 23–24, 210*n*26. *See
also* Catholics; Evangelicalism;
Missionaries; Protestants
Chun Doo Hwan, 56
Churches: authoritarian leadership,
29–30, 236*n*2; as disciplinary
agents, 164, 166–68, 190; double
roles, 187; gender hierarchy, 29–
30, 31–32; inequality within, 124,
125–26; large, 2, 22, 204*n*3, 210*n*23,
215*n*47; lay leaders, 30, 94, 113–15,
125, 216*n*51; patriarchal leadership,
29–30, 113; as performative spaces,

121–26; self-governance, 30–31;
small, 124–25; social functions, 23;
in urban areas, 1, 14, 23. *See also*
Evangelicalism; North River
Church; Protestant denominations; South River Church
Church involvement of women: contradictions in, 186–87, 191–92;
deacons, 31, 110–12, 114–15, 126,
127–29; domestic work, 114–16;
elders, 94, 113–14; evangelism, 19,
111, 207–8*n*14; expectations, 115,
116, 122; history, 19; importance, 3,
111–12; individual variations, 192;
initial, 85; institutional maintenance tasks, 115–16; institutional
roles, 112–16; internal transformation as result, 126–31; as learning
opportunity, 131–32; motivations,
8–9, 111, 117–21, 131–32, 189, 193;
official leadership positions, 113–15;
opportunities for self-expression,
126–31, 193; paradox of, 3–4, 8,
171–76, 187, 190; as pastors, 31, 113,
230*n*2; prayer practice, 83; recognition and rewards as incentives,
121–26, 189; recognition related
to economic class, 125–26; as
resistance, 7, 133, 187; as response
to domestic dilemmas, 8–9, 51, 52,
94–95, 187, 189, 191–92; self-
fulfillment through, 129, 189; in
small churches, 124–25; social
interactions, 117–21, 193; status
rewards, 116, 122–25; time spent,
115, 118. *See also* Bible study; Cell
groups
Clark, Donald N., 30–31
Classes: dominant, 186; elites, 16, 17,
19, 61; identification with middle

class, 35; in South Korea, 35–36, 216–17*n*55; working, 35, 36. *See also* Lower-class women; Middle-class women

Clergy. *see* Pastors

Colombia, Pentecostals in, 7, 162

Colonialism. *see* Japanese occupation

Community of church women, 117–21, 193

Confidence. *see* Self-confidence

Confucianism: in corporate cultures, 57, 219*n*11; delegitimization in Korea, 16, 57; female roles in family, 51, 59, 60–62, 143, 179; feminine ideals, 138, 140; filial piety, 59, 61, 62, 67; gender hierarchy, 32, 51, 59, 67; human relationship principles, 29–30, 58–59, 136–37, 182, 220*n*14; ideal father, 103; importance of learning, 78–79; influence on Korean Protestantism, 29–30, 113, 194, 212*n*33; Neo-, 58–59, 60–62, 66–73, 219–20*n*13; obedience as virtue, 145; tensions with modernity, 57, 58, 136–37

Consent: ideological, 177; to oppression, 8, 9–10, 176–77; to patriarchy, 9–10, 11, 137, 171–72, 176–85, 194–96

Conservative religions. *see* Evangelicalism; Traditionalist religions

Conversions: acceptance of church's gender ideology, 162; activist view, 85, 87, 227*n*4, 230*n*19; adult, 84, 85–91; control theory, 229*n*16; crises as motivation, 86, 87–88, 229*n*16; death of self, 166, 234*n*16; experimentation with, 87; healing experiences, 103, 104, 106, 110; by missionaries, 18, 207*n*9, 207*n*12;

motivations, 8–9, 52; narratives, 49–52, 85–86, 87, 88–91, 105; opening up of self, 95–99; pathways to, 84–95; physical experiences, 104; physical illnesses preceding, 88–91; as rebirth, 101, 104–5, 172–73; relief effect, 101; responses to domestic dilemmas, 85–98; self-transformation, 95, 99–100, 104–5; social factors, 86, 229*n*16; social influence theory, 229*n*16; social processes, 97, 229*n*16; strain theory, 229*n*16; subculture theory, 229*n*16; sudden or gradual, 227–28*n*7; as surrender, 100–104, 105, 174–75; testimonies, 100; theories, 229*n*16; worldview changes, 99–100

Daughters-in-law. *see* Married women; Mothers-in-law

Deacons (*jipsa*): appointments, 30, 114, 125, 126; exhorting, 89–90, 114, 116, 124; female, 31, 110–12, 114–15, 126, 127–29; male, 114, 115, 125; motivations, 122; responsibilities, 114–15, 116

Death of self, 166–68, 234*n*16

Deliverance. *see* Liberation

Democracy, 56, 57, 219*n*9

Deuchler, Martina, 62

Disciplinary agents, churches as, 164, 166–68, 190

Discrimination, gender-based, 68–69, 199, 223*n*30, 224*n*36

Division of labor, 59, 69, 121. *See also* Domestic labor; Gender roles

Divorce, 93, 198, 221*n*23, 232–33*n*6

Domestic abuse, 155, 232–33*n*6

Domesticating programs, 72, 73

Domestic dilemmas: church involvement as response to, 8–9, 51,
52, 94–95, 187, 189, 191–92; conflicts between expectations and
reality, 74, 77, 80, 91; conflicts
with husbands, 77–78, 91–92, 99;
conflicts with mothers-in-law, 78,
86, 89, 91–92, 99; conversions as
response to, 85–98; coping strategies, 107–9; emotional deprivation, 106; emotional responses,
91–94; improvements after conversion, 107; lack of outlets, 93–
94, 96; persistence in contemporary South Korea, 199; physical
illnesses related to, 90–91; socio-
cultural factors, 52–53; sources,
74–80; submission as strategy for
negotiation, 6, 149–58, 162, 165–
66; women blamed for conflicts,
136–41, 164–65
Domesticity: changing expectations
of women, 74–76, 77, 80, 91;
policies encouraging, 68–73; redomestication of women, 172, 187,
189; valued by society, 62, 72–73,
75–76, 143, 179–80, 182–83;
women's preferences for role, 70,
182; workplace roles, 69. *See also*
Housewives
Domestic labor: of church women,
114–16; of daughters-in-law, 60,
78, 89, 92, 180, 228*n*11; improvement in conditions, 75; of middle-
class women, 70, 77, 182; non-
traditional activities, 76–77
Donghap (Presbyterian Church of
Korea), 31, 209*n*20
Dying of self, 166–68, 234*n*16

Economic crisis (1997), 56
Economic development: compressed,
53–56, 57; export-oriented growth,
54–55, 65, 68, 218*n*3; five-year
plans, 55, 217–18*n*2; GDP growth,
55–56; industrialization, 22, 54, 57;
Korean "miracle," 22–23, 53–56,
57; rapid, 57; South Korean policies, 54–56. *See also* Work force
Economy of gratitude, 159–60
Education: of children, 78–79, 139,
236*n*6; costs, 236*n*6; enrollments,
64, 221*n*21; higher, 64–65, 71, 79,
91, 112, 224*nn*33–34; under Japanese, 64, 112, 221*n*21; Korean
system, 64; mission schools, 16,
64, 84, 112, 206*n*5; opportunities
in churches, 131–32; public, 64;
relationship to women's employment, 71; of women, 64, 71, 112–13,
221*n*21
Educational attainment: of Christians, 36; of men, 226*n*44; relationship to income, 71, 226*n*44; of
South Koreans, 64–65; in Taiwan,
65; of women, 65, 91, 126, 224*n*33
Egoism, 138–39, 165, 167
Elders: appointments, 125; female, 94,
113–14; leadership role, 30; male,
125
Elites: Christianity and, 16, 17, 19;
women's roles, 61
Emancipation. *see* Liberation
Emotions: deprivation, 106; expressed by husbands, 152; in
prayer, 97; releasing, 97–99; re-
pressed, 91–94
Empathy, 39–40, 44, 46, 217*n*57
Employment. *see* Workforce

Empowerment: from God, 129; through church involvement, 7, 129, 130, 189, 192; through conversion, 106, 172–73; through surrender, 103–4. *See also* Autonomy; Power

Endurance: cultivation of, 143, 146–48, 174; lack of, 165; questioning by women, 149, 150; of women in past, 141

Equal Employment Opportunity Act of 1987, 66

Equal rights, 66, 199

Ethnographic research: challenges, 44–46; empathy, 39–40, 44, 46, 217*n*57; interviews, 32, 38–39, 41–42; methods, 37–47; objectivity, 39–40, 46–47; participant observation, 32, 37–38, 39–40, 42, 43; researcher role, 44–47; site selection, 34–37

Evangelical church women: ages and marital status, 38; childhood church attendance, 84–85, 86; Christian family origins, 84; contradictions and ambiguities in beliefs, 9–10, 171–76, 187, 189; cultural context, 188–89, 193; female subjectivity, 185–86; in future, 197–200; importance in churches, 3; *jeondo buin* (Bible women), 19; in Latin America, 5–6, 7, 162, 191; proportion of Protestant population, 3; reception of researcher, 40–43; redomestication, 172, 187, 189; seen as socializers, 121; in United States, 6, 179, 191; younger generation, 197–200, 236*n*2. *See also* Church involvement of

women; Conversions; Domestic dilemmas; Married women

Evangelicalism in South Korea: beliefs and practices, 25–29, 35, 203*n*1; church membership numbers, 1–2; demographics of membership, 35–36; direct relationship with God, 95–97, 103; doctrinal rigidity, 212*n*33; double role, 187; experiential orientation, 26–27, 213*n*41; future of, 196–200; growth, 1, 2–3; history, 15–22, 208*n*17; institutional culture, 29–32; obedience to authority, 175; patriarchal ideology, 3–4; proselytizing efforts, 19, 85, 111, 207*n*11, 207–8*n*14, 227*n*3; scholarship on, 2–3; worship services, 26–27, 28

Ewha Hakdang (Ewha Womans University), 112

Exhorting deacons (*gwonsa*), 89–90, 114, 116, 124

Export-oriented growth, 54–55, 65, 68, 218*n*3

Families: central role in society, 184; extended, 63, 67, 79; filial piety, 59, 61, 62, 67; importance to woman's identity, 195, 196; male heads, 156–57, 220*n*15; modified stem, 226*n*43; natal, 61, 70, 84; nuclear, 63, 68, 76, 79, 226*n*45; sizes, 63; status production work, 76–77, 78–79, 235–36*n*12; stem, 63; women's management of relationships, 76; women's responsibilities for cohesion, 182–83, 185, 195. *See also* Gender and family relations; Marriages

Familism: Confucian, 57; definition in South Korean context, 184; modern, 184; in South Korean society, 195

Family Law, 66, 221*n*23

Family planning, 63, 73, 236*n*5

Family seminars: assignments, 153; efforts to reform women, 136, 138–41, 152, 165; obedience and submission taught in, 153–55, 158, 160, 163; purpose, 144–45; teachings on gender and family relations, 137, 154, 163

Fathers, 103. *See also* Husbands

Feminism, 7, 45, 181, 196, 199

Feminist theory, 10, 176, 177–78, 181

Fertility rates, 63, 197

Fieldwork sites and method, 32–39. *See also* Ethnographic research

Filial piety, 59, 61, 62, 67

Forgiveness: dealing with domestic conflicts, 107–9, 147; by God, 105; lack of, 165

Foucault, Michel, 10, 178

Fundamentalist religions. *see* Evangelicalism; Traditionalist religions

Galanter, Marc, 101

Gallagher, Sally K., 6

Gender and family relations: acceptance of church's gender ideology, 162, 171–76; attempts to transform women's behavior and consciousness, 136, 143–48, 164, 166–68, 190; changes in contemporary, 81, 198, 236–37*n*7; changes in postwar period, 57–58, 63–74; Confucian principles, 58–59, 60–62, 67; conservative American views, 6, 199, 233*n*8; evangelical ideology, 3–4, 113, 135, 136–48, 171–76, 191, 233*n*8; in future, 197–200; incentives for women's acceptance of traditional role, 179–80, 182–83, 194–95; opportunities for women, 179–80; patrilineal systems, 59, 60, 179, 224–25*n*37; power of women, 179–80, 182; problems seen by churches, 136–43, 232*n*3; questioning of evangelical teachings, 148–49, 150, 158–59; redomestication of women, 172, 187, 189; strains in, 74; Western influences, 63–64, 233*n*8; women's responses to church teachings, 148–49, 158–59, 186–87; women's violations of gender order, 137–41. *See also* Domestic dilemmas; Obedience; Patriarchy; Submission, female; Subordinate status of women

Gender-based employment discrimination, 68–69, 199, 223*n*30, 224*n*36

Gender consciousness: acceptance of traditional gender roles, 160, 162–64, 172–74, 179–80; church attempts to transform, 136, 164, 190; cultural context, 180–84

Gender hierarchy: acceptance by women, 163, 173, 177–85; in churches, 29–30, 31–32; Confucian principles, 32, 51, 59, 67; criticism of women for violations, 137–38; in marriage, 51, 234*n*15; persistence in modern South Korea, 58, 67; reestablishing, 143. *See also* Subordinate status of women

Gender identity, 172–74, 180–84, 195–96

Gender roles: Confucian relationships, 32, 51, 59, 60–62; conventional, 4, 72–73, 77–78, 135, 160, 162–64, 172–74; criticism of women for violations, 137–38; cultural training of girls, 60, 220*n*17; in evangelical churches, 31–32; family cohesion, 182–83; government policies promoting conventional, 72–73; ideal femininity, 138, 140; inner and outer spheres, 59, 62, 69, 143; male, 156–57; moral responsibilities of women, 182–84; occupational segregation, 68, 69, 222*n*29, 223*n*30; in Unified Silla period, 59–60. *See also* Domesticity; Husbands; Married women; Men; Motherhood; Submission, female; Women

Gender segregation, 59, 60, 68, 69

Gender subjectivities: ambivalent, 185–86; church attempts to transform, 141–42; contemporary, 198, 236*n*4; contradictions and ambiguities, 142–43, 185–86, 195–96; control of, 143; cultural context, 180–84

Gijang. *see* Presbyterian Church in the Republic of Korea

Gilkes, Cheryl Townsend, 191

God: authority, 161–62, 172; dependence on, 102; direct relationship with, 95–97, 103; as Father, 103; forgiveness, 105; as husband or lover, 161–62; love of, 105–9; obedience to, 103, 175

Gojong, King, 17

Goryo dynasty, 60

Gramsci, Antonio, 10

Gratitude, 159–60

Great Revival of 1907, 18, 28, 226–27*n*1

Greenhalgh, Susan, 199

Guilt, 142–43, 183–84

Gwonsa. see Exhorting deacons

Hangeul (Korean writing system), 18, 215–16*n*49

Hapdong (Presbyterian Church of Korea), 209*n*20

Hardacre, Helen, 79

Hartmann, Heidi, 68, 69

Haughtiness, 140–41

Healing: ministries, 228*n*9; as motive for conversion, 88, 110, 193, 228*n*9, 229*n*14; through conversion, 103, 104, 106; through faith, 189; through forgiveness, 107–9

Helplessness, 93, 100, 101, 102, 103, 175

Helpmate role, 116

Higher education, 64–65, 71, 79, 91, 112, 224*nn*33–34. *See also* Education

Holiness churches, 21

Holy Spirit (Ghost): baptism of, 26, 213*n*40, 213*n*42; in Pentecostalism, 26, 213–14*n*42; surrender to, 104

Hospitals, 16, 17

Households, 63. *See also* Families; Gender and family relations; Mothers-in-law

Housewives: domestic labor, 75, 182; full-time, 70; informal labor, 70, 76–77, 225*n*40; non-traditional activities, 76–77; training, 72. *See also* Domesticity

Husbands: attitudes of younger, 198; behavioral changes, 151–52, 155–57, 233*n*13; character changes, 152–53;

church teachings for, 233*n*7; communication with wives, 152; conflicts with, 77–78, 91–92, 99; conventional roles, 77–78; expression of emotions, 152; fatherhood, 103; God as, 161–62; as heads of families, 156–57, 220*n*15; increased family orientation, 155–57; respectfulness, 151–52, 198; spiritual leadership, 156–57; taking responsibility, 156–57; wife's position in family of, 60, 78, 228*n*11. *See also* Gender and family relations; Marriages; Mothers-in-law; Obedience

Identity: family-centered, 195, 196; gender, 172–74, 180–84, 195–96; relational, 176; transformation in conversion, 95, 99–100, 104–5; transformation through church involvement, 126–31

Illnesses: preceding conversions, 88–91, 110; psychosomatic, 90–91, 110. *See also* Healing

IMF. *see* International Monetary Fund

Impatience, 138, 141, 167

Incomes: informal activities, 70, 76–77, 225*n*40; of married women, 77, 236*n*6; relationship to educational attainment, 71, 226*n*44. *See also* Wages

Indigenization, religious, 194

Individualism, 182, 196

Industrialization, 22, 54, 57. *See also* Economic development

Injeong (recognition), 122

Internal transformation, 126–31

International Monetary Fund (IMF), 56

Japan: Ganghwa Treaty, 15; relations with South Korea, 54, 218*n*3; women's workforce participation, 70–71, 223*n*30

Japanese occupation: annexation (1910), 15; Christianity under, 19–21, 209*n*19; cultural assimilation policy, 208–9*n*18; educational system, 64, 112, 221*n*21; Korean resistance, 19–20, 21, 208*n*16; missionaries and, 19, 208*n*15, 212*n*36; protectorate status (1905), 18; Shinto worship, 20–21, 209*n*19

Jeondosa (ministerial interns or nonordained pastors), 113

Jesus: authority, 161; leadership, 230*n*21

Jipsa. see Deacons

Jobs. *see* Work force

Judaism, Orthodox, 7, 199, 205*n*12

Kandiyoti, Deniz, 150, 180–81

Kendall, Laurel, 81

Killing of self, 166–68, 234*n*16

Kim, Dongno, 184

"Kitchen herd," 114–16

KNCC. *see* Korean National Council of Churches

Kondo, Dorinne K., 186

Korea: interest in Western knowledge and culture, 16; nationalism, 19–20; Yi dynasty, 15, 17, 58–59, 205–6*n*2. *See also* Japanese occupation; Missionaries; North Korea; South Korea

Korean Church Women United, 32

Korean National Council of Churches (KNCC), 32

Korean War, 21

Koryo Presbyterian Church, 209*n*20

Labor. *see* Domestic labor; Work force

Latin America: evangelical women, 5–6, 7, 162, 191; Protestantism, 2

Legal status of women, 66, 221*n*23

Lett, Denise, 77

Liberation: meaning for women, 195–96; from patriarchy, 9–10, 186–87; tension with acquiescence to gender oppression, 8, 9–10, 171–72; through conversion, 103, 172–73, 174; through faith, 7, 189–91, 205*n*14; undercut by traditional gender ideology, 172–74, 176

Literacy rates, 64

Love: divine, 105–9; in marriage, 63–64, 151, 164

Lower-class women: church involvement in Latin America, 5–6; conversions, 88, 228*n*9; lack of recognition for church involvement, 125–26; shamanism and, 229*n*15; work of, 61; under Yi dynasty, 220*n*17

Malaysian peasants, 186

Marriages: age differences, 163, 234*n*15; arranged, 225*n*41, 232*n*3; Christian views, 164; companionate, 225*n*41; delayed childbearing, 236*n*5; egalitarian relationships, 63–64, 75, 163, 198; improved relationships after conversion, 107; incompatibility, 232*n*3; lack of preparation for domestic role, 80, 89, 92, 232*n*3; love in, 63–64, 151, 164; sexual relations, 145, 148. *See also* Domestic dilemmas; Gender and family relations; Husbands; Mothers-in-law

Marriage shock, 80

Married women: attitude changes, 147–48; autonomy, 76, 77, 78, 172; educational attainment, 71, 91, 224*n*34; effecting changes in husband's behavior, 151–52, 155–57; expectations, 61, 74–76, 77, 80; filial piety, 61; incomes, 77, 236*n*6; informal income-generating activities, 70, 76–77, 225*n*40; lack of preparation of contemporary girls, 80, 89, 92; moral authority, 160, 161, 195; narratives, 138–39, 140, 146, 151–52, 153, 156, 158–60, 162–64, 167–70; natal families, 61, 84; nation-building role, 73; relations with in-laws, 60–61, 78, 89, 92, 180, 228*n*11; roles, 60–62; sanctions for "evils," 61–62, 220–21*n*19; self-images, 94, 142–43; workforce participation rates, 70, 71, 197, 199, 223*n*31; younger generation, 197–200, 235–36*n*12. *See also* Domestic dilemmas; Domestic labor; Evangelical church women; Gender and family relations; Motherhood; Submission

Martin, David, 30

Media, state-controlled, 72–73

Mega-churches, 2, 22, 29, 204*n*3, 210*n*23, 215*n*47

Men: authority, 161, 172, 173; Christians, 233*n*13; church elders, 125; Confucian gender roles, 59, 103, 220*n*15; deacons, 114, 115, 125; drinking and smoking, 156, 233*n*13; educational attainment, 226*n*44; fathers, 103; as heads of families, 156–57, 220*n*15; power, 185. *See also*

Gender; Husbands; Marriages; Patriarchy

Mental illness, 94

Methodist churches: denominational schisms, 21; female pastors, 31, 113, 230*n*2; large, 2, 204*n*3; leaders, 216*n*51; liberal theology, 35; membership numbers, 24–25. *See also* North River Church

Methodist missionaries: American, 205*n*1; educational and medical work, 112, 206*nn*4–5; female, 230*n*2

Middle class, Korean, 35–36

Middle-class women: family status production work, 76–77; housewives, 70, 76, 182; lack of preparation for domestic role, 80, 89, 91, 232*n*3; workforce participation rates, 70. *See also* Church involvement of women; Domestic dilemmas; Evangelical church women

Minjung theology, 211*n*31

Missionaries: American, 15–16, 205*n*1; Bible-study classes, 215–16*n*49; Bible translations, 18, 206*n*7, 215–16*n*49; Catholic, 15, 205–6*n*2; churches founded, 16; Comity Agreement, 206*n*8; conservative theology, 25, 212*n*32; converts, 18, 207*n*9, 207*n*12; in Korea, 15–18, 19, 21; medical work, 16, 17; organizations, 22, 210*n*24; regional partitions, 21, 206–7*n*8; relations with Japanese colonial government, 19, 208*n*15, 212*n*36; revivals, 212*n*36; rural itineration, 18

Missionary societies. *see* Women's missionary societies

Mission schools, 16, 64, 84, 112, 206*n*5

Modernity: distinction from modernization, 204*n*7; responses to, 5, 56–58; tensions with traditional culture, 57, 58, 80, 136–37, 196–97; Western, 56–58, 197

Modernization: distinction from modernity, 204*n*7; of South Korean society, 196–97. *See also* Economic development

Moffett, Samuel H., 21

Mohanty, Chandra, 181

Moon, Seungsook, 72, 73

Motherhood: child-raising, 80, 139, 145–46; criticism of ambition and greed in, 139; delaying, 236*n*5; education of children, 78–79, 139; emotional bonds, 226*n*45; family planning, 63, 73, 236*n*5; fertility rates, 63, 197; guilt over failings, 183; importance of having sons, 59, 60, 62, 80, 179; nation-building role, 73; number of children, 63; power, 179–80, 182; preparations for role, 72; valued by society, 59, 60, 62, 72–73, 179–80, 182–83, 195. *See also* Children; Married women

Mothers-in-law: changing relationships with daughters-in-law, 236–37*n*7; conflicts with, 78, 86, 89, 91–92, 99; control of daughters-in-law, 60, 78; labor of daughters-in-law, 60, 78, 89, 92, 180, 228*n*11; power and status, 62, 179, 180

Natal families, 61, 70, 84

Neo-Confucianism, 58–59, 60–62, 66–73, 219–20*n*13. *See also* Confucianism

Nevius Plan, 18

North Korea: communist regime, 57; invasion threat, 23; refugees from, 24; repression of Christians, 20, 24

North River Church: Bible-study groups, 121; cell leaders, 167–68; deacons, 110–12, 122, 126, 127–29; description, 33–34; elders, 94; exhorting deacons, 89–90, 114, 116, 124; as fieldwork site, 32, 33–37, 40–44, 45; leaders, 42–43; location, 32, 33–34; member interviews, 85–86, 89–91, 107, 123–24, 127–29, 131–32; membership, 34, 36; missionary societies, 120; pastors, 36–37, 40, 45, 95–96; tithing member lists, 231*n*9

Obedience: acceptance of, 162–63, 169–70; to authority, 145, 175; to church authorities, 175; Confucian principles for women, 61; developing in children, 145–46; docile, 103, 109, 143–46; to God, 103, 175; to husbands, 143–46, 153–55, 158, 165–66, 232–33*n*6; injunctions for women, 143–46, 153–55, 158, 165–66, 232–33*n*6; questioning by women, 150, 158–59; relationship to faith, 166; supreme acts, 159; with a vengeance, 158–59; woman's self-interest in, 154, 155. *See also* Submission

Objectivity, 39–40, 46–47

Occupational segregation, 68, 69, 222*n*29, 223*n*30

Oppression: consent to, 176–77; resistance to, 161, 176–77, 187. *See also* Patriarchy

Ordination of women, 31, 113

Orthodox Jews, 7, 199, 205*n*12

Ortner, Sherry B., 11

Papanek, Hanna, 76

Parents. *see* Children; Families; Fathers; Motherhood

Park Chung Hee, 23–24, 54–56, 217–18*n*2

Participant observation, 32, 37–38, 39–40, 42, 43

Passive resistance, 158–59, 172

Pastors: authority, 29–30; female, 31, 113, 230*n*2; leadership of churches, 29–30; oversupply, 211*n*28; recognition of women's contributions to churches, 123; relations with lay people, 29–30

Patriarchal bargain, 150

Patriarchy: capitalism and, 67–71, 222*n*27, 223*n*30; changes in postwar period, 8, 63–74; in church leadership, 29–30, 113; classic, 180, 233*n*9; consent to, 9–10, 11, 136, 171–72, 176–85, 194–96; contradictory responses of women, 9–10, 185, 186–87; crises of modern, 8–9; frustrations with restrictions, 74, 77, 80, 91; gender oppression, 161, 176, 187; government policies preserving, 72–73; in Korean evangelicalism, 3–4, 135; liberation from, 9–10, 186–87; maintenance of, 171–76, 177–85, 186–87, 190, 194–95; negotiating, 6, 149–58; Neo-Confucian, 58–59, 60–62, 66–73; persistence in modern South Korea, 8–9, 57, 66–73, 199; resistance to, 9–10, 161, 187; traditionalist religions and, 3, 190;

women's interest in preserving, 6, 10, 177–85; women's strategies for dealing with, 150. *See also* Gender and family relations; Subordinate status of women

Patrilineal systems, 59, 60, 179, 224–25*n*37

Penitence. *see* Repentance

Pentecostals: experiential orientation, 26–27; healing ministries, 228*n*9; in Latin America, 7; opposition of other conservative Protestants, 212–13*n*38; revivals, 212*n*36; in South Korea, 25, 212–13*n*38; women, 162, 205*n*14. *See also* Charismatic movements; Evangelicalism

Personality transformation: of husbands, 152–53; through women's church involvement, 126–31

Poststructuralism, 10, 177–78

Power: of African American women in churches, 191; male, 185; of mothers-in-law, 62, 179, 180; poststructuralist analysis, 10, 178; religious, 7, 171–76; of women in families, 10, 179–80, 182. *See also* Empowerment; Patriarchy

Practices: Bible study, 28, 29, 132; evangelical, 25–29, 35, 203*m*; intensity, 2; Pentecostal and charismatic, 26–27; worship services, 26–27, 28. *See also* Prayers

Practice theory, 11

Prayer houses (*gidowon*), 28–29, 215*n*47

Prayers: as aid in submission, 168–69; in cell meetings, 99; communication with God, 95–97, 230*n*22; constant, 95–96; early-morning,

28, 83, 214*n*44; emotions in, 97; fasting, 28; Friday-evening, 28, 82, 83, 214*n*44; healing, 28, 214*n*46; importance of practice, 83, 95–96; practices, 28–29; surrender in, 104; unified, 83, 226–27*m*

Prayer services, 28, 82–83, 214*n*44

Presbyterian churches: conservative theology, 35; denominational schisms, 21, 24, 209*n*20; female pastors, 31; under Japanese rule, 209*n*19; large, 2, 204*n*3; leaders, 30; membership numbers, 24. *See also* South River Church

Presbyterian Church in the Republic of Korea (Gijang), 24, 31, 209*n*20, 210–11*n*27

Presbyterian Church of Korea (Donghap), 31, 209*n*20

Presbyterian Church of Korea (Hapdong), 209*n*20

Presbyterian missionaries, 17, 25, 205*m*, 206*n*4

Professionals, female, 66, 69, 222*n*29

Protestant denominations: in Korea, 2, 24–25, 209–10*n*21; liberal, 31, 35, 211*n*31; regional divisions, 21, 206–7*n*8; schisms, 20, 21–22, 24, 209*n*20, 210*n*22. *See also* Baptist churches; Methodist churches; Missionaries; Presbyterian churches

Protestantism: appeal to Koreans, 17–18; Calvinism, 25; Confucian influence, 29–30, 113, 194, 212*n*33; expansion in Korea, 1, 18–19, 22, 208*m*17, 209–10*n*21; in Latin America, 2; positive perceptions in Korea, 16–17; in urban areas, 23. *See also* Evangelicalism

Protestants: institutional self-reliance, 18, 25, 30–31; lay evangelism, 19, 85, 111, 207*n*11, 207–8*n*14, 227*n*3; in 1950s and 1960s, 21–22; number in South Korea, 1–2; political views, 24, 210*n*26. *See also* Missionaries; Pentecostals

Psychosomatic illnesses, 90–91, 110

Rebirth, 101, 104–5, 172–73. *See also* Conversions

Redomestication, 172, 187, 189. *See also* Domesticity

Relief effect, 101

Religious communities: indigenization, 194; issues in studying, 39–40. *See also* Protestantism; Traditionalist religions

Religious patriarchy, 3–4, 29–30, 113, 135, 190

Repentance, 141, 157, 164, 165, 166

Resistance: church involvement as, 7, 133, 187; to class domination, 186; everyday forms, 178, 186; to gender oppression, 9–10, 161, 176–77, 187; passive, 158–59, 172; romanticization, 11, 176

Revival meetings: contemporary, 22, 28, 210*n*25, 213–14*n*42, 214*n*45; Great Revival of 1907, 18, 28, 226–27*n*1; missionary-sponsored, 212*n*36

Rhee, Syngman, 23–24, 54

Riesebrodt, Martin, 26

Salvation, 101, 104–5, 213*n*40. *See also* Conversions

Sanctified Church, 191

Schools: mission, 16, 64, 84, 112, 206*n*5; mothers' involvement, 79. *See also* Education

Scott, James C., 186

Self: death of, 166–68, 234*n*16; dependence on God, 174–75. *See also* Identity

Self-centeredness. *see* Egoism

Self-confidence, 126–27, 128–29

Self-criticism, 165

Self-cultivation, 131–32

Self-esteem, 106–7, 122–23

Self-fulfillment, 129, 189

Self-transformation, 95, 99–100, 104–5

Seoul: churches, 1, 14; Gangbuk and Gangnam areas, 33; population, 33; Severance Hospital, 17. *See also* North River Church; South River Church

Service worker role, 116

Severance Hospital, 17

Shamanism, 26, 228*n*9, 229*nn*14–15

Shinto, 20–21, 209*n*19

Sin: evangelical understanding, 100, 108; repentance, 141, 157, 164, 165, 166; women's violations of gender order, 138–39, 165

"Smarty" women, 137–38

Smith, Christian, 6

Social change. *see* South Korean society

Social engineering, 72–73

South Korea: anti-government protests, 24, 210–11*n*27; authoritarianism, 54, 57, 219*n*9; constitution, 66; democracy, 56, 57, 219*n*9; military dictatorship, 54–56; opening to external influences, 15–16; pro-American regimes, 23–24; U.S.

occupation, 64. *See also* Economic development

South Korean society: change in contemporary, 196–97, 198, 199–200; church roles, 23; constraints on women's choices, 178–79; educational emphasis, 79; effects of rapid economic development, 22–23, 56–58, 193; familism, 57, 184, 195; heterogeneity, 186–87; importance of family, 67; modernization, 8, 196–97; urban migration, 22–23, 33. *See also* Classes; Confucianism; Gender and family relations; Patriarchy; Workforce

South River Church: cell groups, 36, 98–99, 100, 118–20, 166–67; cell leaders, 126, 132, 143–44; description, 33; divine love theme, 105; family seminar leaders, 137, 146, 148–49, 160; family seminars, 144–45, 158–59, 163; as fieldwork site, 32, 33, 34–37, 40–44, 45; leaders, 42–43; location, 32, 33; member interviews, 48–50, 51–52, 87, 88–89, 92–93, 108, 158–59, 162–63, 183; membership, 33, 36; pastors, 36–37, 40, 45, 105, 175; prayer services, 82–83; programs and activities, 36; training programs, 36, 132

Spirit. *see* Holy Spirit

Spiritual practice. *see* Cell groups; Conversions; Forgiveness; Healing; Prayers; Surrender

Stacey, Judith, 6

Status production work, 76–77, 78–79, 235–36*n*12

Stem families, 63

Strength: obtained through conversion, 106–7; of women, 94, 142–43. *See also* Empowerment

Stress-related illnesses, 90–91, 110

Subjectivities. *see* Gender subjectivities

Submission, female: acceptance, 162–64, 169–70; as acquiescence, 149, 155, 159, 162–64; in church involvement, 116; coexistence with image of strong woman, 142–43; Confucian principles, 61–62; consequences, 157, 172; death of self, 166–68; disciplinary strategies, 166–69; evangelical teachings, 4, 6, 144–45, 153–55, 158–59, 160; to God's authority, 161–62, 172; paradox, 149; passive resistance, 158–59, 172; rhetorical and disciplinary strategies for teaching, 164–69; as strategy for negotiating domestic situations, 6, 149–58, 162, 165–66; subversive gender bargaining acts, 159–62. *See also* Obedience

Subordinate groups, 10, 11

Subordinate status of women: Bible passages supporting, 113, 231*n*7; in churches, 31–32, 113, 116; Confucian principles, 51, 59, 60; consent to, 177–85, 195; in husband's family, 51, 60, 78, 228*n*11; power relations with men, 185. *See also* Gender hierarchy; Patriarchy

Surrender: conversion as, 100–104, 105, 174–75; dying of self, 234*n*16; to Holy Spirit, 104; repeated experiences, 230*n*22

Taiwan: educational attainment, 65; patriarchal family system, 224–25*n*37; women's workforce participation, 70–71

Testimonies, 100

Theological schools, 211*n*28

Tithing, 2, 28, 114, 125–26, 231*n*9

Traditionalist religions: appeal of, 192; empowerment of women, 7; instrumental involvement of women, 162; in Latin America, 5–6, 7, 162; liberating aspects, 7, 189–91, 205*n*14; paradox of women's involvement in, 3; patriarchy supported by, 3, 190; scholarship on women and, 5–7, 10, 162, 176–77, 189–91, 192–94; in United States, 6, 7, 199; women's motivations for involvement, 5–7. *See also* Evangelicalism

Turkey, women's experiences, 181

Turner, Victor, 161

Unification Church, 228*n*8

Unified Silla period, 59–60

United States: conservative gender ideology, 6, 199, 233*n*8; evangelical women, 6, 179, 191; missionaries to Korea, 15–16, 205*n*1; occupation of South Korea, 64; Orthodox Jewish women, 7, 199; relations with Korea, 15, 16, 23–24, 54; traditionalist religions, 6, 7, 199

Urban areas: churches, 1, 14, 23; isolation from extended family, 79; migration to, 22–23, 33. *See also* Seoul

Volunteer labor. *see* Church involvement of women

Wages: family, 68; gender-based inequality, 68–69, 199, 222*n*28; low, 55. *See also* Incomes

Welfare system, 57, 219*n*10

Williams, Raymond, 10

Wives. *see* Married women

Women: blamed for domestic conflicts, 136–41, 164–65; choices, 176, 178–79; education, 64, 65, 71, 91, 112–13, 126, 221*n*21, 224*nn*33–34; equality, 66, 199; ideal femininity, 138, 140; leadership in domestic sphere, 62; ordination of, 31, 113, 230*n*2; rights, 60, 66, 221*n*23; rulers, 60; societal constraints, 178–79; strength, 94, 106–7, 142–43. *See also* Evangelical church women; Gender; Married women; Motherhood; Workforce participation of women

Women's missionary societies (*yeoseongyobu*), 115–16, 120

Women's organizations, 32, 72–73

Work. *see* Church involvement of women; Domestic labor; Workforce participation of women

Workforce: labor disputes, 55, 68–69; manufacturing, 68, 69, 218*n*5, 221*n*22; repressive government policies, 55, 57; segmented industrial structure, 68; South Korean, 55. *See also* Wages

Workforce participation of women: as cheap labor, 68–69; clerical workers, 69, 221*n*22; equal employment opportunity, 66; gender-based discrimination, 68–69, 199, 223*n*30, 224*n*36; increased rates, 65–66, 68, 197, 199, 221*n*22, 223–24*n*32; international comparisons, 70–71, 223*n*32; in Japan, 70–71, 223*n*30; in manufacturing, 68, 69, 221*n*22; of married women, 70, 71, 197, 199, 223*n*31; occupational segregation, 68, 69, 222*n*29, 223*n*30; policies discouraging, 68–73; professionals, 66, 69, 222*n*29; of single women, 70, 72, 198, 223*n*31; in Taiwan, 70–71

Working class, 35, 36. *See also* Lower-class women

Yeoido Full Gospel Church: demographics of membership, 228*m*10; pastor, 212–13*n*38; Pentecostal practices, 27; prayer center, 215*n*47; as world's largest church, 2, 22, 204*n*3

Yeoseongyobu. see Women's missionary societies

Yi dynasty, 15, 17, 58–59, 205–6*n*2

Yi Seungman (Syngman Rhee), 23–24, 54

Harvard East Asian Monographs
(*out-of-print)

*1. Liang Fang-chung, *The Single-Whip Method of Taxation in China*

*2. Harold C. Hinton, *The Grain Tribute System of China, 1845–1911*

3. Ellsworth C. Carlson, *The Kaiping Mines, 1877–1912*

*4. Chao Kuo-chün, *Agrarian Policies of Mainland China: A Documentary Study, 1949–1956*

*5. Edgar Snow, *Random Notes on Red China, 1936–1945*

*6. Edwin George Beal, Jr., *The Origin of Likin, 1835–1864*

7. Chao Kuo-chün, *Economic Planning and Organization in Mainland China: A Documentary Study, 1949–1957*

*8. John K. Fairbank, *Ching Documents: An Introductory Syllabus*

*9. Helen Yin and Yi-chang Yin, *Economic Statistics of Mainland China, 1949–1957*

10. Wolfgang Franke, *The Reform and Abolition of the Traditional Chinese Examination System*

11. Albert Feuerwerker and S. Cheng, *Chinese Communist Studies of Modern Chinese History*

12. C. John Stanley, *Late Ching Finance: Hu Kuang-yung as an Innovator*

13. S. M. Meng, *The Tsungli Yamen: Its Organization and Functions*

*14. Ssu-yü Teng, *Historiography of the Taiping Rebellion*

15. Chun-Jo Liu, *Controversies in Modern Chinese Intellectual History: An Analytic Bibliography of Periodical Articles, Mainly of the May Fourth and Post-May Fourth Era*

*16. Edward J. M. Rhoads, *The Chinese Red Army, 1927–1963: An Annotated Bibliography*

*17. Andrew J. Nathan, *A History of the China International Famine Relief Commission*

*18. Frank H. H. King (ed.) and Prescott Clarke, *A Research Guide to China-Coast Newspapers, 1822–1911*

*19. Ellis Joffe, *Party and Army: Professionalism and Political Control in the Chinese Officer Corps, 1949–1964*

*20. Toshio G. Tsukahira, *Feudal Control in Tokugawa Japan: The Sankin Kōtai System*

*21. Kwang-Ching Liu, ed., *American Missionaries in China: Papers from Harvard Seminars*

*22. George Moseley, *A Sino-Soviet Cultural Frontier: The Ili Kazakh Autonomous Chou*

23. Carl F. Nathan, *Plague Prevention and Politics in Manchuria, 1910–1931*

*24. Adrian Arthur Bennett, *John Fryer: The Introduction of Western Science and Technology into Nineteenth-Century China*

*25. Donald J. Friedman, *The Road from Isolation: The Campaign of the American Committee for Non-Participation in Japanese Aggression, 1938–1941*

*26. Edward LeFevour, *Western Enterprise in Late Ching China: A Selective Survey of Jardine, Matheson and Company's Operations, 1842–1895*

27. Charles Neuhauser, *Third World Politics: China and the Afro-Asian People's Solidarity Organization, 1957–1967*

*28. Kungtu C. Sun, assisted by Ralph W. Huenemann, *The Economic Development of Manchuria in the First Half of the Twentieth Century*

*29. Shahid Javed Burki, *A Study of Chinese Communes, 1965*

30. John Carter Vincent, *The Extraterritorial System in China: Final Phase*

31. Madeleine Chi, *China Diplomacy, 1914–1918*

*32. Clifton Jackson Phillips, *Protestant America and the Pagan World: The First Half Century of the American Board of Commissioners for Foreign Missions, 1810–1860*

*33. James Pusey, *Wu Han: Attacking the Present Through the Past*

*34. Ying-wan Cheng, *Postal Communication in China and Its Modernization, 1860–1896*

35. Tuvia Blumenthal, *Saving in Postwar Japan*

36. Peter Frost, *The Bakumatsu Currency Crisis*

37. Stephen C. Lockwood, *Augustine Heard and Company, 1858–1862*

38. Robert R. Campbell, *James Duncan Campbell: A Memoir by His Son*

39. Jerome Alan Cohen, ed., *The Dynamics of China's Foreign Relations*

40. V. V. Vishnyakova-Akimova, *Two Years in Revolutionary China, 1925–1927*, trans. Steven L. Levine

41. Meron Medzini, *French Policy in Japan During the Closing Years of the Tokugawa Regime*

42. Ezra Vogel, Margie Sargent, Vivienne B. Shue, Thomas Jay Mathews, and Deborah S. Davis, *The Cultural Revolution in the Provinces*

43. Sidney A. Forsythe, *An American Missionary Community in China, 1895–1905*

*44. Benjamin I. Schwartz, ed., *Reflections on the May Fourth Movement.: A Symposium*

*45. Ching Young Choe, *The Rule of the Taewŏngun, 1864–1873: Restoration in Yi Korea*

46. W. P. J. Hall, *A Bibliographical Guide to Japanese Research on the Chinese Economy, 1958–1970*

47. Jack J. Gerson, *Horatio Nelson Lay and Sino-British Relations, 1854–1864*

Harvard East Asian Monographs

48. Paul Richard Bohr, *Famine and the Missionary: Timothy Richard as Relief Administrator and Advocate of National Reform*

49. Endymion Wilkinson, *The History of Imperial China: A Research Guide*

50. Britten Dean, *China and Great Britain: The Diplomacy of Commercial Relations, 1860–1864*

51. Ellsworth C. Carlson, *The Foochow Missionaries, 1847–1880*

52. Yeh-chien Wang, *An Estimate of the Land-Tax Collection in China, 1753 and 1908*

53. Richard M. Pfeffer, *Understanding Business Contracts in China, 1949–1963*

*54. Han-sheng Chuan and Richard Kraus, *Mid-Ching Rice Markets and Trade: An Essay in Price History*

55. Ranbir Vohra, *Lao She and the Chinese Revolution*

56. Liang-lin Hsiao, *China's Foreign Trade Statistics, 1864–1949*

*57. Lee-hsia Hsu Ting, *Government Control of the Press in Modern China, 1900–1949*

*58. Edward W. Wagner, *The Literati Purges: Political Conflict in Early Yi Korea*

*59. Joungwon A. Kim, *Divided Korea: The Politics of Development, 1945–1972*

60. Noriko Kamachi, John K. Fairbank, and Chūzō Ichiko, *Japanese Studies of Modern China Since 1953: A Bibliographical Guide to Historical and Social-Science Research on the Nineteenth and Twentieth Centuries, Supplementary Volume for 1953–1969*

61. Donald A. Gibbs and Yun-chen Li, *A Bibliography of Studies and Translations of Modern Chinese Literature, 1918–1942*

62. Robert H. Silin, *Leadership and Values: The Organization of Large-Scale Taiwanese Enterprises*

63. David Pong, *A Critical Guide to the Kwangtung Provincial Archives Deposited at the Public Record Office of London*

*64. Fred W. Drake, *China Charts the World: Hsu Chi-yü and His Geography of 1848*

*65. William A. Brown and Urgrunge Onon, translators and annotators, *History of the Mongolian People's Republic*

66. Edward L. Farmer, *Early Ming Government: The Evolution of Dual Capitals*

*67. Ralph C. Croizier, *Koxinga and Chinese Nationalism: History, Myth, and the Hero*

*68. William J. Tyler, tr., *The Psychological World of Natsume Sōseki*, by Doi Takeo

69. Eric Widmer, *The Russian Ecclesiastical Mission in Peking During the Eighteenth Century*

*70. Charlton M. Lewis, *Prologue to the Chinese Revolution: The Transformation of Ideas and Institutions in Hunan Province, 1891–1907*

71. Preston Torbert, *The Ching Imperial Household Department: A Study of Its Organization and Principal Functions, 1662–1796*

72. Paul A. Cohen and John E. Schrecker, eds., *Reform in Nineteenth-Century China*

73. Jon Sigurdson, *Rural Industrialism in China*

74. Kang Chao, *The Development of Cotton Textile Production in China*

75. Valentin Rabe, *The Home Base of American China Missions, 1880–1920*

*76. Sarasin Viraphol, *Tribute and Profit: Sino-Siamese Trade, 1652–1853*

77. Ch'i-ch'ing Hsiao, *The Military Establishment of the Yuan Dynasty*

78. Meishi Tsai, *Contemporary Chinese Novels and Short Stories, 1949–1974: An Annotated Bibliography*

*79. Wellington K. K. Chan, *Merchants, Mandarins and Modern Enterprise in Late Ching China*

80. Endymion Wilkinson, *Landlord and Labor in Late Imperial China: Case Studies from Shandong by Jing Su and Luo Lun*

*81. Barry Keenan, *The Dewey Experiment in China: Educational Reform and Political Power in the Early Republic*

*82. George A. Hayden, *Crime and Punishment in Medieval Chinese Drama: Three Judge Pao Plays*

*83. Sang-Chul Suh, *Growth and Structural Changes in the Korean Economy, 1910–1940*

84. J. W. Dower, *Empire and Aftermath: Yoshida Shigeru and the Japanese Experience, 1878–1954*

85. Martin Collcutt, *Five Mountains: The Rinzai Zen Monastic Institution in Medieval Japan*

86. Kwang Suk Kim and Michael Roemer, *Growth and Structural Transformation*

87. Anne O. Krueger, *The Developmental Role of the Foreign Sector and Aid*

*88. Edwin S. Mills and Byung-Nak Song, *Urbanization and Urban Problems*

89. Sung Hwan Ban, Pal Yong Moon, and Dwight H. Perkins, *Rural Development*

*90. Noel F. McGinn, Donald R. Snodgrass, Yung Bong Kim, Shin-Bok Kim, and Quee-Young Kim, *Education and Development in Korea*

*91. Leroy P. Jones and Il SaKong, *Government, Business, and Entrepreneurship in Economic Development: The Korean Case*

92. Edward S. Mason, Dwight H. Perkins, Kwang Suk Kim, David C. Cole, Mahn Je Kim et al., *The Economic and Social Modernization of the Republic of Korea*

93. Robert Repetto, Tai Hwan Kwon, Son-Ung Kim, Dae Young Kim, John E. Sloboda, and Peter J. Donaldson, *Economic Development, Population Policy, and Demographic Transition in the Republic of Korea*

94. Parks M. Coble, Jr., *The Shanghai Capitalists and the Nationalist Government, 1927–1937*

95. Noriko Kamachi, *Reform in China: Huang Tsun-hsien and the Japanese Model*

96. Richard Wich, *Sino-Soviet Crisis Politics: A Study of Political Change and Communication*

97. Lillian M. Li, *China's Silk Trade: Traditional Industry in the Modern World, 1842–1937*

98. R. David Arkush, *Fei Xiaotong and Sociology in Revolutionary China*

*99. Kenneth Alan Grossberg, *Japan's Renaissance: The Politics of the Muromachi Bakufu*

100. James Reeve Pusey, *China and Charles Darwin*

101. Hoyt Cleveland Tillman, *Utilitarian Confucianism: Chen Liang's Challenge to Chu Hsi*

102. Thomas A. Stanley, *Ōsugi Sakae, Anarchist in Taishō Japan: The Creativity of the Ego*

103. Jonathan K. Ocko, *Bureaucratic Reform in Provincial China: Ting Jih-ch'ang in Restoration Kiangsu, 1867–1870*

104. James Reed, *The Missionary Mind and American East Asia Policy, 1911–1915*

105. Neil L. Waters, *Japan's Local Pragmatists: The Transition from Bakumatsu to Meiji in the Kawasaki Region*

106. David C. Cole and Yung Chul Park, *Financial Development in Korea, 1945–1978*

107. Roy Bahl, Chuk Kyo Kim, and Chong Kee Park, *Public Finances During the Korean Modernization Process*

108. William D. Wray, *Mitsubishi and the N.Y.K, 1870–1914: Business Strategy in the Japanese Shipping Industry*

109. Ralph William Huenemann, *The Dragon and the Iron Horse: The Economics of Railroads in China, 1876–1937*

*110. Benjamin A. Elman, *From Philosophy to Philology: Intellectual and Social Aspects of Change in Late Imperial China*

111. Jane Kate Leonard, *Wei Yüan and China's Rediscovery of the Maritime World*

112. Luke S. K. Kwong, *A Mosaic of the Hundred Days:. Personalities, Politics, and Ideas of 1898*

*113. John E. Wills, Jr., *Embassies and Illusions: Dutch and Portuguese Envoys to K'ang-hsi, 1666–1687*

114. Joshua A. Fogel, *Politics and Sinology: The Case of Naitō Konan (1866–1934)*

*115. Jeffrey C. Kinkley, ed., *After Mao: Chinese Literature and Society, 1978–1981*

116. C. Andrew Gerstle, *Circles of Fantasy: Convention in the Plays of Chikamatsu*

117. Andrew Gordon, *The Evolution of Labor Relations in Japan: Heavy Industry, 1853–1955*

*118. Daniel K. Gardner, *Chu Hsi and the "Ta Hsueh": Neo-Confucian Reflection on the Confucian Canon*

119. Christine Guth Kanda, *Shinzō: Hachiman Imagery and Its Development*

*120. Robert Borgen, *Sugawara no Michizane and the Early Heian Court*

121. Chang-tai Hung, *Going to the People: Chinese Intellectual and Folk Literature, 1918–1937*

*122. Michael A. Cusumano, *The Japanese Automobile Industry: Technology and Management at Nissan and Toyota*

123. Richard von Glahn, *The Country of Streams and Grottoes: Expansion, Settlement, and the Civilizing of the Sichuan Frontier in Song Times*

124. Steven D. Carter, *The Road to Komatsubara: A Classical Reading of the Renga Hyakuin*

125. Katherine F. Bruner, John K. Fairbank, and Richard T. Smith, *Entering China's Service: Robert Hart's Journals, 1854–1863*

126. Bob Tadashi Wakabayashi, *Anti-Foreignism and Western Learning in Early-Modern Japan: The "New Theses" of 1825*

127. Atsuko Hirai, *Individualism and Socialism: The Life and Thought of Kawai Eijirō (1891–1944)*

128. Ellen Widmer, *The Margins of Utopia: "Shui-hu hou-chuan" and the Literature of Ming Loyalism*

129. R. Kent Guy, *The Emperor's Four Treasuries: Scholars and the State in the Late Chien-lung Era*

130. Peter C. Perdue, *Exhausting the Earth: State and Peasant in Hunan, 1500–1850*

131. Susan Chan Egan, *A Latterday Confucian: Reminiscences of William Hung (1893–1980)*

132. James T. C. Liu, *China Turning Inward: Intellectual-Political Changes in the Early Twelfth Century*

*133. Paul A. Cohen, *Between Tradition and Modernity: Wang T'ao and Reform in Late Ching China*

134. Kate Wildman Nakai, *Shogunal Politics: Arai Hakuseki and the Premises of Tokugawa Rule*

*135. Parks M. Coble, *Facing Japan: Chinese Politics and Japanese Imperialism, 1931–1937*

136. Jon L. Saari, *Legacies of Childhood: Growing Up Chinese in a Time of Crisis, 1890–1920*

137. Susan Downing Videen, *Tales of Heichū*

138. Heinz Morioka and Miyoko Sasaki, *Rakugo: The Popular Narrative Art of Japan*

139. Joshua A. Fogel, *Nakae Ushikichi in China: The Mourning of Spirit*

140. Alexander Barton Woodside, *Vietnam and the Chinese Model: A Comparative Study of Vietnamese and Chinese Government in the First Half of the Nineteenth Century*

*141. George Elison, *Deus Destroyed: The Image of Christianity in Early Modern Japan*

142. William D. Wray, ed., *Managing Industrial Enterprise: Cases from Japan's Prewar Experience*

*143. T'ung-tsu Ch'ü, *Local Government in China Under the Ching*

144. Marie Anchordoguy, *Computers, Inc.: Japan's Challenge to IBM*

145. Barbara Molony, *Technology and Investment: The Prewar Japanese Chemical Industry*

146. Mary Elizabeth Berry, *Hideyoshi*

147. Laura E. Hein, *Fueling Growth: The Energy Revolution and Economic Policy in Postwar Japan*

148. Wen-hsin Yeh, *The Alienated Academy: Culture and Politics in Republican China, 1919–1937*

149. Dru C. Gladney, *Muslim Chinese: Ethnic Nationalism in the People's Republic*

150. Merle Goldman and Paul A. Cohen, eds., *Ideas Across Cultures: Essays on Chinese Thought in Honor of Benjamin L Schwartz*

151. James M. Polachek, *The Inner Opium War*

152. Gail Lee Bernstein, *Japanese Marxist: A Portrait of Kawakami Hajime, 1879–1946*

Harvard East Asian Monographs

*153. Lloyd E. Eastman, *The Abortive Revolution: China Under Nationalist Rule, 1927–1937*

154. Mark Mason, *American Multinationals and Japan: The Political Economy of Japanese Capital Controls, 1899–1980*

155. Richard J. Smith, John K. Fairbank, and Katherine F. Bruner, *Robert Hart and China's Early Modernization: His Journals, 1863–1866*

156. George J. Tanabe, Jr., *Myōe the Dreamkeeper: Fantasy and Knowledge in Kamakura Buddhism*

157. William Wayne Farris, *Heavenly Warriors: The Evolution of Japan's Military, 500–1300*

158. Yu-ming Shaw, *An American Missionary in China: John Leighton Stuart and Chinese-American Relations*

159. James B. Palais, *Politics and Policy in Traditional Korea*

*160. Douglas Reynolds, *China, 1898–1912: The Xinzheng Revolution and Japan*

161. Roger R. Thompson, *China's Local Councils in the Age of Constitutional Reform, 1898–1911*

162. William Johnston, *The Modern Epidemic: History of Tuberculosis in Japan*

163. Constantine Nomikos Vaporis, *Breaking Barriers: Travel and the State in Early Modern Japan*

164. Irmela Hijiya-Kirschnereit, *Rituals of Self-Revelation: Shishōsetsu as Literary Genre and Socio-Cultural Phenomenon*

165. James C. Baxter, *The Meiji Unification Through the Lens of Ishikawa Prefecture*

166. Thomas R. H. Havens, *Architects of Affluence: The Tsutsumi Family and the Seibu-Saison Enterprises in Twentieth-Century Japan*

167. Anthony Hood Chambers, *The Secret Window: Ideal Worlds in Tanizaki's Fiction*

168. Steven J. Ericson, *The Sound of the Whistle: Railroads and the State in Meiji Japan*

169. Andrew Edmund Goble, *Kenmu: Go-Daigo's Revolution*

170. Denise Potrzeba Lett, *In Pursuit of Status: The Making of South Korea's "New" Urban Middle Class*

171. Mimi Hall Yiengpruksawan, *Hiraizumi: Buddhist Art and Regional Politics in Twelfth-Century Japan*

172. Charles Shirō Inouye, *The Similitude of Blossoms: A Critical Biography of Izumi Kyōka (1873–1939), Japanese Novelist and Playwright*

173. Aviad E. Raz, *Riding the Black Ship: Japan and Tokyo Disneyland*

174. Deborah J. Milly, *Poverty, Equality, and Growth: The Politics of Economic Need in Postwar Japan*

175. See Heng Teow, *Japan's Cultural Policy Toward China, 1918–1931: A Comparative Perspective*

176. Michael A. Fuller, *An Introduction to Literary Chinese*

177. Frederick R. Dickinson, *War and National Reinvention: Japan in the Great War, 1914–1919*

178. John Solt, *Shredding the Tapestry of Meaning: The Poetry and Poetics of Kitasono Katue (1902–1978)*

179. Edward Pratt, *Japan's Protoindustrial Elite: The Economic Foundations of the Gōnō*

180. Atsuko Sakaki, *Recontextualizing Texts: Narrative Performance in Modern Japanese Fiction*

181. Soon-Won Park, *Colonial Industrialization and Labor in Korea: The Onoda Cement Factory*

182. JaHyun Kim Haboush and Martina Deuchler, *Culture and the State in Late Chosŏn Korea*

183. John W. Chaffee, *Branches of Heaven: A History of the Imperial Clan of Sung China*

184. Gi-Wook Shin and Michael Robinson, eds., *Colonial Modernity in Korea*

185. Nam-lin Hur, *Prayer and Play in Late Tokugawa Japan: Asakusa Sensōji and Edo Society*

186. Kristin Stapleton, *Civilizing Chengdu: Chinese Urban Reform, 1895–1937*

187. Hyung Il Pai, *Constructing "Korean" Origins: A Critical Review of Archaeology, Historiography, and Racial Myth in Korean State-Formation Theories*

188. Brian D. Ruppert, *Jewel in the Ashes: Buddha Relics and Power in Early Medieval Japan*

189. Susan Daruvala, *Zhou Zuoren and an Alternative Chinese Response to Modernity*

*190. James Z. Lee, *The Political Economy of a Frontier: Southwest China, 1250–1850*

191. Kerry Smith, *A Time of Crisis: Japan, the Great Depression, and Rural Revitalization*

192. Michael Lewis, *Becoming Apart: National Power and Local Politics in Toyama, 1868–1945*

193. William C. Kirby, Man-houng Lin, James Chin Shih, and David A. Pietz, eds., *State and Economy in Republican China: A Handbook for Scholars*

194. Timothy S. George, *Minamata: Pollution and the Struggle for Democracy in Postwar Japan*

195. Billy K. L. So, *Prosperity, Region, and Institutions in Maritime China: The South Fukien Pattern, 946–1368*

196. Yoshihisa Tak Matsusaka, *The Making of Japanese Manchuria, 1904–1932*

197. Maram Epstein, *Competing Discourses: Orthodoxy, Authenticity, and Engendered Meanings in Late Imperial Chinese Fiction*

198. Curtis J. Milhaupt, J. Mark Ramseyer, and Michael K. Young, eds. and comps., *Japanese Law in Context: Readings in Society, the Economy, and Politics*

199. Haruo Iguchi, *Unfinished Business: Ayukawa Yoshisuke and U.S.-Japan Relations, 1937–1952*

200. Scott Pearce, Audrey Spiro, and Patricia Ebrey, *Culture and Power in the Reconstitution of the Chinese Realm, 200–600*

201. Terry Kawashima, *Writing Margins: The Textual Construction of Gender in Heian and Kamakura Japan*

202. Martin W. Huang, *Desire and Fictional Narrative in Late Imperial China*

203. Robert S. Ross and Jiang Changbin, eds., *Re-examining the Cold War: U.S.-China Diplomacy, 1954–1973*

204. Guanhua Wang, *In Search of Justice: The 1905–1906 Chinese Anti-American Boycott*

205. David Schaberg, *A Patterned Past: Form and Thought in Early Chinese Historiography*

206. Christine Yano, *Tears of Longing: Nostalgia and the Nation in Japanese Popular Song*

207. Milena Doleželová-Velingerová and Oldřich Král, with Graham Sanders, eds., *The Appropriation of Cultural Capital: China's May Fourth Project*

208. Robert N. Huey, *The Making of 'Shinkokinshū'*

209. Lee Butler, *Emperor and Aristocracy in Japan, 1467–1680: Resilience and Renewal*

210. Suzanne Ogden, *Inklings of Democracy in China*

211. Kenneth J. Ruoff, *The People's Emperor: Democracy and the Japanese Monarchy, 1945–1995*

212. Haun Saussy, *Great Walls of Discourse and Other Adventures in Cultural China*

213. Aviad E. Raz, *Emotions at Work: Normative Control, Organizations, and Culture in Japan and America*

214. Rebecca E. Karl and Peter Zarrow, eds., *Rethinking the 1898 Reform Period: Political and Cultural Change in Late Qing China*

215. Kevin O'Rourke, *The Book of Korean Shijo*

216. Ezra F. Vogel, ed., *The Golden Age of the U.S.-China-Japan Triangle, 1972–1989*

217. Thomas A. Wilson, ed., *On Sacred Grounds: Culture, Society, Politics, and the Formation of the Cult of Confucius*

218. Donald S. Sutton, *Steps of Perfection: Exorcistic Performers and Chinese Religion in Twentieth-Century Taiwan*

219. Daqing Yang, *Technology of Empire: Telecommunications and Japanese Expansionism, 1895–1945*

220. Qianshen Bai, *Fu Shan's World: The Transformation of Chinese Calligraphy in the Seventeenth Century*

221. Paul Jakov Smith and Richard von Glahn, eds., *The Song-Yuan-Ming Transition in Chinese History*

222. Rania Huntington, *Alien Kind: Foxes and Late Imperial Chinese Narrative*

223. Jordan Sand, *House and Home in Modern Japan: Architecture, Domestic Space, and Bourgeois Culture, 1880–1930*

224. Karl Gerth, *China Made: Consumer Culture and the Creation of the Nation*

225. Xiaoshan Yang, *Metamorphosis of the Private Sphere: Gardens and Objects in Tang-Song Poetry*

226. Barbara Mittler, *A Newspaper for China? Power, Identity, and Change in Shanghai's News Media, 1872–1912*

227. Joyce A. Madancy, *The Troublesome Legacy of Commissioner Lin: The Opium Trade and Opium Suppression in Fujian Province, 1820s to 1920s*

Harvard East Asian Monographs

228. John Makeham, *Transmitters and Creators: Chinese Commentators and Commentaries on the Analects*

229. Elisabeth Köll, *From Cotton Mill to Business Empire: The Emergence of Regional Enterprises in Modern China*

230. Emma Teng, *Taiwan's Imagined Geography: Chinese Colonial Travel Writing and Pictures, 1683–1895*

231. Wilt Idema and Beata Grant, *The Red Brush: Writing Women of Imperial China*

232. Eric C. Rath, *The Ethos of Noh: Actors and Their Art*

233. Elizabeth Remick, *Building Local States: China During the Republican and Post-Mao Eras*

234. Lynn Struve, ed., *The Qing Formation in World-Historical Time*

235. D. Max Moerman, *Localizing Paradise: Kumano Pilgrimage and the Religious Landscape of Premodern Japan*

236. Antonia Finnane, *Speaking of Yangzhou: A Chinese City, 1550–1850*

237. Brian Platt, *Burning and Building: Schooling and State Formation in Japan, 1750–1890*

238. Gail Bernstein, Andrew Gordon, and Kate Wildman Nakai, eds., *Public Spheres, Private Lives in Modern Japan, 1600–1950: Essays in Honor of Albert Craig*

239. Wu Hung and Katherine R. Tsiang, *Body and Face in Chinese Visual Culture*

240. Stephen Dodd, *Writing Home: Representations of the Native Place in Modern Japanese Literature*

241. David Anthony Bello, *Opium and the Limits of Empire: Drug Prohibition in the Chinese Interior, 1729–1850*

242. Hosea Hirata, *Discourses of Seduction: History, Evil, Desire, and Modern Japanese Literature*

243. Kyung Moon Hwang, *Beyond Birth: Social Status in the Emergence of Modern Korea*

244. Brian R. Dott, *Identity Reflections: Pilgrimages to Mount Tai in Late Imperial China*

245. Mark McNally, *Proving the Way: Conflict and Practice in the History of Japanese Nativism*

246. Yongping Wu, *A Political Explanation of Economic Growth: State Survival, Bureaucratic Politics, and Private Enterprises in the Making of Taiwan's Economy, 1950–1985*

247. Kyu Hyun Kim, *The Age of Visions and Arguments: Parliamentarianism and the National Public Sphere in Early Meiji Japan*

248. Zvi Ben-Dor Benite, *The Dao of Muhammad: A Cultural History of Muslims in Late Imperial China*

249. David Der-wei Wang and Shang Wei, eds., *Dynastic Crisis and Cultural Innovation: From the Late Ming to the Late Qing and Beyond*

250. Wilt L. Idema, Wai-yee Li, and Ellen Widmer, eds., *Trauma and Transcendence in Early Qing Literature*

251. Barbara Molony and Kathleen Uno, eds., *Gendering Modern Japanese History*

252. Hiroshi Aoyagi, *Islands of Eight Million Smiles: Idol Performance and Symbolic Production in Contemporary Japan*

253. Wai-yee Li, *The Readability of the Past in Early Chinese Historiography*

254. William C. Kirby, Robert S. Ross, and Gong Li, eds., *Normalization of U.S.-China Relations: An International History*

255. Ellen Gardner Nakamura, *Practical Pursuits: Takano Chōei, Takahashi Keisaku, and Western Medicine in Nineteenth-Century Japan*

256. Jonathan W. Best, *A History of the Early Korean Kingdom of Paekche, together with an annotated translation of* The Paekche Annals *of the* Samguk sagi

257. Liang Pan, *The United Nations in Japan's Foreign and Security Policymaking, 1945–1992: National Security, Party Politics, and International Status*

258. Richard Belsky, *Localities at the Center: Native Place, Space, and Power in Late Imperial Beijing*

259. Zwia Lipkin, *"Useless to the State": "Social Problems" and Social Engineering in Nationalist Nanjing, 1927–1937*

260. William O. Gardner, *Advertising Tower: Japanese Modernism and Modernity in the 1920s*

261. Stephen Owen, *The Making of Early Chinese Classical Poetry*

262. Martin J. Powers, *Pattern and Person: Ornament, Society, and Self in Classical China*

263. Anna M. Shields, *Crafting a Collection: The Cultural Contexts and Poetic Practice of the* Huajian ji 花間集 *(Collection from Among the Flowers)*

264. Stephen Owen, *The Late Tang: Chinese Poetry of the Mid-Ninth Century (827–860)*

265. Sara L. Friedman, *Intimate Politics: Marriage, the Market, and State Power in Southeastern China*

266. Patricia Buckley Ebrey and Maggie Bickford, *Emperor Huizong and Late Northern Song China: The Politics of Culture and the Culture of Politics*

267. Sophie Volpp, *Worldly Stage: Theatricality in Seventeenth-Century China*

268. Ellen Widmer, *The Beauty and the Book: Women and Fiction in Nineteenth-Century China*

269. Steven B. Miles, *The Sea of Learning: Mobility and Identity in Nineteenth-Century Guangzhou*

270. Lin Man-houng, *China Upside Down: Currency, Society, and Ideologies, 1808–1856*

271. Ronald Egan, *The Problem of Beauty: Aesthetic Thought and Pursuits in Northern Song Dynasty China*

272. Mark Halperin, *Out of the Cloister: Literati Perspectives on Buddhism in Sung China, 960–1279*

273. Helen Dunstan, *State or Merchant? Political Economy and Political Process in 1740s China*

274. Sabina Knight, *The Heart of Time: Moral Agency in Twentieth-Century Chinese Fiction*

275. Timothy J. Van Compernolle, *The Uses of Memory: The Critique of Modernity in the Fiction of Higuchi Ichiyō*

276. Paul Rouzer, *A New Practical Primer of Literary Chinese*

277. Jonathan Zwicker, *Practices of the Sentimental Imagination: Melodrama, the Novel, and the Social Imaginary in Nineteenth-Century Japan*

278. Franziska Seraphim, *War Memory and Social Politics in Japan, 1945–2005*

279. Adam L. Kern, *Manga from the Floating World: Comicbook Culture and the* Kibyōshi *of Edo Japan*

280. Cynthia J. Brokaw, *Commerce in Culture: The Sibao Book Trade in the Qing and Republican Periods*

281. Eugene Y. Park, *Between Dreams and Reality: The Military Examination in Late Chosŏn Korea, 1600–1894*

282. Nam-lin Hur, *Death and Social Order in Tokugawa Japan: Buddhism, Anti-Christianity, and the* Danka *System*

283. Patricia M. Thornton, *Disciplining the State: Virtue, Violence, and State-Making in Modern China*

284. Vincent Goossaert, *The Taoists of Peking, 1800–1949: A Social History of Urban Clerics*

285. Peter Nickerson, *Taoism, Bureaucracy, and Popular Religion in Early Medieval China*

286. Charo B. D'Etcheverry, *Love After* The Tale of Genji: *Rewriting the World of the Shining Prince*

287. Michael G. Chang, *A Court on Horseback: Imperial Touring & the Construction of Qing Rule, 1680–1785*

288. Carol Richmond Tsang, *War and Faith:* Ikkō Ikki *in Late Muromachi Japan*

289. Hilde De Weerdt, *Competition over Content: Negotiating Standards for the Civil Service Examinations in Imperial China (1127–1279)*

290. Eve Zimmerman, *Out of the Alleyway: Nakagami Kenji and the Poetics of Outcaste Fiction*

291. Robert Culp, *Articulating Citizenship: Civic Education and Student Politics in Southeastern China, 1912–1940*

292. Richard J. Smethurst, *From Foot Soldier to Finance Minister: Takahashi Korekiyo, Japan's Keynes*

293. John E. Herman, *Amid the Clouds and Mist: China's Colonization of Guizhou, 1200–1700*

294. Tomoko Shiroyama, *China During the Great Depression: Market, State, and the World Economy, 1929–1937*

295. Kirk W. Larsen, *Tradition, Treaties and Trade: Qing Imperialism and Chosŏn Korea, 1850–1910*

296. Gregory Golley, *When Our Eyes No Longer See: Realism, Science, and Ecology in Japanese Literary Modernism*

Harvard East Asian Monographs

297. Barbara Ambros, *Emplacing a Pilgrimage: The Ōyama Cult and Regional Religion in Early Modern Japan*

298. Rebecca Suter, *The Japanization of Modernity: Murakami Haruki between Japan and the United States*

299. Yuma Totani, *The Tokyo War Crimes Trial: The Pursuit of Justice in the Wake of World War II*

300. Linda Isako Angst, *In a Dark Time: Memory, Community, and Gendered Nationalism in Postwar Okinawa*

301. David M. Robinson, ed., *Culture, Courtiers, and Competition: The Ming Court (1368–1644)*

302. Calvin Chen, *Some Assembly Required: Work, Community, and Politics in China's Rural Enterprises*

303. Sem Vermeersch, *The Power of the Buddhas: The Politics of Buddhism During the Koryŏ Dynasty* (918–1392)

304. Tina Lu, *Accidental Incest, Filial Cannibalism, and Other Peculiar Encounters in Late Imperial Chinese Literature*

305. Chang Woei Ong, *Men of Letters Within the Passes: Guanzhong Literati in Chinese History, 907–1911*

306. Wendy Swartz, *Reading Tao Yuanming: Shifting Paradigms of Historical Reception (427–1900)*

307. Peter K. Bol, *Neo-Confucianism in History*

308. Carlos Rojas, *The Naked Gaze: Reflections on Chinese Modernity*

309. Kelly H. Chong, *Deliverance and Submission: Evangelical Women and the Negotiation of Patriarchy in South Korea*